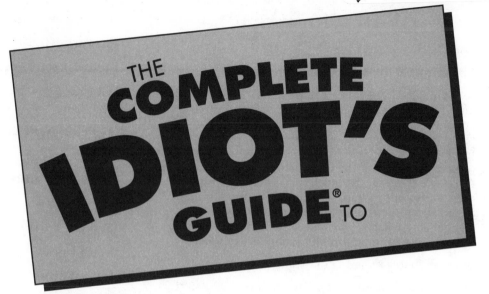

THE **COMPLETE IDIOT'S GUIDE**® TO

Microsoft®
Office 2000

by Joe Kraynak

que®

201 West 103rd Street, Indianapolis, Indiana 46290

The Complete Idiot's Guide to Microsoft® Office 2000

Trademarks

Warning and Disclaimer

Executive Editor

Jim Minatel

Acquisitions Editors

Jill Byus
Don Essig

Development Editor

Benjamin Milstead

Managing Editor

Brice Gosnell

Project Editor

Kevin Laseau

Copy Editors

Bonnie Lawler
Michael Dietsch

Indexer

Kevin Cline

Proofreader

Benjamin Berg

Technical Editor

Don Roche

Interior Design

Glenn Larsen

Cover Design

Mike Freeland

Illustrator

Judd Winnick

Layout Technicians

Brandon Allen
Stacey DeRome
Timothy Osborn
Staci Somers

Contents at a Glance

Table of Contents

xiii

XV

About the Author

Joe Kraynak has been writing and editing computer books and other technical material for over ten years. His long list of computer books include *The Complete Idiot's Guide to PCs*, *The Big Basics Book of Windows 98*, *10 Minute Guide to Excel*, *Easy Internet*, and *Windows 95 Cheat Sheet*. Joe graduated from Purdue University in 1984 with a Master's degree in English and a strong commitment to making computers and software easily accessible to the average user.

Dedication

To my son, Nick, for asking all the right questions.

Acknowledgments

Special thanks to Jill Byus and Don Essig (acquisitions editors) for choosing me to write this book and for expertly dealing with contract details and all that other messy stuff; to Ben Milstead (development editor) whose insightful comments and questions significantly enhanced this book; and to Kevin Laseau and Benjamin Berg for shepherding this book through the production cycle.

Don Roche (technical editor) deserves special kudos not only for checking the step-by-step instructions, but also for adding some great tips that have made this book more than worth the manufacturer's suggested retail price. A special round of applause goes to the illustrators and page layout crew for transforming my loose stack of files, figures, and printouts into such an attractive, bound book.

Tell Us What You Think!

As the reader of this book, *you* are our most important critic and commentator. We value your opinion and want to know what we're doing right, what we could do better, what areas you'd like to see us publish in, and any other words of wisdom you're willing to pass our way.

As an executive editor for the Desktop Applications team at Que Publishing, I welcome your comments. You can fax, email, or write me directly to let me know what you did or didn't like about this book—as well as what we can do to make our books stronger.

Please note that I cannot help you with technical problems related to the topic of this book, and that due to the high volume of mail I receive, I might not be able to reply to every message.

When you write, please be sure to include this book's title and author as well as your name and phone or fax number. I will carefully review your comments and share them with the author and editors who worked on the book.

Fax: 317.581.4666

Email: office_que@mcp.com

Mail: Executive Editor
Desktop Applications
Que Publishing
201 West 103rd Street
Indianapolis, IN 46290 USA

Introduction

Your Office in the Year 2000

Computers have revolutionized the traditional office. Gone are the days of manual typewriters, adding machines, ledger books, and desktop rolodexes. In the modern office, these familiar tools have been replaced with word processing applications, spreadsheets, computerized databases, and electronic address books. Even the relatively recent day planners are migrating to the PC.

And that's not all. Currently, the computer revolution is also changing the way we communicate and collaborate. Instead of typing, printing, copying, and manually distributing memos and other paper documents, we distribute memos and exchange messages via email. Instead of publishing reports, we may place them on a network or Web server. Digital communications even allow us to hold virtual conferences and collaboration sessions over network and intranet connections.

Mastering the New Age with Microsoft Office 2000

To master this new age, a simple word processing or spreadsheet application is no longer sufficient. We need a new set of tools—a suite of applications that not only work together, but also allow us to collaborate on projects, exchange ideas and information via email, and make our presence known on the Web. We need Microsoft Office 2000.

Office 2000 extends the capabilities of its former versions by adding tools that make it even easier to collaborate on projects over a network, take advantage of intranets, exchange email within a company and over the Internet, and publish Web pages. With Office 2000 and the right training on how to use its components individually and together, you will be well equipped to master this age of information and communication.

Welcome to *The Complete Idiot's Guide to Microsoft Office 2000 Professional*

The Complete Idiot's Guide to Microsoft Office 2000 Professional is your key to success with Office 2000. It explains the new versions of the Microsoft Office programs: Word, Excel, PowerPoint, Access, Outlook, and Publisher—including all the spiffy things you can do with them. This book covers everything from word processing to spreadsheet number crunching, from database management to graphics, and from slide shows to appointment books. And that's not all—for a limited time only, we'll tell you how to make the programs work together so you can tackle even bigger tasks. You'll also learn how to unleash these various tools through email and on the Web.

Specifically, this book is going to help you do the following:

➤ Grasp the basics of Office 2000 (and use its help system when you get into a jam).

➤ Master the ins and outs of using Office 2000 to create documents of all kinds, design graphic presentations with pizzazz, make spreadsheets using formulas and functions, keep an electronic calendar, and much more.

➤ Use the Office 2000 applications for practical, home-office purposes, such as creating newsletters, paying bills, and managing a budget.

➤ Get the most out of Office 2000, by using all of the products together. Here, you will learn how to transform a Word document into a PowerPoint presentation, drop an Excel spreadsheet or graph into a Word document, or even merge a list of addresses from an Access database into a form letter created in Word.

➤ Communicate more effectively with people in your company and around the world, through email. You will learn how to send messages, documents, and files right from the Office 2000 applications instead of using a separate email program.

➤ Publish professional looking pages on the Web. You will learn how to transform Word documents, Excel spreadsheets, and PowerPoint presentations into brilliant Web pages!

The Unconventional Conventions

To make this book a little easier to use, we took it upon ourselves to follow a few conventions. Anything you need to type appears in bold, like this:

Type **this entry**

If there's any variable information to be typed in, such as your own name or a file name, it appears in italic, like this:

Type *this number*

In addition, you'll find boxed information (like the examples below) scattered throughout the book to help you with terminology, boring technical background, shortcuts, and other tips. You certainly don't have to read these little boxes, although I did work hard putting them together for you. If you want to understand more about a topic, you might find these boxes helpful. But in case you don't, they're sort of tucked out of the way so you can quickly skip them.

Techno Talk

These boxes contain technical twaddle that will make you drowsy. Read them only if you're planning to appear on Jeopardy! Look to these boxes when you want to find definitions and explanations of technical words and operations.

Check This Out!

Hey, you'll like reading these boxes. They contain tips, tricks, shortcuts, and other suggestions on how you can cheat your way through a long, boring procedure. Plus, I'll throw in fascinating tidbits for you, just to keep things exciting.

Web Work!

If you see a Techno Talk box that's labeled Web Work, be ready to learn how to use one of the exciting (not to mention new) Office 2000 Web features.

New! Office 2000

To quickly discover the differences between Office 97 and Office 2000, scan the margins for this icon. Although this icon won't point out *all* the differences in the new version, it will point out the most innovative and exciting new features.

Part 1

Microsoft Office 2000 Over Easy

When you first drive a new car off the dealer's lot, you usually don't know that much about it. The salesperson takes three minutes out of his busy life to show you how to turn on the lights and the windshield wipers, scan for FM radio stations, and gives you confusing instructions on how to set and cancel cruise control. It takes a couple weeks to figure out all the little things such as how to turn on the air conditioner, open the glove compartment, and keep your airbag from acting as a lethal weapon.

It's the same with a new program. You need to know what's new about it, why it places that extra toolbar on your desktop, and how to navigate the help system when you back yourself into a corner. This part teaches you all that and a little more so that you can sit behind the wheel of Office 2000 with complete confidence.

Chapter 1

10-Minute Guide to Office 2000 Professional

> ## In This Chapter
>
> ➤ Running the Office 2000 applications
>
> ➤ Using and configuring the Shortcut bar
>
> ➤ Saving and opening files
>
> ➤ Learning some fancy mouse moves

You're no idiot. You've probably poked around in several Windows applications, and you have a general idea of how they work. You are quite capable of opening pull-down menus and clicking buttons, and you didn't shell out seventeen bucks to be told what you already know. So I'm not going to give you the step-by-boring-step tutorial of how to use Windows or Windows applications. Instead, this chapter provides you with a brief overview of how to run the various Office 2000 applications, as well as some tips that can help you perform the basics a little faster.

Running Your Office Applications

The installation procedure places icons for the Office 2000 applications on the Windows **Start**, **Programs** menu. Just open the menu and click the name of the application you want to run. You can also run some of the applications by using the Microsoft Office Shortcut bar (explained in the following section).

If you use a particular Office 2000 application frequently, consider placing a shortcut to it on the Windows desktop. Right-drag the icon from the Start, Programs menu to a blank area of the desktop, release the mouse button, and click **Create Shortcut(s)**

Here. This places a copy of the icon on the desktop. Click the icon to run the application.

Web Work!

The Office 2000 installation installs Microsoft's Web browser, Internet Explorer 5, on your PC. It also adds a shortcut to the Windows desktop, named Connect to the Internet. Click this icon and follow the onscreen instructions to start a new Internet account or to enter connection settings for your existing account.

Scooting Up to the Shortcut Bar

Microsoft Office comes with its very own toolbar, called the *Shortcut bar*, which typically pops up on the right side or top of the Windows desktop whenever you start Windows. The Shortcut bar contains buttons for creating new documents, composing email messages, setting appointments, and performing other common tasks.

If the Shortcut bar does not appear, you can turn it on: click **Start**, **Programs**, **Office Tools**, **Microsoft Office Shortcut Bar**. The first time you choose to display the Shortcut bar, Office setup prompts you to install it from the CD; insert the Office CD and click **OK** to install it. The Microsoft Office Shortcut Bar dialog box asks if you want the Shortcut bar to run automatically on startup. Click the desired button—**Yes** or **No**. The following figure shows the Shortcut bar in action. The list following the figure describes the buttons. Later in this chapter, I'll show you how to move the bar.

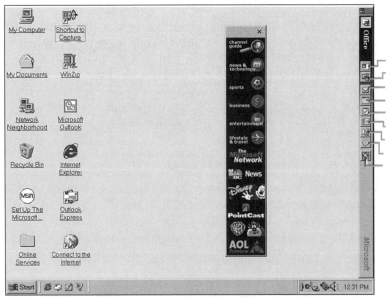

The Shortcut Bar is your one-stop shop for everything Office 2000.

New Office Document
Open Office Document
New Message
New Appointment
New Task
New Contact
New Journal Entry
New Note
Microsoft FrontPage

New Office Document. Enables you to create a document using a template. The application that runs depends on the type of document that you choose to create—for instance, if you choose a presentation, PowerPoint runs.

Open Office Document. Enables you to open and start editing a document that has already been created and stored on your computer or on the network. By default, Office looks in the C:\My Computer folder for Office documents.

New Message. Displays a window that you can use to create and send an email message.

New Appointment. Enables you to add an appointment to your schedule. Outlook can display a reminder before the scheduled date and time, if you choose.

New Task. Displays a dialog box that enables you to add a task to your to-do list (as if you didn't have enough to do). Again, this button runs Outlook.

New Contact. Enables you to add a person's name, address, phone number, email address, and all sorts of other information to your address book in Outlook.

New Journal Entry. Prompts you to enter information about something that you have done during the day, about an email message that you sent or received, or about anything else that you want to record in Outlook.

New Note. Places an electronic "sticky note" on your screen, compliments of Outlook.

Microsoft FrontPage. Runs Microsoft's Web page creation and editing program, FrontPage. For details on creating and publishing Web pages with your Office applications, including FrontPage, see Chapter 25, "Creating and Publishing Your Own Web Pages."

ScreenTip Tip

When you rest the mouse pointer on a button in the Shortcut bar or in any toolbar, a box pops up displaying the name of the button. This is called a *ScreenTip*. To change the name of the button, right-click the button and choose **Rename**. To turn off a button, right-click it and choose **Hide Button**.

Activating Other Shortcut Bars

The Shortcut bar initially displays the Office toolbar, which contains buttons mostly for Outlook tasks. You can turn on other toolbars to enable quick access to other files and programs on your computer. To turn a toolbar on or off, right-click a blank area of the Shortcut bar and choose any of the following toolbars:

➤ *Favorites.* Displays icons for Web pages that you added to your list of favorites in Internet Explorer (assuming that you cruise the Web with Internet Explorer).

➤ *Programs.* Turns on the toolbar equivalent of the Windows Start, Programs menu.

➤ *Accessories.* Displays icons for applications on the Start, Programs, Accessories submenu.

➤ *Desktop.* Turns on a toolbar that displays the shortcuts on the Windows desktop.

Whenever you turn on a toolbar, an icon for that bar appears in the Shortcut bar and the toolbar's buttons appear. Only one toolbar's buttons are shown at a time. You can display the buttons of another toolbar (assuming that you turned it on earlier) by clicking its icon (shown in the following figure).

If you need more or different buttons, give your toolbar a swift click.

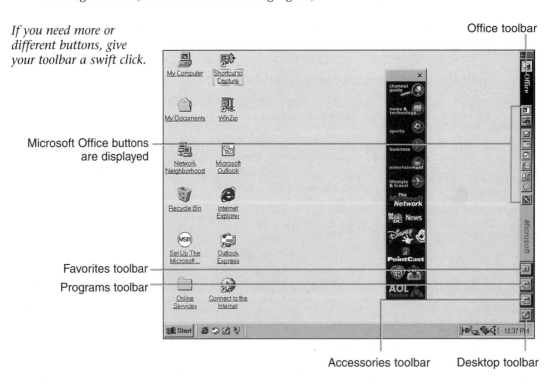

Office toolbar

Microsoft Office buttons are displayed

Favorites toolbar
Programs toolbar

Accessories toolbar   Desktop toolbar

Customizing the Shortcut Bar

The first thing you may want to know about the Shortcut bar is how to move it. Drag any blank area of the Shortcut bar to the desired position on your screen: left, right, top, bottom, or (to make it most intrusive) smack dab in the middle. To turn off the Shortcut bar, right-click its title bar (at the top or left end of the Shortcut bar) and click **Exit**.

If you have a genuine affection for the Shortcut bar and decide to leave it on, you can customize it in all sorts of ways. My favorite option is Auto Hide, which tucks the Shortcut bar out of the way as you work in an application. To turn on Auto Hide, right-click a blank area of the Shortcut bar and click **Auto Hide**. Whenever you need the Shortcut bar, slide the mouse pointer over to the right side of the screen (or wherever you moved the bar) to display it. If AutoHide is grayed out (inactive), Auto Fit in Title Bar Area is on; see the accompanying Check This Out.

For additional customization options, right-click a blank area of the Shortcut bar and click **Customize**. The View tab appears up front, giving you options for changing the appearance and behavior of the Shortcut bar. I'm not going to bore you with all the details. Just be sure that if you have more than one toolbar turned on, you choose the toolbar that you want to customize from the **Toolbar** drop-down list before you start changing settings.

Another tab that you should check out is the Buttons tab. It contains a list of buttons that you can turn on or off. A check in the box next to a button indicates that the button is turned on. You can add icons for commonly used files or folders by clicking the **Add File** or **Add Folder** button. You can also move buttons by clicking the button and then clicking the **Move** up or down arrow (or simply **Alt**+drag a button on the Shortcut bar to the desired location).

Check This Out

Let's Get Fancy

Do you see all that wasted space in your Office application's title bar? You can squeeze the Shortcut bar in there. In the Customize dialog box, on the View tab, under Options, turn on **Auto Fit into Title Bar Area** and click **OK**. You can now drag the Shortcut bar into the title bar of your Office application when the window is maximized. If the window is not maximized, the Shortcut bar appears at the top of the Windows desktop.

Getting Help in Dialog Boxes

Dialog boxes are typically packed with cryptic options. To determine what an option does, right-click its name and select **What's This?,** or click the question mark icon in the upper-right corner of the dialog box and click the option's name. A small text box appears describing the option.

Saving, Naming, and Opening the Files You Create

Whichever Office application you use, the first thing you need to know is how to create, save, and open files.

To create a new file in most of the Office applications, click the **New** button or open the **File** menu and choose **New**. The New button slaps a new document window on your screen, no questions asked. File, New opens a dialog box that enables you to choose a template (a prefab document, such as a business letter) with which to start. (You'll learn more about templates in later chapters.)

To save a file in any of the Office 2000 applications, open the **File** menu and choose **Save** (or click the **Save** button on the toolbar). The first time you save a file, the application prompts you to name it and specify where you want it stored. Select the folder in which you want to store the file, as shown in the following figure. Type a name for the file in the **File name** text box. (Don't type a period or a file name extension; the application adds the correct extension.)

The Save Options

By default (unless you changed it), all Office applications save files to the My Documents folder and look to that folder whenever you enter the Open command. To use a different folder as the default folder for one of the Office applications, open the Office application's **Tools** menu and choose **Options**. Click the **File Locations** tab, click **Documents**, click the **Modify** button, and select the desired folder.

Double-click a folder to select it.　Select a drive from this list.

The first time you save a file, you must name it.

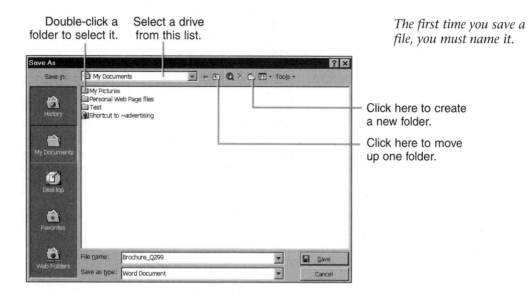

Click here to create a new folder.

Click here to move up one folder.

You should save your file every ten minutes or so to protect your work in the event of a power outage or system crash. After you've named a file, saving your changes is easy: just click the **Save** button. Your application remembers the name and location of the file, and saves it automatically.

To work on an existing file, you must open it in the application that you used to create it. You can enter the **File**, **Open** command (or click the **Open** button) and use the Open dialog box to select the file, but the following methods are easier:

➤ The Windows **Start**, **Documents** menu contains a list of the 15 documents on which you've most recently worked. Select the file from this list.

➤ The **File** menu in the Office application displays the names of the last few files on which you worked. Select the file from the bottom of the File menu.

➤ Click the **Open Office Document** button in the Shortcut bar, and then locate and double-click the name of the file you want to open.

➤ If you edit the document on a regular basis, drag its icon from My Computer or Windows Explorer onto the Microsoft Office Shortcut bar or the Windows desktop. To open the document, click its icon.

Streamlined Installation

Microsoft not only streamlined the interface, but it also pared down the installation. The Office installation omits many features to save space on your hard drive and installs those features only when you choose to use them. It's a good idea to keep your Office CD in your CD-ROM drive as you use the Office applications.

Working with the Smart New Office Interface

If you upgraded from a previous version of Office, you probably noticed that Microsoft completely revamped the Save and Open dialog boxes. The dialog boxes now include a *Places* bar on the left that contains icons for commonly used folders. To quickly change folders, you click the folder's icon. The History folder contains icons for the fifty most recently opened files.

Microsoft has also streamlined the Office menus and toolbars and given them some intelligence. The toolbars and menus initially list only the most commonly used commands and display a double-headed arrow for expanding the menus or toolbars. Click the double-headed arrow to view additional commands or options. As you work, your Office applications automatically bump up the commands you enter most often to place them near the top of the menu or the left side of the toolbar.

The streamlined interface displays only the commands you use most.

Click the double-headed arrow to view more buttons.

Drag a toolbar down to view it as a separate toolbar.

Rest the mouse pointer on the double-headed arrow to view more options.

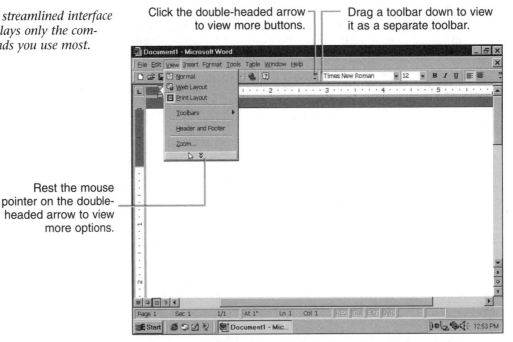

I Liked It Better Before

If the streamlined interface doesn't appeal to you, you can return to the old dumb interface. In your Office application, choose **Tools**, **Customize** and enter your preferences on the **Options** tab.

Not-So-Basic Mouse Moves

Newer baby books now list mouse skills as a stage of human development that falls somewhere between walking and holding down a full-time job. "Click," "double-click," and "drag" are standard words in any grade schooler's vocabulary. Some new mouse moves, however, might confuse even a well-educated adult:

➤ *Right-click pop-up menus.* Sometimes the quickest way to act on existing text (or any other object in a document, including graphics) is to select it and then right-click the selected text or object to display a menu. Pop-up menus are great because they present options that are used only for the selected text or object.

➤ *Right-dragging.* When you right-drag, a pop-up menu appears when you release the mouse button. This menu usually provides options for moving the selected object, pasting a copy of it, or creating a *hyperlink* to it.

➤ *Scraps.* You can drag selected text onto a blank area of the Windows desktop to create a *scrap.* You can then drag the scrap into a document to paste it into that document.

Hyperlink

Hyperlinks are specially formatted icons or bits of text that point to other files. These files may be stored on your hard drive, on the network drive, or on the Internet. When you click a hyperlink, Windows finds and runs the application needed to play the file and opens the file in that application. (See Chapter 25, "Creating and Publishing Your Own Web Pages," for more information.)

➤ *Funky selection moves.* Everyone knows that you can drag over text to select it. Most applications, however, offer additional ways to select with the mouse. In Word, for example, you can double-click a word to select it or triple-click inside a paragraph to select it. (I point out these special selection techniques in the chapters that deal with the individual applications.)

➤ *Selection boxes.* If you paste pictures or other objects on a page, most applications enable you to select two or more objects by dragging a box around them.

16

Chapter 2

When in Doubt, Ask for Help

In This Chapter

➤ Have your personal Office Assistant hunt down information for you

➤ Turn off your Office Assistant when he starts getting on your nerves

➤ Find a topic in the table of contents

➤ Search an onscreen index of Help topics

Online help systems: You love 'em or you hate 'em. Either they're impossible to find and navigate, or they're like some overzealous philanthropist who just won't leave you alone.

In Office 97, Microsoft finally found a middle ground with the Office Assistant, an animated character who answers your questions and knows when to get out of the way. In Office 2000, Microsoft has fine-tuned the Office Assistant and built a more automated help system. In this chapter, you learn how to get the help you need.

Meeting Your Office Assistant

Whenever you start one of the Office applications, an Office Assistant pops up to let you know that help is just a click away. As you type, edit, format, and enter commands, this animated character keeps an eye on what you're doing and remains ready to lend a hand.

When you need help, all you have to do is click your Office Assistant or the help button, and your Assistant jumps into action, displaying a list of four or five Help topics that pertain to what you are currently doing (or at least what your Assistant *thinks* you are doing). If you just entered the File, Print command, for example, your Assistant displays topics that deal with printing. At this point, you have the following options:

➤ If the topic with which you need help is in the list, click it to display information and instructions for that topic.

➤ If the desired topic is not listed, click **See more** at the bottom of the list to display additional topics.

➤ If your Assistant has no suggestions for the type of help you need, type your question in the text box below the list and click the **Search** button. When you start typing, your Assistant whips out a notepad and starts jotting down your question. When you click the Search button, the Assistant returns a list of topics that should answer your question. Click the desired topic.

➤ To turn off the Assistant, right-click the Assistant and click the **Hide** option. To beckon your Assistant, press **F1** or click the **Help** button (the question mark button) on the right end of the Standard toolbar.

Your Office Assistant can usually track down the help you need.

The Help button   Click here to see more topics.   If the desired topic appears, click it.

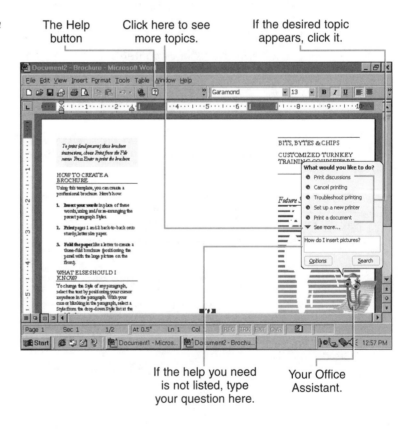

If the help you need is not listed, type your question here.

Your Office Assistant.

Although the Office Assistant is nearly perfect, you can make it even better. To enter your preferences, right-click your Assistant and select **Options** or **Choose Assistant**. Both commands open the Office Assistant dialog box, which includes the following two tabs:

➤ The Options tab allows you to specify when you want the Assistant to leap into action and how you want it to perform its job. To determine what an option does, right-click its name and select **What's This?**

➤ The Gallery tab allows you to choose a different animated character to use as your Office Assistant. Enter your preference and click **OK**. (You may have to insert your Office CD to install the character.)

Because the Office Assistant is a shared tool, any preferences you enter control the appearance and behavior of your Assistant in all Office applications.

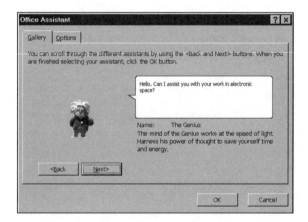

You can replace your Assistant with another animated character.

Finding Help Topics in the Table of Contents

If you find it demeaning to have a cartoon character show you how to use your applications, you can opt for a more traditional approach and look for help in the table of contents. To use the standard Help window, first turn off the Assistant:

1. Right-click your Assistant and choose **Options**.

2. Click **Use the Office Assistant**, to remove the check mark.

3. Click **OK**.

With the Office Assistant disabled, press **F1** or click the **Help** button in the Standard toolbar. This displays the Help Window. If the Contents tab is hiding in the back, click it to bring it up front. Then, click the following icons to view the help you need:

➤ A closed book icon next to a topic means there's a more detailed list of topics. Click the plus sign next to the icon to expand the list of topics.

➤ An opened book icon next to a topic means the topic is selected. You can close the book and collapse the list of subtopics by clicking the minus sign next to the book icon.

➤ A question mark icon next to a topic means there's detailed text to view about the topic. Click the topic or icon to display specific information in the pane on the right.

To change the relative size of the panes, drag the bar that separates the panes to the left or right. To completely hide the left pane and provide additional room for displaying information, click the **Hide** button in the toolbar.

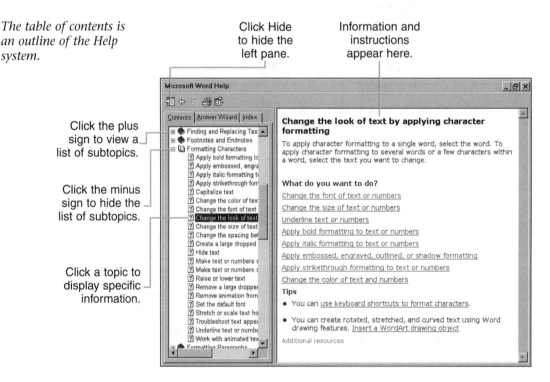

The table of contents is an outline of the Help system.

Click Hide to hide the left pane.

Information and instructions appear here.

Click the plus sign to view a list of subtopics.

Click the minus sign to hide the list of subtopics.

Click a topic to display specific information.

In addition to displaying information and step-by-step instructions, the right pane may also contain highlighted text, called *links*, that point to related information or call up a definition box. Click the link to display additional information. To go back to the previous help screen, click the **Back** button. If the instructions contain a Show Me button, click the button to make the help system perform the task for you.

Getting Help from the Answer Wizard

The Answer Wizard is a cross between the Office Assistant and a standard Help window. It allows you to ask a question in plain English without having to deal with an intrusive Assistant. To get help from the Answer Wizard, take the following steps:

1. Click the **Help** button in the Standard toolbar or press **F1**.
2. Click the **Answer Wizard** tab.
3. Type your question.
4. Press **Enter** or click the **Search** button. A list of topics that match your inquiry appear in the Select Topic to Display list.
5. Double-click the desired topic.

Searching the Index for Specific Help

Most users of technical documentation rank a thorough and well-organized index as the most important part of the documentation. With that in mind, you may find the online Help system index a most valuable tool. To use it, click the **Help** button in the Standard toolbar and click the **Index** tab. In the Type Keywords text box at the top of the Index tab, type a few letters of the topic for which you're looking. As you type, the list of keywords scrolls down to

Web Work!

If you can't find the help you need, get help from Microsoft's Web site. If you are connected to the Internet and you have a Web browser installed, open the **Help** menu and click **Office on the Web**. This connects you to Microsoft's Web site, which contains additional information, technical assistance, free files, and other goodies.

What's This?

Earlier in this chapter, you learned how to get help in a dialog box by right-clicking an option and clicking **What's This?** You can obtain similar help for any toolbar button or other control in your application's window. Open the **Help** menu and select **What's This?** (or press **Shift+F1**), and a question mark attaches itself to the mouse pointer. Now click the button or other control for which you want help. A box pops up describing the control. Pressing **Esc** or clicking outside the help box makes it go away.

show topics whose names match what you have typed so far. Double-click the desired keyword. Scroll down the **Choose a Topic** list and double-click the desired topic.

You can quickly look up information using the Index.

Start typing here.

A list of topics that match what you've typed so far.

Double-click the desired topic.

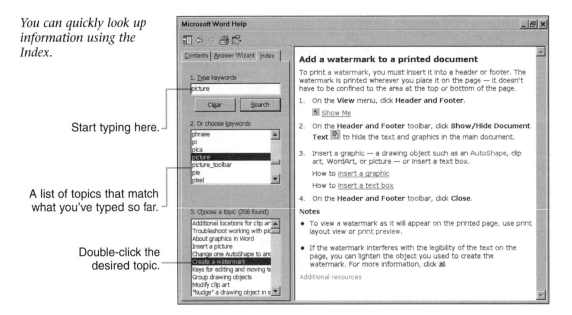

Part 2

Whipping Up Word Documents

Every office needs a good word processor, and Microsoft Word is one of the best. Its standard text layout tools enable you to easily set margins, indent text, and drop pictures and graphs anywhere on a page. The Table feature gives you the power to easily align chunks of text in columns and rows. The Spelling and Grammar checkers provide you with a professional, online proofreader that can catch errors as you type.

In this part, you learn how to use these tools and others to crank out high-quality documents with minimal effort. In addition, you learn to create and print your own fancy newsletters and résumés.

Chapter 3

Making and Editing Word Documents

In This Chapter

➤ Using prefab documents with wizards and templates

➤ Typing, copying, and moving chunks of text

➤ Becoming a 500 word-per-minute typist with AutoText

➤ Finding and replacing bits of text

Microsoft Word has been the superhero of word processing programs for several years now, kicking sand in the face of the former giant, WordPerfect, and pummeling ambitious newcomers such as WordPro. Its powerful features have won over several generations of computer users.

Even with this power, Microsoft has not forgotten the simple tasks that we need to perform, such as typing a letter, printing addresses on envelopes, and arranging text in columns. While beefing up Word with advanced features, Microsoft has continued to make it easier to perform these routine tasks.

In this chapter, you see several of these improvements in action as you learn the basics of creating and editing your documents.

Starting with the Boilerplate Special

If you're in a hurry to create a document and you don't have time to design and format your own, use one of Word's *templates* or *wizards*. A *template* is a ready-made document; all you have to do is add text. A *wizard* is a series of fill-in-the-blank dialog boxes that lead you through the process of creating a custom document, enabling you to specify design preferences and enter chunks of text.

Word's templates and wizards are found in the New dialog box, shown in the following figure. To get there, open the **File** menu and select **New**. (Clicking the New button on the Standard toolbar won't open the New dialog box. You need to use the File menu to open it.) The New dialog box contains several tabs full of wizards and templates. Click the tab for the type of document you want to create, and then double-click the desired template or wizard.

The New dialog box gives you access to document wizards and templates.

Click a tab.

The Preview area displays the currently selected template.

Click a template or wizard to select it or double-click to start a new document.

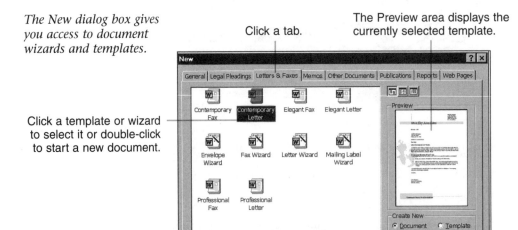

What happens next depends on whether you selected a template or a wizard. If you selected a wizard, a dialog box appears, prompting you to make a selection. Simply follow the wizard's instructions, click the **Next** button until you've reached the last dialog box, and click **Finish**. The wizard creates the document and returns you to the Word window where you can further customize the document or print it as is.

If you picked a template, Word opens the template in its own document window, where you can start editing it. Many templates have placeholders that indicate the type of information you must enter. For example, if you use a letter template, [Click here and type recipient's address] appears next to the greeting. Do whatever the placeholder instructs. (Whether you use a Wizard or template to create your document, Word creates a new document, which you must name and save.)

Placeholders tell you what to do to customize the template.

The template can't do all the work!

[Screenshot of Microsoft Word document]

> Document2 - Microsoft Word
>
> File Edit View Insert Format Tools Table Window Help
>
> Times New Roman   8   **B** *I* U
>
> [Click here and type return address]
>
> ## Company Name Here
>
> March 17, 2000
>
> [Click **here** and type recipient's address]
>
> Dear Sir or Madam:
>
> Type your letter here. For more details on modifying this letter template, double-click ⊠. To return to this letter, use the Window menu.
>
> Sincerely,
>
> [Click **here** and type your name]
> [Click **here** and type job title]
>
> Page 1   Sec 1   1/1   At 0.5"   Ln 1   Col 1   REC TRK EXT OVR

Inserting, Typing Over, and Deleting Text

If you don't know your home keys from your house keys, you should probably take a typing course. Once you know how to type, typing in Word is easy–just do it. The following are a few tips that help if you're making the transition from a typewriter to a computer keyboard:

No Preview?

Office installs some templates only when you choose to use them. The first time you choose a template, Word may not display it, because it hasn't been installed. The next time you use the template, it appears in the Preview area.

➤ Don't press **Enter** at the end of a line. Word wraps the lines for you as you type. If the text disappears off the left or right side of the window, zoom out (explained in "Changing Views," later in this chapter).

➤ A blinking vertical bar, called the *insertion point*, indicates where text is inserted as you type.

➤ At the end of the document, a short horizontal line marks the end of the document. You can't type or insert anything below this line. (As you type, the line automatically moves down.)

Click and Type

Word sports a new feature called Click and Type that allows you to type anywhere inside a document, providing an easy way to control the position of your text without having to press the Enter key. Just double-click wherever you want to insert text and start typing. (Click and Type works only in Print Layout view. See "Changing Views," later in this chapter.)

➤ Move the mouse pointer (shaped like an I-beam) where you want to start typing, and then click. The text you type is inserted, and any existing text moves to the right to make room for the new text.

➤ To replace text, drag over it and start typing.

➤ To delete text to the right of the insertion point, press the **Delete** (**Del**) key. To delete to the left, press the **Backspace** key.

➤ Don't use a lot of tabs to align text in columns. (Chapter 5, "Aligning Your Text with Columns and Tables," explains a much easier way.)

Move the insertion point, and start typing.

The insertion point shows where the text you type will appear.

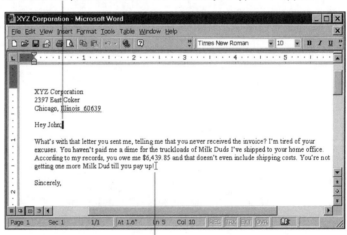

Place the I-beam pointer where you want the insertion point and click.

What's with the Red Pen?

As you type, you may get a strange feeling that your sixth-grade English teacher is inside your computer, underlining your spelling mistakes. Whenever you type a string of characters that does not match a word in Word's spelling dictionary, Word draws a squiggly red line under the word to flag it for you so that you can immediately correct it. (You can turn this feature on or off as desired. See Chapter 7, "Checking Your Spelling and Grammar," for details.)

Typing Text Has Never Been Easier!

I promised early on to teach you how to type 500 words per minute. The trick is to use AutoText. With AutoText, you can assign a term, quote, paragraph, or any other block of text to a couple of unique characters. For example, you might create an AutoText entry that inserts "Democratic National Convention" whenever you type **dnc**.

To create an AutoText entry, type the block of text for which you want to create an AutoText entry, and then drag over the text to select it. Open the **Insert** menu, point to **AutoText**, and click **New** (or just press **Alt+F3**). The Create AutoText dialog box prompts you to type a name for the entry. Type a short unique name for the entry and click **OK**. To insert the block of text, simply type the unique name you assigned to the text and press **F3** or start typing the unique name, and when a ScreenTip appears, showing the complete entry, press the **Spacebar** or the **Enter** key.

AutoText toolbar

The AutoText toolbar makes it easier to create and insert AutoText entries. To turn on the toolbar, right-click any toolbar and select AutoText. This toolbar offers three buttons: click AutoText to display the AutoCorrect dialog box; click All Entries to display a list of AutoText entries you've created; click New to transform selected text into a new AutoText entry.

You can insert or delete AutoText entries via the AutoCorrect dialog box. To display this box, open the **Insert** menu, point to **AutoText**, and click **AutoText**. To delete an entry, choose its name and click the **Delete** button.

Scroll, Scroll, Scroll Your Document

As you type, the screen fills up, and your text starts scrolling off the top as Word "feeds you more paper." Eventually, you need to move back up to that text to edit it or at least read it. The easiest way to move is to point and click with your mouse. To move farther, use one of the following scrollbar methods:

➤ Drag the scroll box up or down. As you drag, a box pops up showing the page number Word will display when you release the mouse button.

➤ Click an arrow at the end of the scrollbar to scroll one line in the direction of the arrow. Hold down the mouse button to scroll continuously.

➤ Click inside the scrollbar above or below the scroll box to scroll up or down one screenful of text.

➤ Click the **Previous Page** or **Next Page** button (bottom of the scrollbar) to flip one page at a time. The dot between the two page buttons gives you additional options to scroll through a document's notes, graphics, or edits. When you flip pages, the insertion point doesn't move–you must click where you want it. (You can quickly flip back to the insertion point by pressing the left or right arrow key.)

Use the scrollbar to move quickly through your document.

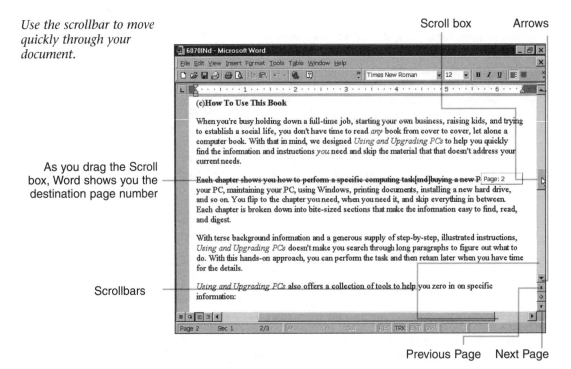

Scroll box   Arrows

As you drag the Scroll box, Word shows you the destination page number

Scrollbars

Previous Page   Next Page

Changing Views

When you start out in Word, it usually displays huge pages that look more like blocky billboard signs than typewritten pages. You might want to see more of your text (to give your thoughts some context) or zoom in when you're styling text. To zoom in, open the **Zoom** drop-down list in the Standard toolbar and click the desired zoom setting. If the Zoom drop-down list is not displayed, click the More Buttons button at the end of the Standard toolbar, as shown in the following figure. You can click inside the text box and type your own setting (zoom percentage).

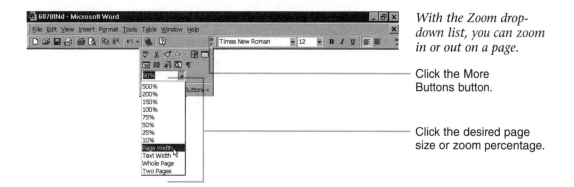

With the Zoom drop-down list, you can zoom in or out on a page.

Click the More Buttons button.

Click the desired page size or zoom percentage.

Word also offers various views of a page, each of which is designed to help you perform a specific task. To change to a view, open the **View** menu and click one of the following view options (buttons for these views are also available in the lower-left corner of the document window):

➤ *Normal* (**Ctrl+Alt+N**) shows your document as one continuous document. In Normal view, Word hides complex page formatting, headers, footers, objects with wrapped text, floating graphics, and backgrounds. Scrolling is smooth because this view uses the least amount of memory.

➤ *Web Layout* displays a document as it will appear when displayed in a Web browser. In Web layout view, Word displays Web page backgrounds, wraps the text to fit inside a standard browser window, and positions the graphics as they will appear when viewed online.

➤ *Print Layout* (**Ctrl+Alt+P**), formerly known as Page Layout, provides a more realistic view of how your pages will appear in print. Print Layout displays graphics, wrapping text, headers, footers, margins, and drawn objects. This uses a lot of memory, however, and may make scrolling a little jerky.

➤ *Outline* (**Ctrl+Alt+O**) allows you to quickly reorganize your document by dragging headings from one location to another in the document.

10 Ways to Select Text

Before you can do anything with the text you just typed, you must select it. You can always just drag over text to select it, but Word offers several quicker ways to select text. The following table outlines these techniques.

Table 3.1   Selecting Text with Your Mouse.

To Select This	Do This
Single word	Double-click the word.

continues

Table 3.1   Selecting text with your mouse. Continued

To Select This	Do This
Sentence	Ctrl+click anywhere in the sentence.
Paragraph	Triple-click anywhere in the paragraph. Alternatively, position the pointer to the left of the paragraph until it changes to a right-pointing arrow, and then double-click.
One line of text	Position the pointer to the left of the line until it changes to a right-pointing arrow, and then click. (Drag to select additional lines.)
Several paragraphs	Position the pointer to the left of the paragraphs until it changes to a right-pointing arrow. Then double-click and drag up or down.
Large block of text	Click at the beginning of the text, scroll down to the end of the text, and Shift+click.
Entire document	Position the pointer to the left of any text until it changes to a right-pointing arrow. Then triple-click.
Entire document shortcut	Press **Ctrl+A.**
Extend selection	Hold down the **Shift** key while using the arrow keys, Page Up, Page Down, Home, or End.

You can quickly select blocks of text by positioning the mouse pointer in the selection area.

Click to select one line.

In the selection area, the mouse pointer points up and to the right.

Drag to select multiple lines.

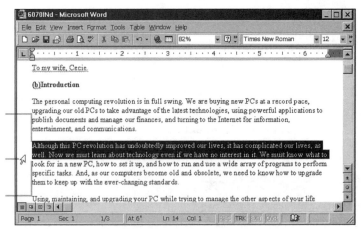

Dragging, Cutting, and Copying Text

You don't select text for the sheer joy of seeing it highlighted. You usually want to do something with it, such as copy or move it. In Word, the easiest way to copy or move text is to drag it. To move text, position the mouse pointer over any part of the selected text, hold down the left mouse button, and drag the text to where you want it inserted. To copy the text, hold down the **Ctrl** key while you're dragging it. If you drag text with the right mouse button, when you release the mouse button, a menu pops up asking if you want to move or copy the text.

Although the drag-and-drop method is the fastest way to copy and move small chunks of text a short distance, you may find it awkward for working with larger blocks of text, for moving text from one document to another, or for moving text a long distance in the same document. Word offers the Cut, Copy, and Paste commands, which are better able to handle these tasks.

Improved Clipboard

 Office 2000 empowers the Windows Clipboard to store more than one cut or copied chunk of data. When you cut or copy two or more selections, the Clipboard toolbar appears, displaying an icon for each copied or cut selection. To paste the data, click its icon. To paste all of the cut or copied selections, click the **Paste All** button. If the Clipboard toolbar does not appear, right-click any toolbar and click **Clipboard**.

 To cut or copy text, select it, and then click either the **Cut** or the **Copy** button in the toolbar. (You can also access these commands by opening the **Edit** menu or by right-clicking the selected text.) When you select the Cut or Copy command, the selected text is placed on the Windows Clipboard. You can then move the insertion point to where you want the text inserted and use the **Paste** command (or button) to paste the text into a different place in the current document, into another Word document, or into a document in just about any other Windows application.

Juggling Two or More Documents

Word enables you to work with more than one document at a time. Whenever you open a document or create a new one, Word opens it in its own window. All the other windows are hidden under the current window, just like a deck of cards. To switch from one window to another, open the **Window** menu and select the desired document.

One of the best new features of Office 2000 is that it now displays an icon for each open document in the Windows taskbar. To switch from one document to another, simply click the button for the desired document in the taskbar.

If you have two documents open, you might want to display them both at the same time, so you can easily drag and drop between them. To arrange the windows, open the **Window** menu and select **Arrange All**. You can also do this with more than two windows, but then your screen starts looking like some twisted mosaic.

The Ol' Find and Replace Trick

If you have used any word processing program, you know that the program can search your document for unique words and phrases and replace those words or phrases with other text. In Word, both the Find and Replace commands are located on your Edit menu.

33

To search for text without replacing it, open the **Edit** menu and choose **Find**. Type the word or phrase that you want to find and click **Find Next**. Word finds the specified text and highlights it. To find the next occurrence of the text, click **Find Next**. When you are done searching, click **Cancel** to close the Find and Replace dialog box.

To have Word replace text with other text, take the following steps:

1. Open the **Edit** menu and choose **Replace**.
2. In the **Find What** text box, type the word or phrase that you want to replace and type the replacement word or phrase in the **Replace With** box. (For additional replacement options, click the **More** button.)
3. To start the search and replace, click the **Find Next** button.
4. Word highlights the first occurrence of the text that it finds and gives you the opportunity to replace the word or skip to the next occurrence. Click one of the following buttons to tell Word what you want to do:

    Find Next. Skips this text and moves to the next occurrence. (You can close the Find dialog box and use the double-headed arrow buttons below the vertical scrollbar to quickly skip to the next or previous occurrence of the word or phrase.)

    Replace. Replaces this text and moves to the next occurrence.

    Replace All. Replaces all occurrences of the specified text with the replacement text–and does not ask for your okay.

    Cancel. Aborts the operation.

On Second Thought: Undoing Changes

If you enjoy the slash-and-burn, never-look-back approach to editing your documents, you may just decide to live with whatever changes that you enter. If you're a little more hesitant, and you get that sinking feeling whenever you delete a sentence, you will feel safe knowing that Word has an Undo feature that enables you to take back any of the most recent edits that you've made.

To undo the most recent action, open the **Edit** menu and choose **Undo**, or click the **Undo** button in the Standard toolbar. You can continue to click the **Undo** button to undo additional actions.

The Undo button doubles as a drop-down list that enables you to undo an entire group of actions. To view the list, click the drop-down arrow to the right of the Undo button. Then click the last action that you want to undo. Be careful, Word undoes the last selected action and all actions above it in the list; you cannot pick and choose one action from the list.

To recover from an accidental undo, use the Redo button (just to the right of Undo). It works just like the Undo button: Click the **Redo** button to restore the most recently undone action, or click the drop-down arrow to the right of the Redo button and select one or more actions from the list. (You may need to click the More Buttons button to access the Redo button.)

Chapter 4

Giving Your Text a Makeover

In This Chapter

➤ Making your text big and bold, like in magazines

➤ Aligning text left, right, and center

➤ Making bulleted and numbered lists

➤ Fancy text with WordArt text boxes

➤ Automated formatting with styles

You need to breathe some life into your document, spice it up with some big bold headings, drop in a few bulleted lists, maybe even add some color. (You do have a color printer, don't you?) In this chapter, you learn how to use Word's formatting tools to give your document that much-needed face-lift.

Fast and Easy Formatting with the Toolbar

The easiest way to format text is to use Word's Formatting toolbar. In case you haven't noticed this toolbar, it's the one with the B I U buttons in the middle of it. The following table lists the buttons and drop-down lists that appear in this toolbar by default and provides a brief description of each. For additional buttons, click the **More Buttons** button (the double-headed arrow) at the right end of the toolbar or drag the vertical line that's to the left of the Font drop-down list down to place the toolbar on a line of its own.

Table 4.1   Get to Know Your Formatting Toolbar

Control	Description
Style	Enables you to select a style that contains several format settings. For example, in the Normal template, the Heading1 style uses Arial 14-point bold text. To learn more, skip ahead to "Baby, You've Got Style(s)," later in this chapter.
Font	Provides typefaces from which you can choose. The typeface is the design of the characters.
Font Size	Enables you select the size of the characters.
B Bold	Makes text bold.
I Italic	Italicizes text.
U Underline	Underlines text.
Align Left	Pushes the left side of the paragraph against the left margin.
Center	Centers the paragraph between the left and right margins.
Align Right	Pushes the right side of the paragraph against the right margin.
Justify	Spreads the text evenly between the left and right margins, as in newspaper columns.
Numbering	Creates a numbered list.
Bullets	Creates a bulleted list.
Decrease Indent	Decreases the distance that the text is indented from the left margin.
Increase Indent	Increases the distance that the text is indented from the left margin.
Borders	Draws a box around the paragraph.
Highlight	Highlights the text (you can select a different color from the drop-down list).
A Font Color	Changes the color of the text.

You can use any of the buttons in the Formatting toolbar to format your text before or after you type it. To format on-the-fly, use the Formatting toolbar to set your preferences, and start typing. If you have already typed the text, select it (as explained in Chapter 3, "Making and Editing Word Documents") and use the tools to apply formatting to the text.

Two More Formatting Tricks

The Formatting toolbar is pretty cool, but there are a couple of other formatting shortcuts that you can use to dazzle your friends and impress your boss. The first is to right-click selected text and choose one of the formatting options (Font, Paragraph, or Bullets and Numbering) in the pop-up menu. This displays the dialog box for applying the desired format.

The second trick is much cooler. Use the Format Painter to copy the format of the text without copying the text itself. First, drag over the text whose format you want to use. Then click the **Format Painter** button (you may have to click the More Buttons button to access the Format Painter). Now, for the grand finale, drag over the text to which you want to apply the format you just copied. Voilà!

Visiting the Font Smorgasbord

The Font and Type Size lists are great for some light text formatting, but you're not going to start your own magazine with those limited choices. You need more power! You need the Font dialog box—a box overflowing with fonts, sizes, and enhancements such as strikethrough, superscript, and double-underlining.

Using the Font dialog box is simple. You drag over the text you want to format, right-click the selected text, and choose **Font** (or open the **Format** menu and choose **Font**). The

Check This Out

Paint the Town

Double-click the **Format Painter** button to keep it on so that you can paint the copied format to several text selections. When you're finished, click the **Format Painter** button to turn it off.

Font dialog box spreads out like a table full of choice grub. Just point and click to pick the desired font, size, and attributes. In addition, the Font dialog box contains a Character Spacing tab that lists options for controlling the space between characters. Use those options to scrunch the characters together or spread them out.

The Font dialog box offers you all the text enhancements you need.

Select a size.

Select a font.

Select a color.

Select enhancements.

The Preview box shows your text with its new look.

Network News

Check This Out

Animated Text!

If you're creating a document to share electronically with colleagues or friends, consider using Word's Animated text feature. In the Font dialog box, click the **Text Effects** tab and select the desired effect. When someone opens the document, the text does a little jig.

Paragraph Formatting: Line Spacing and Indents

After playing with fonts, paragraph formatting is going to seem a little on the boring side; however, you need to know how to shove paragraphs around on a page. First, if you want to format more than one paragraph, select the paragraphs. (To format a single paragraph, you don't have to select the whole thing; just make sure that the insertion point is somewhere inside the paragraph.) Next, right-click any portion of the selected paragraph(s) and click **Paragraph** (or choose **Format**, **Paragraph**). The Paragraph dialog box appears, giving you the following five options:

➤ *Alignment.* Sets the paragraph left, right, or center, or justifies it. You can also do this with the alignment buttons in the Formatting toolbar.

➤ *Indentation.* Enables you to indent the left or right sides of the paragraph. This is useful for setting off long quotes and other chunks of text from surrounding text.

➤ *Spacing Before and After.* Enables you to set the amount of space that you want between the current paragraph and the one preceding or following it. Setting the spacing this way is more accurate than trying to set the spacing by pressing the Enter key repeatedly.

➤ *Line Spacing.* Sets the space between lines of text within the paragraph. Just as on a typewriter, you can choose single-space, double-space, or other settings.

Align left, right, centered, or justified.

The Paragraph dialog box controls indents, line spacing, and the space between paragraphs.

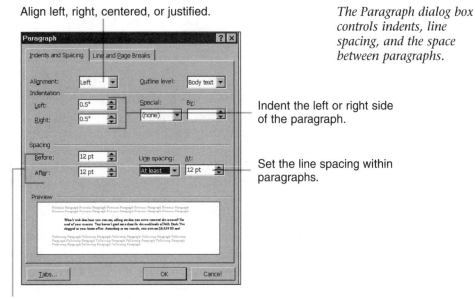

Indent the left or right side of the paragraph.

Set the line spacing within paragraphs.

Set the distance between paragraphs.

Ruling Your Indented Servants

Some people are good at judging measurements for the indents they want to create. Other people are men. We men need to see our indents in context to know whether they are right. For us, Word offers the horizontal ruler (just above the document viewing area). If the ruler isn't on your screen, some joker turned it off. Open the **View** menu and select **Ruler**. The ruler contains four markers (three triangles and a rectangle below the lower-left triangle), which you can drag to do the following:

➤ Drag the upper left triangle to the right to indent the first line of the paragraph.

➤ Drag the lower left triangle to indent the rest of the lines in the paragraph.

➤ Drag the rectangle that's below the lower left triangle to move both left triangles at the same time (but retain their positions relative to one another). The lower left triangle is glued to the rectangle, so the two always stay together. This indents all the lines of the paragraph.

➤ Drag the rightmost triangle to indent all the lines of the paragraph in from the right margin.

Use this picture as your guide to indents.

Drag to indent the first line only.

Drag to indent all but the first line.

Drag to indent the right side of the paragraph.

Drag to indent all lines in the selected paragraph(s).

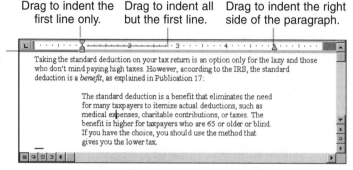

Check This Out

More tab control

For more control over the look and behavior of your tab stops, open the Format menu and select Tabs. The Tabs dialog box enables you to set tab stops in inches, clear tab stops, and add leaders to tab stops. A leader is a string of characters that lead up to the text at the tab stop like this:

Keeping Tabs on Your Tabs

By default, regular paragraphs have tab stops at every half inch. That is, whenever you press the Tab key, the insertion point moves a half inch to the right. It's tempting to just keep pressing the Tab key until you've nudged the insertion point to where you want it. Don't. Instead, set the tab stops yourself, and press the Tab key only once to get there.

The easiest way to set tab stops is to use the horizontal ruler. At the far-left end of the ruler is a tab type symbol, which should be shaped like the letter L. Rest the mouse pointer on it to see which type of tab it is set to insert. Click it to pick the type of tab you want to set—Left, Center, Right, or Decimal (for aligning a column of numbers on the decimal point). Click inside the lower half of the horizontal ruler where you want the tab stop inserted. An icon representing the tab stop appears on the ruler. To move a tab stop, drag it to a new position. To delete a tab stop, drag it off the ruler.

Click this button to select the tab stop type.

Click inside the bottom of the ruler to set the tab stop.

The easiest way to set tab stops is to use the horizontal ruler.

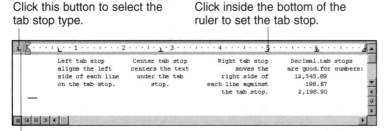

Rest the mouse pointer on this button to see the selected tab stop type.

The Painted Word: Using Text As Art

Fancy fonts are great for headings and running text, but sometimes you need something a little different. Maybe you want to add a curving banner to the top of a page or set off a block of text in its own box. Word offers a couple of tools that you can use to create these special effects: WordArt and text boxes.

Inserting WordArt Objects

With WordArt, you can create three-dimensional text objects that curve, angle up or down, and even lean back. To insert a WordArt object on a page, move the insertion point where you want the object inserted. Open the **Insert** menu, point to **Picture**, and choose **WordArt**. The WordArt Gallery appears, displaying a bunch of styles from which to choose. Click the desired style and click **OK**. In the Edit WordArt Text dialog box, type your text and choose the desired font, font size, and attributes (bold or italic). Click **OK**. Word creates the object, places it on the page along with the WordArt toolbar, and changes to Print Layout view (which is required for displaying graphics). At first, the WordArt object lays over any text on your page, but you can change its properties, as explained later, to make text wrap around the object.

The WordArt object is essentially a graphic object. When it first appears and whenever you click it, small squares called *handles* appear around it, and the WordArt toolbar appears. You can drag a handle to change the size of the object. If you move the mouse pointer over the object, the pointer appears as a four-headed arrow. You can drag the object to move it.

In addition to changing the object's size and position, you can use buttons in the WordArt toolbar to modify the object, as shown in the following table.

Table 4.2   WordArt Toolbar Buttons

Button	Description
Insert WordArt	Inserts another WordArt object on the page.
Edit Text	Enables you to edit the text used in the WordArt object.
WordArt Gallery	Enables you to select a different style for this WordArt object from the WordArt Gallery.
Format WordArt	Displays a dialog box that enables you to change the WordArt object's size and position, control how surrounding text wraps around the object, change the object's color, and much more.
WordArt Shape	Enables you to pick a different shape for the object.
Free Rotate	Displays round handles around the object, which you can drag to spin the object on the page.
Text Wrapping	Controls the way surrounding text wraps around the WordArt object.
WordArt Same Letter Heights	Displays all the characters in the object (uppercase or lowercase) at the same height.
WordArt Vertical Text	Displays characters running from the top to the bottom, instead of left to right.
WordArt Alignment	Doesn't do anything if you have only one line of text. With two or more lines of text, this button enables you to align the text left, right, center, or to justify it (so that it spreads out to touch both sides of the imaginary WordArt box).
WordArt Character Spacing	Enables you to change the space between characters in the WordArt object.

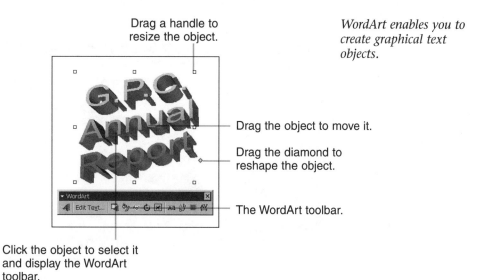

Drag a handle to resize the object.

WordArt enables you to create graphical text objects.

Drag the object to move it.

Drag the diamond to reshape the object.

The WordArt toolbar.

Click the object to select it and display the WordArt toolbar.

Setting Off Text in Text Boxes

Word is becoming more and more like a desktop publishing program with each new release. Word even offers text boxes, which you can use to set off a block of text from surrounding text. You've probably seen text boxes used in your favorite magazines to set off quotes or add a brief summary of the article. Because the text is in a box of its own, it captures the reader's attention.

To create a text box in Word, position the insertion point where you want the text box placed, open the **Insert** menu, and click **Text Box**. The mouse pointer turns into a crosshair pointer, which you drag on your page to create the text box. Word inserts the box and displays the Text Box toolbar. Type your text in the box, and use the Formatting toolbar to style the text. As with WordArt, the text box is surrounded by handles that you can drag to change the size or dimensions of the box.

On the left end of the Text Box toolbar are two Link buttons—**Create Text Box Link** and **Break Forward Link**. These buttons enable you to continue the contents of one text box inside another text box on the same page or on another page. To create a link, make two text boxes and insert or type the desired text in the first text box. Then click the **Create Text Box Link** button and click inside the second text box. If the story doesn't fit in that text box, you can create a third text box and link to it. The **Break Forward Link** button enables you to break the link between text boxes without losing text.

One last text box trick, and I'll let you move on. Activate the Drawing toolbar (right-click any toolbar and select **Drawing**). All the way to the right are two buttons called **Shadow** and **3-D**. To add a drop shadow to the text box, click the **Shadow** button and select the desired shadow. To give your text box a three-dimensional look such as the one in the following figure, click the **3-D** button and select a 3D effect.

Get out your 3D glasses, and turn on the Drawing toolbar.

A text box in 3D

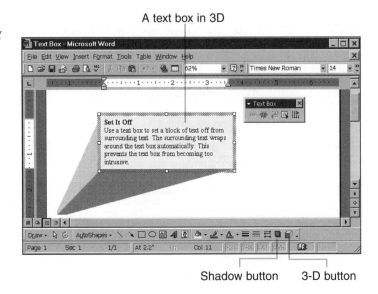

Shadow button   3-D button

If you drop a text box on top of existing text, you notice that it hides the text under it. If you prefer, you can have the existing text wrap around the text box so that you can see all the text. To enter text wrap and other format settings for your text box, open the **Format** menu, select **Text Box,** and enter your preferences.

Baby, You've Got Style(s)

You go to a lot of trouble creating a wardrobe for your documents. Maybe you've designed the perfect title, created some great-looking bulleted lists, and spent way too much time playing with the various levels of headings. You don't want to do all that work over again, and you don't have to. Instead, you can save your format settings as *styles* and apply the styles to the text in any other documents you create.

A style is a group of format settings. For example, if you create a heading using 18-point Arial bold italic type that's centered, you have to apply all those formats separately the first time you format the heading. If you then create a style for that heading, however, and name it, say, Attitude, you can apply all those format settings to some other text by selecting the Attitude style from the style list.

Even better, you can modify a style and have your changes affect all the text that you have formatted using that style. For instance, if you decide that you want to bump the Attitude type size down from 18-point to 16-point, all you have to do is change the Attitude style. All the headings that you've formatted using that style are then automatically changed from 18-point to 16-point.

The two types of styles are paragraph and character. A *paragraph style* applies paragraph and character formatting to all the characters in the paragraph. Paragraph formatting includes alignment, indents, line spacing, space before and after the paragraph, and so on. Character formatting controls the font, size, and character attributes, such as bold and italic. A *character style* applies format settings only to selected text; it does not apply formatting to all the text in a paragraph. The style list (on the Formatting toolbar) marks paragraph styles with a ¶ and character styles with an a.

Applying Character and Paragraph Styles

Word's templates all come with a set of styles that you can apply to your paragraphs and text. To apply a paragraph style, click anywhere in the paragraph to which you want to apply the style, open the **Style** drop-down list, and click the desired style (you may need to click the More Buttons icon to display the Style drop-down list). To apply a character style, drag over the text to which you want to apply the style, open the **Style** drop-down list, and click the desired style.

If the drop-down list doesn't include the desired style, open the **Format** menu and

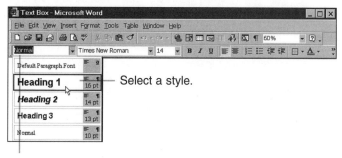

Pick a style from the Style list.

Select a style.

Style list.

select the **Style** command. Open the **List** drop-down list and click **All Styles**. This displays a list of even more ready-made Word styles and styles that you have created (which you do in the next section).

Creating Your Own Styles

An easy way to create your own paragraph style is to use the **Style** box on the toolbar. (You can't use this box to create a character style.) First, set up the paragraph on which you want to base your style; include any special formatting that you want to use. Make sure that your insertion point is somewhere in that paragraph, and then click in the **Style** box in the Formatting toolbar. Enter a new style name, being careful not to duplicate an existing name. Click anywhere outside of the box or press **Enter**, and you have created a new style. You can now apply it by name to new paragraphs that you add to your document.

To create a character style, you can't use the Style box on the Formatting toolbar. You

Check This Out

Displaying the Style Bar

You can display the names of paragraph styles used in your document on the left side of the document window. Open the **Tools** menu, choose **Options**, and click the **View** tab. Under Outline and Normal options, use the **Style Area Width** spin box to set the style area to .5" or more.

must use the Style dialog box, as covered in these steps:

1. Open the **Format** menu and select **Style** to display the Style dialog box.

2. Click the **New** button.

3. In the **Name** text box, type the desired name for the style.

4. Open the **Style Type** list box and select **Character**.

5. Open the **Format** menu at the bottom of the dialog box and select **Font** to change the appearance of the text. This displays the Font dialog box.

6. Use the Font dialog box to select the desired character formatting and click **OK**. This returns you to the Style dialog box.

7. You can use the **Shortcut Key** button to assign a keystroke to this style. You can then quickly apply the style by selecting your text and pressing the keystroke.

8. Click **Close** to save your new style.

Chapter 5

Aligning Your Text with Columns and Tables

In This Chapter

➤ Using columns to create your own newsletters

➤ Understanding section breaks

➤ Aligning text in columns and rows

➤ Drawing a table with your mouse—cool!

Text is fairly orderly. As you type, the text lines up and marches right along with the insertion point. However, when you need text to break rank and arrange itself in rows and columns, it isn't very cooperative.

Should you give up? No! Word has a whole box full of text-alignment tools for taking control of stubborn text and making it line up the way you want it to. With Word's text boxes, columns, and tables, you can make newspaper columns that snake across the page from top to bottom, accent documents with small chunks of text, and create perfectly aligned tables. This chapter shows you how to use Word's advanced text-alignment tools to make your text behave.

Creating Your Own Newspaper Columns

Although text boxes (discussed in the previous chapter) provide excellent control over columns of text, enabling you to flow an article from one page to another, for basic newsletters you may want to use a more standard feature: *newspaper columns*. Newspaper columns divide the text into two or more columns that wrap the text from the bottom of one column to the top of the next column, just like a newspaper or magazine.

Before you create columns, figure out where you want the columns to start and end. Maybe you want the entire document divided into columns, or perhaps you want to apply columns to only a portion of the document. Whichever you choose, take the following steps to create your columns:

1. Position the insertion point where you want the columns to start, or drag over the text that you want to lay out in columns. (To format the entire document with columns, it doesn't matter where the insertion point is within the document.)

2. Open the **Format** menu and choose **Columns**. The Columns dialog box appears, prompting you to specify the number of columns to use. (To quickly create columns, click the **Columns** button in the Standard toolbar and drag over the desired number of columns.)

3. Select one of the preset column styles at the top, and specify additional preferences as desired to modify the style. You can click the **Line Between** option to insert a vertical line between the columns. (For uniform columns, make sure **Equal Column Width** is checked.)

4. Open the **Apply To** drop-down list and choose the desired option: **This Section**, **Selected Text, This Point Forward**, or **Whole Document**. If you selected text in Step 1, your only choices are Selected Text (the default option), Selected Sections, and Whole Document. If you did not select text, your choices are This Section, This Point Forward, and Whole Document.

5. Click **OK**. Word automatically changes to Print Layout view, to display the columns as they will appear in print.

If you decide later to return the columns to normal text (turn columns off), position the insertion point where the columns start and repeat the steps for setting columns. This time, pick the **One** column option from the Presets list. You can change the column layout anywhere inside the document; for instance, you might want to shift from two columns on one page to three columns on the next.

Whenever you create columns, the horizontal ruler displays markers for controlling the column boundaries. To quickly change the width of a column, drag its marker. (When the mouse pointer is over a column width marker, the pointer appears as a double-headed arrow.) To display the column width measurements in the ruler, hold down the **Alt** key while dragging.

You can also adjust the column widths by resetting the columns. To do so, move the insertion point to where the columns begin, open the **Format** menu, and select **Columns**. Enter the desired measurements for the width of each column. (Remember that you can make all the columns the same width by turning on Equal Column Width.)

Newsletter Title

To place a title at the top of your newsletter, type the title at the top of the first column and highlight it. Perform the previous set of steps to change the number of columns to one.

Drag a column marker to change the column width.

The easiest way to resize a column is to drag its marker.

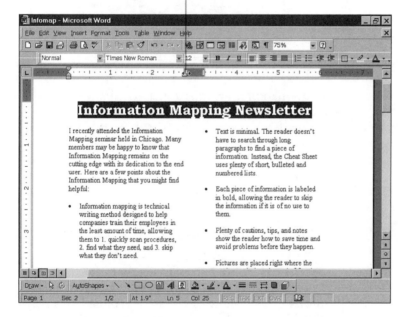

Avoiding Gridlock with Tables

The most useful page layout tool in any word processing program is the Table feature. This tool enables you to align blocks of text side by side not only to create tables packed with small bits of information, but also to create professional-looking résumés, exams, study guides, and documentation. If you ever have trouble placing two items side by side in a document, the solution is usually a table. The following figure shows a table used to create a résumé.

A table disguised as a résumé.

	Susan K. Shiffer 1603 North Emerson Chicago, Illinois 60631 Home Phone: (312) 555-5555
Goals	To teach and share my love and knowledge of the Spanish language and culture in an environment that will further enrich and develop my personal and academic skills.
Education May, 1983 May, 1980	*Purdue University, West Lafayette, Indiana* Master of Arts in Spanish Literature. Bachelor of Arts in Spanish/Education.
Sept., 1978- June, 1979	*University of Madrid, Spain.* Concentrated on all aspects of peninsular Spanish culture, including History, Economics, Architecture, Literature, and Art.
Sept., 1974- Jan., 1975	*University of the Americas, Cholula, Mexico* Emphasis on furthering language skills, plus first-hand cultural exchanges.
Honors 1980	Delta Kappa Pi (Spanish Honorary Society) Distinguished Student Award, Purdue University. Dean's List and Honor Roll throughout my undergraduate career.
Special Projects/ Publications 1984	Presentation, "How to Organize a Successful Foreign Language Week," at the IFLTA Fall Conference.
Jan., 1983	Critical review of Gail L. Nemetz-Robinson's book, *Issues in Second Language and Cross-Cultural Education: The Forest Through the Trees.* Published in *The Canadian Modern Language Review,* Vol. 39, No.2, Jan., 1983.
1982	Graduate Assistant of Purdue's summer study program at the Universidad-Iberoamericana in Mexico City.
1981	Assistant Instructor for Purdue's "Super Saturday" educational program. Language instruction for exceptional children, ages 6-12.

The key to Word tables is that the information is organized in a systematic fashion. Like a well-designed city, a table is a grid consisting of *rows* and *columns* that intersect to form *cells.* The following sections teach you four techniques for creating your own tables. Later sections in this chapter show you how to insert text and pictures in the cells that make up the table, and how to change the look and layout of the cells.

Setting Your Table with a Dialog Box

For more control over the structure and appearance of your table, use the Insert Table dialog box. Open the **Table** menu, point to **Insert**, and click **Table.** Then, enter your preferences in the Insert Table dialog box. To give your table a professional look, click the **AutoFormat** button and select a predesigned format from the **Formats** list.

Using the Insert Table Button

The easiest way to create a table is to use the **Insert Table** button in the Standard toolbar. When you click the **Insert Table** button, Word opens a menu showing a graphic representation of the columns and rows that make up a table. Drag down and to the right to highlight the number of rows and columns that you want your table to have (you'll learn how to insert and delete columns and rows later). Drag beyond the bottom or right side of the drop-down box to expand the table grid. When you release the mouse button, Word inserts the table.

The Insert
Table button.

*Create a table of uniform
row height and column
width.*

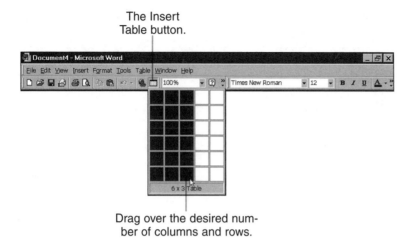

Drag over the desired number of columns and rows.

Drawing a Table with Your Mouse

If you're looking for a more intuitive way to create a table, just draw it. Word offers a table drawing tool that enables you to create the overall table outline and then chop the table into little pieces by adding row and column lines.

To draw a table, open the **Table** menu and select **Draw Table**. The mouse pointer turns into a pencil, the Tables and Borders toolbar appears, and Word switches to Page Layout view. Drag a rectangle of the desired length and width where you want the table to appear. When you release the mouse button, Word inserts a one-cell table. You can then drag vertical and horizontal lines across the table (within the original rectangle), using the pencil pointer to create columns and rows (see the following figure). You can also draw a table by drawing individual cells side-by-side and on top of one another, as opposed to sectioning off a large cell.

The Tables and Borders Toolbar

Whenever you choose to draw a table, the Tables and Borders toolbar appears. You can start drawing a table with simple lines, or you can select options from the tool-bar (such as line color and thickness) before you start drawing.

You can now draw tables.

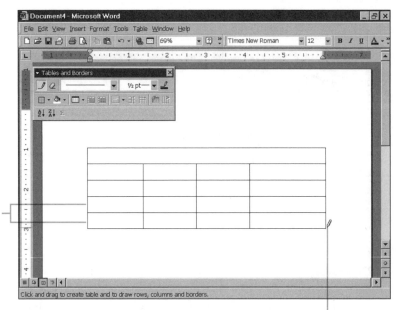

You can drag the mouse pointer inside the table box to create vertical and horizontal lines that define rows and columns.

Drag the mouse pointer to create the table.

Aligning Graphics and Text

Although tables are traditionally used to align blocks of text, they're excellent for aligning pictures with text as well. Just place the insertion point in the cell where you want the picture to appear and select the **Insert**, **Picture** command.

Transforming Existing Text into a Table

Creating a table using tabs is like performing brain surgery with a meat cleaver; tabs just don't give you enough control over your columns and rows. If, however, you're reading this after having set up a table with tabs or inserting one from another program, don't despair. You can recover from your ill-conceived mistake by converting your tabular table into a bona fide table.

First, drag over all the text that you want to include in the table. Then, open the **Table** menu and point to **Convert**, and click **Text to Table**. The Convert Text to Table dialog box appears, prompting you to specify the number of columns and rows and to enter other preferences. Make the desired selections and click **OK**. Word converts the text to a table, and you can start modifying it if necessary.

Moving Around Inside Your Table

Navigating a table with the mouse is fairly straightforward. You click inside a cell to move the insertion point to that cell. You can also use the keyboard to quickly move from cell to cell. Table 5.1 lists the keystrokes to use for moving around in a table.

Table 5.1   Moving Around in a Table

Press	To
Tab	Move to the next cell. At the end of the table, creates a new row and moves to its first cell.
Shift+Tab	Move to the previous cell in the table.
Alt+Home	Move to the first cell in the row you're in.
Alt+PgUp	Move to the top cell in the column you're in.
Alt+End	Move to the last cell in the row you're in.
Alt+PgDn	Move to the bottom cell in the column you're in.

You select text inside a table the same way that you select text in a paragraph—by dragging over it. To select an entire row, move the mouse pointer to the left of the row (outside the table) until the mouse pointer points to the right, and then click. To select a column, move the mouse pointer over the topmost line of the column until the pointer points down, and then click. To select multiple columns or rows, drag the mouse when the pointer is pointing down or to the right. To move selected columns or rows, you can drag and drop them to the desired location. You can also select a row, a column, or the entire table by choosing the desired option from the Table, Select submenu.

Performing Reconstructive Surgery on Your Table

A table never turns out perfect the first time. Maybe you want more space between the topmost row and the rest of the table or you need to shade some of the cells or add lines to divide the columns and rows. In the following sections, you learn all the tricks for restructuring and enhancing your table.

Adjusting the Row Height and Column Width

The easiest way to adjust the row height and column width is to drag the lines that divide the columns and rows. When you move the mouse pointer over a line, the pointer changes into a double-headed arrow; that's when you can start dragging. If you hold down the **Alt** key and drag, the horizontal or vertical ruler shows the exact row height or column width measurement. (You can also drag the column or row markers inside the rulers to change the row height and column width.)

Inserting and Deleting Columns and Rows

When you start typing entries in a table, you may find that you have either too many rows or columns or too few. This problem is easy to correct:

➤ To insert one or more rows, click in the row where you want the new row added (or drag over the desired number of rows) and choose **Table**, **Insert**, **Rows Above** or **Rows Below**.

➤ To insert one or more columns, first select an existing column (to insert two columns, select two columns). Then choose **Table**, **Insert**, **Columns to the Left** or **Columns to the Right**.

➤ To delete rows or columns, drag over the rows or columns you want to delete and choose **Table**, **Delete**, **Rows** or **Columns**. (If you press the Delete key instead, Word removes only the contents of the rows or columns.)

Splitting and Joining Cells

Although not quite as exciting as splitting atoms, splitting cells and joining them (fusion, I guess) can keep you entertained for hours—and give you a great deal of control over your tables. The following figure shows some instances in which you might want to join cells to create a single cell that spans several rows or columns.

You can join cells to form a single cell, or split one cell into many.

A column heading can span two or more columns.

A row heading might span several rows.

Snack Table					
	Quantity	Calories	Total Fat	Cholesterol	Sodium
Snack Type	Chips Ahoy (4 Cookies)	200	10g	0mg	27g
	Fritos (1 ¼ oz. Bag)	200	13g	0mg	200mg
	Pringles (1 can)	160	11g	0mg	340mg
	Cheese Crackers (1 pkg.)	130	8g	15mg	340mg

To join cells, drag over the cells that you want to transform into a single cell, open the **Table** menu, and select **Merge Cells**. Word transforms the multiple cells into a single-cell organism.

To split a cell into two or more cells, select the cell that you want to split, open the **Table** menu, and select **Split Cells**. The Split Cells dialog box appears, asking you to specify the number of rows and columns you want to split the cell into. Enter your preferences and click **OK**. After the cells are split, you may have to drag the borders to adjust the width and height of the cells.

Split Tables

Word now allows you to split an entire table in two. With the insertion point in the row where you want the table split, open the **Table** menu and click **Split Table**. You can't split a table vertically by columns.

Giving Your Table a Face-Lift with Borders and Shading

Tables are bland at first sight; however, Word offers several seasonings, such as and borders and shading, that can add spice to your tables. By far, the easiest way to embellish your table is to use the AutoFormat feature. Click anywhere inside the table, open the **Table** menu, and select **Table AutoFormat**. Select the desired design for your table and click **OK**.

If you don't like the prefab table designs that Word has to offer, you can design the table yourself using the Borders and Shading dialog box. To change the borders or add shading to the entire table, make sure that the insertion point is somewhere inside the table; you don't have to select the entire table. To add borders or shading to specific cells, select the cells. Then open the **Format** menu and select **Borders and Shading**.

The Borders and Shading dialog box has three tabs, two of which you can use to format your table: the **Borders** tab and the **Shading** tab. On the **Borders** tab, select any of the border arrangements on the left, or create a custom border by inserting lines of a specific thickness, design, and color.

To create your own lines, first, select a line style, thickness, and color from the options in the center of the dialog box. Next, open the **Apply to** drop-down list, and choose **Table** (to apply the lines to the entire table) or **Cell** (to apply lines only to selected cells). In the Preview area (just above the Apply to list), click the buttons or click locations in the preview to insert lines.

To shade cells with color or gray shading, click the **Shading** tab. In the Fill grid, click the color that you want to use to shade the table or selected cells. Under Patterns, click a color and percentage to add a pattern of a different color to the shading. For example, you might choose green as the fill and use a 50% yellow pattern to brighten the green. When you finish entering all your border and shading preferences, click **OK** to apply the changes to your table.

You can select a pre-designed border arrangement or create your own.

Select a line style, thickness, and color.

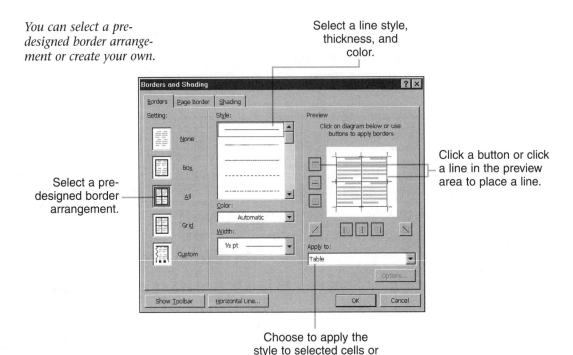

Select a pre-designed border arrangement.

Click a button or click a line in the preview area to place a line.

Choose to apply the style to selected cells or the entire table.

Use the Tables and Borders Toolbar

For quick formatting, use the Tables and Borders toolbar. To display the toolbar, right-click any toolbar and click **Tables and Borders**. In addition to buttons for formatting tables, this toolbar contains the **Eraser** button, which allows you to quickly erase the lines that define cell boundaries.

Sorting and Summing Table Entries

Tables commonly contain entries that you need to sort alphabetically or numerically. If you create a table of phone numbers for people and places that you frequently call, for example, you may want to sort the list alphabetically to make it easy to find people when you need to. You might also create a table with numerical entries that you need to total. Word offers a couple of tools that can help.

To sort entries in a table, first select the entire table (or the portion that contains the entries you want to sort). If you have a row at the top that contains descriptions of the contents in each column, make sure it is *not* selected; otherwise, it is sorted along with the other rows.

Open the **Table** menu and select **Sort**. Then open the **Sort By** drop-down list and select the column that contains the entries to sort by (for example, if you want to sort by last name and the last names are in the second column, select Column 2). Open the **Type** drop-down list and select the type of items you want to sort (**Number**, **Text**, or **Date**). Select the desired sort order: **Ascending** (1,2,3 or A,B,C) or **Descending** (Z,Y,X or 10,9,8). Click **OK** to sort the entries.

Although a Word table is not designed to perform the complicated mathematical operations that an Excel spreadsheet can handle, tables can add a column of numbers. Click inside the cell directly below the column of numbers that you want to add, open the **Table** menu, and click **Formula**. By default, the Formula dialog box is set up to total the values directly above the current cell. Click **OK** to total the numbers.

Chapter 6

Spicing It Up with Graphics, Sound, and Video

In This Chapter

➤ Decorating your text-heavy pages with pictures

➤ Inserting audio and video clips

➤ Moving and sizing your pictures

➤ Drawing your own masterpieces

To catch the attention of today's media-savvy audience and effectively convey your ideas and insights, you must now know how to communicate visually as well as verbally. You must use graphics both to attract the reader and to convey information. And if you really want to captivate the audience of the future with your digital documents, you will have to dazzle them with multimedia elements, as well.

In this chapter, you learn how to use several tools in Word to add graphics, sound, and video to your documents.

Inserting Pictures, Sounds, and Video Clips from the Gallery

Maybe you can hold your own in a doodling contest or sketch Gumby and Pokey in your sleep; but chances are that you probably don't have the talent, ambition, or determination to become a professional artist. Fortunately, Word has gathered a collection of clip art, audio recordings, and video clips that you can use to transform your bland text into a dazzling multimedia document.

Web Work!

If you're connected to the Internet (currently online) and you have Internet Explorer installed, you can download additional clips from Microsoft's Web site. Click the **Clips Online** button in the toolbar at the top of the Clip Art window.

To insert an item from the gallery, first insert your Microsoft Office CD into the CD-ROM drive. The CD contains additional clips that were not installed when you installed Office. Open the **Insert** menu, point to **Picture**, and click **Clip Art**. The Insert ClipArt window appears, displaying several tabs full of images, sound clips, and video clips.

Click the desired tab and click the icon for the desired category. (You can click the **Back** button in the upper left corner of the window to go back to the category list.) When you find the clip you want, click the clip and then click the **Insert Clip** button.

The Microsoft Clip Gallery enables those who lack artistic talent to pretend.

Click here to back up.

Click here to get additional clips from Microsoft's Web site.

Each tab lists a different media type.

Click the desired clip.

Choose Insert Clip.

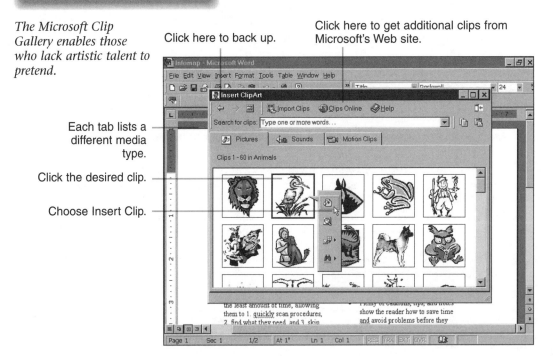

Although clip art is the staple of home grown paper publications, electronic publishing is becoming more and more popular. People are publishing multimedia pages on the Web, setting up interactive kiosks on their networks, and exchanging multimedia documents. To give your documents another dimension, consider inserting audio or video clips into your documents. If you have the Office CD loaded in your CD-ROM drive, choose **Insert**, **Picture**, **Clip Art**, click the **Sounds** or **Motion Clips** tab, and choose the desired clip. You can also insert clips stored on your hard disk by using the **Insert**, **File** or **Insert**, **Object** command.

If you encounter an electronic document that contains audio or video clips (on the Web, on your network, or via email), an icon marks the presence of the media clip. Double-click the icon to play the clip.

Inserting Scanned Images On-the-Fly

If you have a scanner, you can insert a scanned image directly into your document. To insert a scanned image, select **Insert**, **Picture**, **From Scanner or Camera**, and then use your scanner to scan in the desired image. The first time you choose to scan an image, Word prompts you to install the feature from your Office CD. Insert the CD and follow the instructions to install the feature. Then, follow the onscreen instructions to scan the image. The steps vary depending on your scanner and the scanning software you have installed.

Importing Graphics Files

To insert a graphic image that's stored on your disk, open the **Insert** menu, point to **Picture**, and click **From File**. The Insert Picture dialog box appears, prompting you to select the graphics file. By default, this dialog box is set up to display *all* the graphics file types that Word supports, which may include file types that you have no intention of using. You can narrow the list by selecting a specific graphics file type from the **Files of Type** drop-down list.

Use this dialog box just as you would use the Open dialog box to open a document file. Select the drive, folder, and name of the graphics file that you want to insert and click the **Insert** button.

Moving Pictures Around on a Page

Pictures never land right where you want them on a page. You usually have to shove the picture around a little to give your page some balance. To move a picture, click the picture and then drag it to the desired location. When you release the mouse button, Word plops the picture in the current location.

Nudge It

To fine-tune the position of an image, use the arrow keys to nudge it.

Drag the picture to the desired location in the document.

You move pictures by dragging them.

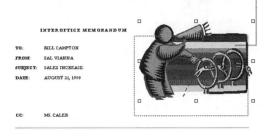

What happens to the surrounding text depends on the text wrapping setting for this picture. By default, the picture is set to have text appear above it and below it, but not on either side. To change the way text wraps around a picture, right-click the picture and select **Format Picture** or **Format Object**. Click the **Layout** tab and select the desired wrapping style. For additional wrapping options, click the **Advanced** button to display the Advanced Layout dialog box.

The Advanced Layout dialog box also contains a Picture Position tab, which allows you to fine-tune the position of the picture on a page and control whether the picture moves with its surrounding text (so you can keep the picture on the same page as the text that refers to it). In the Advanced Layout dialog box, click the **Picture Position** tab, enter your preferences, and click **OK**.

Check This Out

Copying and Cutting Pictures

The Cut, Copy, and Paste commands on the Edit menu work for pictures as well as text. You can also copy a picture by holding down the Ctrl key and dragging it, or you can right-click a picture and select the desired command from the pop-up menu.

Resizing and Reshaping Your Pictures

Pictures rarely fit in. Either they're so large that they take over the entire page, or they're too dinky to make any impression at all. Changing the size of a picture is a fairly standard operation. When you click the picture, squares (called *handles*) surround it. You can drag the squares to change the picture's size and dimensions:

➤ Drag a top or bottom handle to make the picture taller or shorter.

➤ Drag a side handle to make the picture skinny or fat.

➤ Drag a corner handle to change both the height and width proportionally.

➤ Hold down the **Ctrl** key while dragging to increase or decrease the size from the center out. If you hold down the Ctrl key while dragging a handle on the right side out, for example, the picture gets fatter on both the left and right sides.

For more control over the size and dimensions of an image, right-click the image, click **Format Picture** (or **Format Object**), and click the **Size** tab. This page of options enables you to enter specific measurements for your picture. (The Size tab also has an option called Lock Aspect Ratio, which is on by default. This ensures that when you change the height or width of a picture, the corresponding dimension is resized proportionally. That way, you don't turn a tall thin person into a short fat person.)

Drag a handle to resize
or reshape a picture.

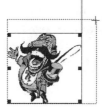

You can use the handles around an object to resize it.

Touching Up a Picture with the Picture Toolbar

The Picture toolbar is like a graphics program built right into your desktop. With about ten buttons, this toolbar enables you to adjust the picture's brightness and contrast, crop the image (to use only a portion of it), transform a color picture into grayscale or black-and-white, add a border around the picture, and even change the way text wraps around it:

 Insert Picture. Enables you to insert a graphics file from disk.

 Image Control. Displays a menu that enables you to transform a color image into grayscale, black and white, or a watermark (a ghost image that can lie on top of text without hiding it).

More Contrast. Is like a TV control that increases the contrast of the image.

Less Contrast. Decreases the contrast in an image.

 More Brightness. Makes the image brighter.

 Less Brightness. Makes the image darker.

 Crop. Turns the mouse pointer into a cropping tool. Move the pointer over one of the handles and drag it to chop off a portion of the picture. You can use the cropping tool to uncrop a cropped picture, as well.

63

Line Style. Enables you to add a border around the picture.

 Text Wrapping. Does the same thing as the options on the Layout tab described earlier, but this control is a lot easier to use.

 Format Picture (or Format Object). Displays the Format Picture or Format Object dialog box, which offers plenty of options for changing the appearance and layout of the image.

 Set Transparent Color. Makes the selected color in a picture transparent so that the background of the page (paper) or screen shows through. Click this button, and then click the color you want to make transparent. (This button is unavailable for most clip art images.)

 Reset Picture. Changes the options back to their original settings in case you mess up while entering changes.

Sketching Custom Illustrations

Word offers a Drawing toolbar that offers several tools that you can use to create your own drawings, logos, flow charts, illustrations, and other simple graphics. You can also use these tools to modify and enhance existing drawings. To turn on the Drawing toolbar, click the **Drawing** button or right-click any toolbar and choose **Drawing**. The following sections show you how to use the drawing tools to create your own custom illustrations.

Creating Drawings with Simple Lines and Shapes

Technical illustrators typically have a collection of rulers and templates that they use to draw lines, ovals, rectangles, curves, triangles, and other shapes. They assemble these very basic geometric shapes to create complex illustrations. This is the same technique you use to create drawings in Word.

The Drawing toolbar enables you to place five different geometrical objects on a page: a line, an arrow, an oval, a rectangle, and an AutoShape (a predrawn object, such as a diamond, heart, or starburst). In addition, you can use the Shadow and 3D tools to transform two-dimensional objects, such as squares, into three-dimensional objects, such as cubes.

You follow the same procedure for drawing any of these objects. Click the button for the object you want to draw (or choose a shape from the AutoShapes menu), and then drag the mouse on the page to create the object. For more control over the drawing tool, use the following techniques:

➤ Hold down the **Ctrl** key while dragging to draw the object out from an imaginary center point. Without the Ctrl key, you drag the object out from its corner or starting point.

➤ Hold down the **Shift** key while dragging to create a uniform shape (a perfect square or circle).

➤ Hold down **Ctrl+Shift** while dragging to draw the object out from its center point and create a uniform shape.

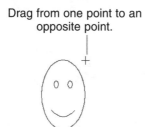

Drag from one point to an opposite point.

Click a drawing tool and then drag the object into existence.

After you have an object on the page, you can use some of the other buttons in the Drawing toolbar to change qualities of the object, such as its fill color and the color and width of the line that defines it. First select the shape whose qualities you want to change. Then use the following buttons to change the object's qualities:

 Free Rotate. Enables you to spin the object. When you click this button, little green circles surround the selected object. Drag a circle clockwise or counterclockwise to spin the object.

 Fill Color. Colors inside the lines (as you would in a coloring book). Click the button to fill the object with the color that's shown. To change the fill color, click the arrow next to this button and select a color from the menu.

 Line Color. Changes the color of the line that defines the shape. Click the button to use the color that's shown. To change the color, click the arrow next to this button and select a color from the menu.

 Font Color. Is for text boxes only. Drag over the text inside the box, open Font Color, and select the desired color.

 Line Style. Displays a menu from which you can choose the line thickness and style that you want to use for the line that defines the shape.

65

Dash Style. Enables you to use dashed lines instead of solid lines.

 Arrow Style. Works only for arrows that you have drawn. Select the arrow, and then use this menu to pick the type of arrow that you want to use or to change the direction it points.

 Shadow. Works only for ovals, rectangles, AutoShapes, and other two-dimensional objects (including text boxes). This menu contains various drop-shadow styles that you can apply to objects.

 3D. Works for ovals, rectangles, AutoShapes, and text boxes. It turns rectangles into blocks and ovals into cylinders. What it does to AutoShapes, you have to see for yourself.

Graphics and Text

You can add some interesting special effects to a document by combining text with AutoShapes. For sales brochures or announcements, for example, you might consider placing small bits of text inside a starburst. Just lay a text box on top of the starburst.

Working with Layers of Objects

Working with two or more drawing objects on a page is like playing with a Colorforms toy; you know, those storyboards with the vinyl characters you stick on and peel off to create various scenes? The trouble with these objects is that when you place one on top of another, the top object blocks the bottom one and prevents you from selecting it. You have to flip through the deck to find the object that you want. Word offers a couple of drawing tools that can help you flip through the stack and create groups of objects, which makes it easier to maneuver them.

The first thing you need to do is reorder the objects. You can send an object that's up front back one layer or all the way to the bottom of the stack, or you can bring an object from the back to the front. First, click the object that you want to move (if possible). Some objects are buried so deep that you can't get to them. In such a case, you have to move objects from the front to the back to get them out of the way until you find the one you want.

After selecting the object that you want to move, right-click it, point to **Order**, and select the desired movement: **Bring to Front**, **Send to Back**, **Bring Forward**, **Send Backward**, **Bring in Front of Text**, or **Send Behind Text**.

Working with Two or More Objects as a Group

After you've created a drawing or a portion of a drawing consisting of several shapes, it becomes difficult to move this loose collection of shapes or to resize it. If you drag one object, you ruin its relative position with the other objects. Similarly, if you need to shrink or enlarge the drawing, you shouldn't have to resize each object separately. And you don't have to. Word enables you to group two or more objects so that you can move and resize them as if they were a single object.

To create a group, click the **Select Objects** button in the Drawing toolbar and drag a selection box around all the objects that you want to include in the group (or just Shift+click each object). Handles appear around all the selected objects. (When dragging a selection box, make sure the box completely surrounds all desired objects; if a portion of an object is outside the box, it may not get selected.)

Next, right-click one of the selected objects, point to **Grouping** and click **Group** (or open the **Draw** menu in the Drawing toolbar and select **Group)**. The handles around the individual objects disappear, and a single set of handles appears around the group. You can now drag a handle to resize all the objects in the group, or you can drag any object in the group to move the group.

To turn off grouping so that you can work with an individual object, open the **Draw** menu again and click **Ungroup**. After you're done working with the individual object, you can regroup the objects by opening the **Draw** menu and selecting **Regroup**.

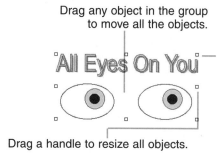

Drag any object in the group
to move all the objects.

*You can group two or
more objects and treat
them as a single object.*

A single set
of handles appears
around the group.

Drag a handle to resize all objects.

Check This Out

Try This!

If you insert a picture from your hard disk using Insert, Object, you may be able to select the image, ungroup its component parts, and edit the image. Unfortunately, this doesn't work with the Office clip art.

67

Editing Existing Pictures

Suppose one of your friends or colleagues sent you a graphic or you copied one off the Internet. You like the overall design, but it needs a few minor adjustments. You definitely don't want to redraw it from scratch. The solution? Insert the graphic into a Word document (as explained earlier in this chapter) and double-click it. This opens the picture in a drawing window.

When Word displays the picture in the drawing window, gray lines surround the picture. These define the object's boundaries; whatever is inside the gray lines will be inserted as a picture into your document. Anything outside the lines will be chopped off. To change the position of these lines, drag the markers in the vertical and horizontal toolbars.

After you've set up the markers, use the buttons in the Drawing toolbar to add shapes to the existing drawing. Keep in mind that you can use the Picture toolbar to modify the existing picture. When you're done, click the **Close Picture** button.

Chapter 7

Checking Your Spelling and Grammar

In This Chapter

➤ Proofreading for lazy people

➤ Check spelling and grammar as you type

➤ Use AutoCorrect to automatically correct common typos

➤ Use a thesaurus to find just the right word

In this era of electronic communications in which people are sharing documents, rifling off email messages, and having virtual meetings with chat programs, written communications skills are becoming much more important. No matter how well you speak, if your writing is unclear and packed with typos and grammatical errors, your colleagues and customers are going to think you're a dolt.

Word offers a couple of tools that can help you clean up your writing. The spelling checker can catch most of your spelling errors and typos; the grammar checker can help you avoid passive voice and other grammatical no-no's; and the thesaurus can help you think up just the right word. In this chapter, you learn how to use these tools and a few others to clean up your prose.

What About the Other Office Applications?

The spelling checker is shared among all Office applications, including Excel and PowerPoint. So if you need to check your spreadsheets and presentations for spelling errors and typos, refer to this chapter for instructions.

Looking for Mis Spellings

Word provides more than one way for you to check your spelling. Word can check your spelling on-the-fly as you type, or after you're done typing. You can also customize the spelling checker to have it skip over special character strings such as acronyms (NAACP, for instance) and Internet addresses (such as www.mcp.com). The following sections show you what to do.

Spell-Checking on the Go

By default, Word is set up to check for possible spelling errors as you type. If you type a word that does not have a matching entry in Word's spelling dictionary, Word displays a squiggly red line below the word. You have several options at this point:

➤ Ignore the line.

➤ Backspace over the misspelled word and type the correct spelling.

➤ Right-click the word in question to display a pop-up menu that may contain suggested corrections. If you see the correct spelling, click it.

➤ Right-click the word and select **Ignore All** to have Word remove its annoying red squiggly line and tell it not to question the spelling of this word in this document again.

➤ Right-click the word and select **Add** to add the word to Word's spelling dictionary. After the word is in the dictionary, Word does not question its spelling in any document again.

➤ Right-click the word, point to **AutoCorrect**, and select the correct spelling of the word. (See "Making Word Automatically Correct Your Typos," later in this chapter, for details.)

Right-click the word to display a list of suggested corrections.

Right-click the questionable word.

You can select the correct spelling if it's listed.

If the word is spelled correctly, you can add it to the dictionary.

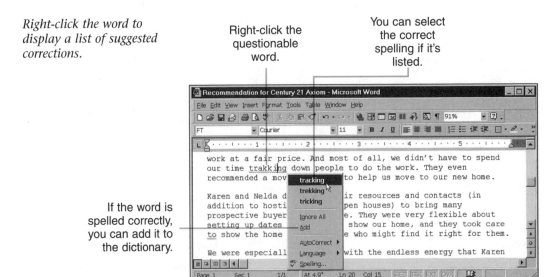

Personally, I find it offensive to see squiggly red lines popping up as I type. They give me flashbacks to grade school, where good writing meant every word was spelled correctly and you followed the grammar rules. To turn off automatic spell checking, open the **Tools** menu, select **Options**, and click the **Spelling & Grammar** tab. Click **Check Spelling As You Type** to remove the check from the box, and then click **OK**. If you turn off this option, be sure to check the document's spelling before you print it, as explained in the following section.

Spell-Checking Just Before You Hand It In

If you took my advice and turned off the check-as-you-type option, you can use Word to perform one of these last-minute spell checks for you. To do so, open the **Tools** menu and select **Spelling and Grammar** or click the Spelling and Grammar button in the Standard toolbar. Word starts checking your document and stops on the first questionable word. The Spelling and Grammar dialog box displays the word in red and usually displays a list of suggested corrections. You have several options:

➤ Double-click the word in the Not in Dictionary text box, type the correction, and click **Change**.

➤ Click **Ignore** if the word is spelled correctly and you want to skip it just this once. Word stops on the next occurrence of the word.

➤ Click **Ignore All** if the word is spelled correctly but is not in the dictionary and you want Word to skip any other occurrences of this word in this document.

➤ Click **Add** to add the word to the dictionary so that the spelling checker never questions it again in any of your Office documents (the dictionary is shared by all Office applications).

➤ If the word is spelled incorrectly and the Suggestions list displays the correct spelling, click the correct spelling and click **Change** to replace only this occurrence of the word.

➤ To replace this misspelled word and all other occurrences of the word in this document, click the correct spelling in the Suggestions list and click **Change All**.

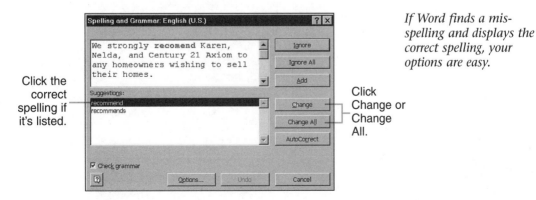

Click the correct spelling if it's listed.

Click Change or Change All.

If Word finds a misspelling and displays the correct spelling, your options are easy.

When Word completes the spelling check, it displays a dialog box telling you so. Click **OK**.

Check a Word

To check the spelling of a single word or paragraph, double-click the word or triple-click the paragraph to select it before you start the spelling checker. When Word is done checking the selection, it displays a dialog box asking if you want to check the rest of the document.

Customizing the Spelling Checker

The spelling checker is your flunky. You tell it what to do and how to do it, and the spelling checker carries out your instructions. To display the spelling checker options, either click the **Options** button during a spelling check, or open the **Tools** menu, click **Options**, and click the **Spelling & Grammar** tab.

Most of the options on this tab are self-explanatory, but a couple might give you trouble, such as Hide Spelling Errors in This Document. This option tells Word to hide the squiggly red lines under questionable words as you type. Always Suggest Corrections tells Word to display a list of possible corrections for any questionable word. You should probably keep this option on. If any other options confuse you, right-click the option and select **What's This?**

You can tell the spelling checker how to do its job.

The spelling checker options

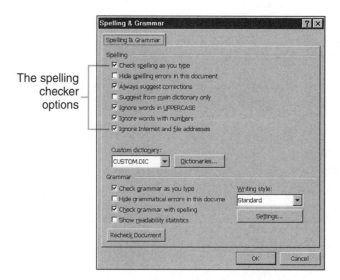

Making Word Automatically Correct Your Typos

One of my favorite features in Word is AutoCorrect. I type **teh**, and Word inserts **the**. I start a sentence with a lowercase character, and AutoCorrect capitalizes it. Now *that's* a feature!

To create an AutoCorrect entry on-the-fly, simply choose the AutoCorrect option when the spelling checker stops on a questionable word. When you create an AutoCorrect entry, you pair a commonly misspelled (or mistyped) word with its correct spelling. Whenever you type the misspelling and follow it with a space or punctuation mark, Word automatically inserts the correction.

You can edit the list of paired words to create additional AutoCorrect entries or to delete entries. Open the **Tools** menu and choose **AutoCorrect**. The AutoCorrect dialog box appears, displaying a list of options for controlling the behavior of AutoCorrect and displaying a list of AutoCorrect pairs. Set your preferences using the check box options at the top of the dialog box.

To create a new AutoCorrect pair, click in the **Replace** text box and type the text that you want Word to automatically replace. Tab to the **With** text box, and type the text with which you want Word to replace it. You can type more than one word in either or both text boxes, and you can choose to have the replacement text formatted. When you're done, click the **Add** button. To remove a pair from the list, click the pair and then click the **Delete** button.

Type the typo here.

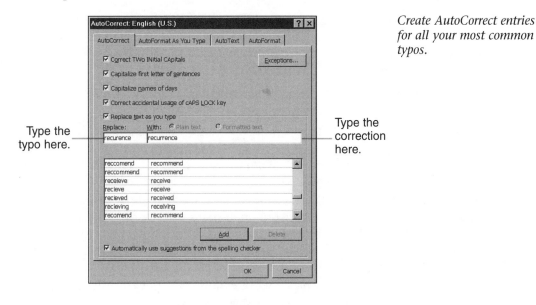

Type the correction here.

Create AutoCorrect entries for all your most common typos.

Create Your Own Shorthand

You can create your own shorthand by using AutoText entries (explained in Chapter 3, "Making and Editing Word Documents"), but then you have to type and press the F3 key to insert a word or phrase. Instead of creating AutoText entries, create an AutoCorrect entry, so you won't have to press F3.

Write Good with the Grammar Checker

Grammar checkers are easy to fool. If you write short subject-verb sentences without contractions, the grammar checker ranks your writing skills right up there with Dr. Seuss and Forrest Gump. The grammar checker doesn't care whether your writing is entertaining, insightful, or even well organized. As long as you don't break any rules, you're a genius. In addition, grammar checkers aren't always right and often suggest changes that are downright absurd.

With that in mind, I'm going to keep this section brief. The grammar checker options are similar to those of the spelling checker (and they're on the same tab). To change them, open the **Tools** menu, select **Options**, and click the **Spelling & Grammar** tab. Enter your preferences of the following:

➤ *Check Grammar As You Type.* Draws a green squiggly line under questionable phrases and sentences.

➤ *Hide Grammatical Errors in This Document.* Hides the green squiggly lines as you type.

➤ *Check Grammar with Spelling.* Tells Word to check both grammar and spelling at the same time whenever you choose to spell check a document.

➤ *Show Readability Statistics.* Displays a message at the end of the grammar check showing the reading level required to understand your writing. For instance, if you're writing a children's book and the readability statistics show that you're writing for college kids, you might need to simplify your vocabulary and sentence structure.

➤ *Writing Style.* Enables you to pick a set of grammatical rules for various types of writing, such as technical, formal, or casual writing.

➤ *Settings.* Enables you to turn individual grammar rules on or off.

➤ *Recheck Document.* Rechecks the document using the preferences you just entered.

Word's Helpful, Useful, Beneficial Thesaurus

Suppose you're writing your letter of resignation to your supervisor, and you can't think of a less offensive word than "stupid." The dictionary's no help, and you can't really ask around the office. What do you do? Take the following steps to look up alternative words in the thesaurus:

1. Click the word to place the insertion point somewhere inside it.

2. Open the **Tools** menu, point to **Language**, and click **Thesaurus** (or just press **Shift+F7**). Word displays the Thesaurus dialog box, providing a list of alternative words or phrases.

3. If the Meanings list has more than one word, click the word that most closely matches your intended meaning. If you look up "stupid," for example, the Meanings list displays "unintelligent," "dim," "brainless," and so on. The Replace with Synonym list displays suggested replacement words.

4. If the Replace with Synonym list contains a word that's pretty close to the one that you want but just not quite it, click the word and click the **Look Up** button or double-click the word. (If the list of synonyms that you get next is worse than the previous list, click the **Previous** button.)

5. When you find the word you want or a word that's as close as the thesaurus can find, click it and click the **Replace** button. (The Replace with Synonym list may also include antonyms, cleverly marked with "(antonym)" following the word.

2. Click a word and click **Look Up** to display its synonyms.

The thesaurus can help you find the perfect word.

1. Click a meaning that's close.

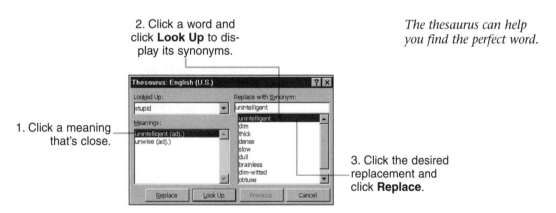

3. Click the desired replacement and click **Replace**.

Chapter 8

Creating Mailing Labels and Form Letters

In This Chapter

➤ Addressing an envelope with your printer

➤ Laying out and printing address labels

➤ Creating your very own personalized form letters

➤ Doing mass mailings with mail merge

Face it, you're a mail junkie. Your motivation to wake up in the morning comes only from the possibility that you might receive a piece of mail addressed specifically to you. You stare out the window to catch the familiar gait of your mail carrier. You're on a first-name basis with the UPS delivery person. You just can't get enough. And you know that the only way to get mail is to send mail.

This chapter shows you how to use a couple of features that can help you address your paper mail correspondence. You learn how to easily print addresses on envelopes or mailing labels and merge a form letter with a list of names and addresses to create a stack of personalized letters for mass mailings.

Quick and Easy Letters

The easiest way to write and format a letter is to use the Letter Wizard. Choose **File**, **New**, click the **Letters & Faxes** tab, and double-click **Letter Wizard**. Or, create a new document, open the **Tools** menu, and choose **Letter Wizard**. The Letter Wizard dialog box displays a fill-in-the-blank form that you can use to specify your preferences and enter information such as the inside address, the salutation, and the closing.

Addressing an Envelope or Mailing Label

Most of the letters I receive from friends and family members have obviously been typed and printed using a computer; but for some strange reason, they arrive in handwritten envelopes. I guess it just takes too much time and effort to position the two addresses on the front of that skinny little envelope. Fortunately, Word can print addresses for you on envelopes or mailing labels.

Addressing an Envelope

To print an address on an envelope, open the **Tools** menu, click **Envelopes and Labels**, and make sure that the Envelopes tab is up front. Type the recipient's name and address in the **Delivery Address** text box. (If you already wrote your letter, Word lifts the recipient's address from the letter and inserts it in the Delivery Address text box.) Tab to the **Return Address** text box and type your address. You can format selected text in the Delivery or Return Address text boxes by highlighting the text and pressing the key combination for the desired formatting—for example, Ctrl+B for bold. You can also right-click the text and choose **Font** for additional formatting options.

Enter the delivery and return addresses.

Type the recipient's name and address here.

Type your name and address here.

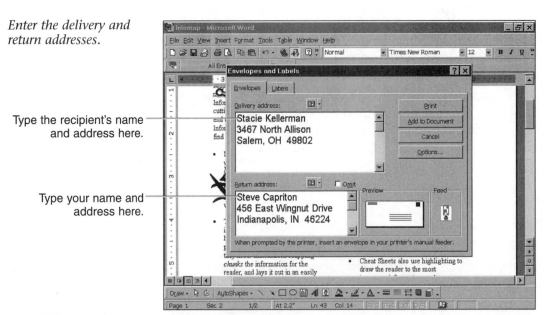

Before you print, click the **Options** button. This displays the Envelope Options dialog box, which allows you to specify the envelope size and the fonts for the delivery and return addresses. The Printing Options tab allows you to specify how the envelopes feed into your printer. Enter your preferences and click the **OK** button.

If you need to manually load the envelope into your printer, load away. All printers are different; check your printer's documentation to determine the proper loading technique. When the envelope is in position, click the **Print** button to print it.

Addressing a Mailing Label

To print a single label or a whole page of labels with the same address or other information, open the **Tools** menu, select **Envelopes and Labels**, and make sure the **Labels** tab is up front. In the Address text box, type the name and address you want printed on the mailing label. (You can print your return address by clicking the **Use Return Address** check box, instead.)

Dry Run

Before printing on a relatively expensive envelope or a sheet of mailing labels, print the envelope or mailing labels on a normal sheet of paper to check the position of the print. You can then make adjustments without wasting costly supplies.

Under Print, specify whether you want to print a single label (and specify the location of the label on the label sheet) or a full page of labels.

Click the **Options** button, use the Label Options dialog box to specify the type of label on which you are printing, and click **OK**. Load the sheet of labels into your printer and click the **Print** button.

Make a Personal Address Book

Just above the text boxes in which you type the delivery and return addresses (for either an envelope or a mailing label) is the Insert Address button. Click this button to create an address book containing the names and addresses of people to whom you commonly send letters. You can then quickly insert a person's address by clicking the arrow next to the button and choosing the person's name. You can also use the address book in mail merges, as explained in the next section.

Merging Your Address List with a Form Letter

You've been getting them for years from Publisher's Clearing House, Reader's Digest, MasterCard, Visa, window installers, and even America Online, all addressed to you (or some guy named Current Resident), selling you products you don't need and dreams of being someone you're not.

Now it's your turn. The following sections show you how to do your own mass mailings right from your desktop.

First You Need Some Data

To perform a mail merge, you need a letter and a list of the names, addresses, and other information you want to insert in the letter. Let's start with the list of names and addresses (hence referred to as the *data source*). You can use any of the following several data sources for the mail merge:

➤ An Outlook address book. (See Chapter 22, "Keeping Track of Dates, Mates, and Things to Do.")

➤ An Access database.

➤ An Excel spreadsheet with column headings.

➤ A Word table. The first row must contain headings describing the contents of the cells in that column. Each row contains information about an individual. See the following figure.

You can use a Word table or Excel spread-sheet as your data source.

A field name can be as many as 40 characters, no spaces, and must begin with a letter.

Each cell contains a piece of information.

Each row, called a record, contains information for one person.

Title	FirstName	LastName	Address	City	State	ZIPCode
Mr.	Mary	Abolt	8517 Grandview Avenue	San Diego	CA	77987
Ms.	Carey	Bistro	987 N. Cumbersome Lane	Detroit	MI	88687
Ms.	Adrienne	Bullow	5643 N. Gaylord Ave.	Philadelphia	PA	27639
Mr.	Chuck	Burger	6754 W. Lakeview Drive	Boston	MA	56784
Mr.	Nicholas	Capetti	1345 W. Bilford Ave.	New Orleans	LA	12936
Ms.	Gary	Davell	76490 E. Bilmew	New York	NY	76453
Mr.	Kathy	Estrich	8763 W. Cloverdale Ave.	Paradise	TX	54812
Ms.	Joseph	Fugal	2764 W. 56th Place	Chicago	IL	60678
Mr.	Marie	Gabel	8784 N. Demetrius Blvd.	Miami	FL	88330
Mr.	Lisa	Kasdan	8976 Westhaven Drive	Orlando	FL	88329
Ms.	William	Kennedy	5567 Bluehill Circle	Indianapolis	IN	46224
Ms.	Marion	Kraft	1313 Mockingbird Lane	Los Angeles	CA	77856
Ms.	John	Kramden	5401 N. Bandy	Pittsburgh	PA	27546
Mr.	Mitch	Kroll	674 E. Cooperton Drive	Seattle	WA	14238
Mr.	Gregg	Lawrence	5689 N. Bringshire Blvd.	Boston	MA	56784
Mr.	Allison	Milton	32718 S. Visionary Drive	Phoenix	AZ	97612
Ms.	Barry	Strong	908 N. 9th Street	Chicago	IL	60643

Then You Need a Form Letter

How you compose your form letter is your business. You can type it from scratch, use a template, or seek help from the Letter Wizard. Omit any information that Word obtains from the data source during the merge, such as the person's name and address. After you complete the letter, you insert field label codes into the letter (one for the person's name, one for the address, and so on). During the merge operation, these codes pull information from the data source and insert it in each letter.

Now You Can Merge

Once you have your form letter and data source, let the fun begin! This is a long process; but if you follow me step by step, you can pull off this merge thing without a hitch:

1. Create or open your form letter.

2. Crank down the **Tools** menu and select **Mail Merge**. The Mail Merge Helper dialog box appears; it leads you through the merge operation.

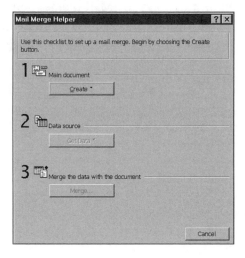

The Mail Merge Helper dialog box leads you through the three-step process.

3. Click **Create** (under Main Document), select **Form Letters**, and click **Active Window**. This tells Word to use your letter as the main document in the merge.

4. Under Data Source, click **Get Data**. Then select one of the following options and perform the necessary steps to select the source of data that you want to use for the merge:

   Create Data Source. Leads you through the process of creating a Word table containing the data that you want to merge with your form letter.

   Open Data Source. Enables you to select an Excel spreadsheet file, another Word file (which contains a properly formatted table), a text file, or a database file (created in Access, Paradox, dBASE, or FoxPro) as your data source.

   Use Address Book. Displays a dialog box asking whether you want to use your personal address book or an address book created in Outlook.

   Header Options. Enables you to use one file that contains the names of the data fields and another file that contains the data entries themselves. You can live a full life without ever selecting this option.

5. The Microsoft Word dialog box appears, telling you that your form letter has no merge fields (as if you didn't know). Click **Edit Main Document**. Word returns you to your form letter and displays the Mail Merge toolbar.

6. Position the insertion point where you want to insert a piece of data from the database. For example, you might move the insertion point just below the date to insert the person's name and address.

7. Open the **Insert Merge Field** drop-down list in the Mail Merge toolbar and click the name of the field you want to insert. This inserts a code (such as <<FirstName>>) that will pull specified data (a person's first name, in this case) from the data source and inserts it into your letter.

8. Repeat step 7 to insert additional merge field codes. Add punctuation between the codes as necessary. For example, if you are assembling codes to create an inside address, you need to add spaces and commas in the following way:

   <<Title>> <<FirstName>> <<LastName>>
   <<Address>>
   <<City>>, <<State>> <<ZIP>>

9. If your database contains information that you want to insert in the salutation or body of the letter, insert a field merge code wherever you want that information to appear. You might, for example, use the following salutation:

   Dear <<Title>> <<LastName>>,

Select a field name to insert a code in your letter.

Click the **Mail Merge Helper** button to display the Mail Merge Helper dialog box at any time.

Insert codes to pull entries from the data source into your letter.

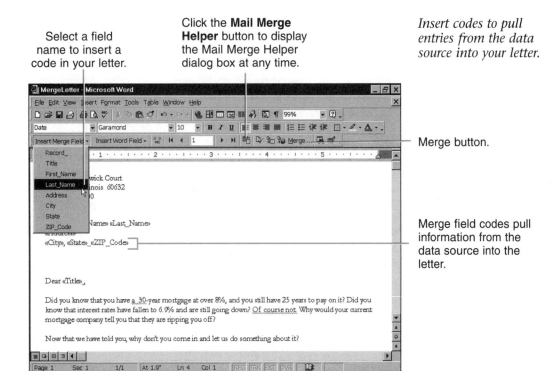

Merge button.

Merge field codes pull information from the data source into the letter.

10. Click the **Merge** button. The Merge dialog box appears, offering the following options for controlling how Word merges the form letter and data source:

    Merge To. Enables you to merge to the printer, to a new document, or to your email program. It's a good idea to merge to a new document so that you can check for errors before printing. You can also flip through the merged document and personalize the form letters that Word generates.

    Records to Be Merged. Enables you to select a range of records (so you can create letters for only selected records in the data source).

    When Merging Records. Tells Word whether or not to insert blank lines when a particular field in a record is blank.

    Query Options. Displays a dialog box that enables you to sort the merged letters or create letters for a specific collection of records.

11. Enter your merge preferences, and then click the **Merge** button. If you choose to merge to the printer, Word starts printing the letters. If you choose to merge to a new file, Word opens a new document window and places the merged letters in this window. You can then print them.

Other Data That You Can Merge

If your data source contains specific information about each person, you can insert that information into the body of your letter. A financial advisor, for instance, might keep a list of clients along with the dates of their last appointments. The advisor could then insert something such as, "The last time we discussed your finances was on <<LastDate>>. We should meet soon to reevaluate your financial situation."

Using Mail Merge to Do Mailing Labels

Now that you have a stack of letters, you need to address them. You can do this by using a mailing label as your main document and merging it with the database. Perform the same steps that you performed in the previous section; but in step 3, open the **Create** menu and select **Mailing Labels**.

After you select the data source to use, click the Set Up Main Document button to display the Label Options dialog box, asking you to specify the type and size of the mailing labels on which you intend to print. This dialog box contains a long list of label manufacturers and label types. If the label type on which you're printing is in the list, select it. Enter your preferences and click **OK**.

The Mail Merge Helper then displays the Create Labels dialog box, which enables you to insert the merge field codes for creating the label. Click the **Insert Merge Field** button to insert the codes. Type any required punctuation between codes. To change the font used for the label, drag over the codes, right-click the selection, and click **Font**.

You can use mail merge to create pages of address labels.

Use this button to insert merge codes.

Type commas and spaces as needed.

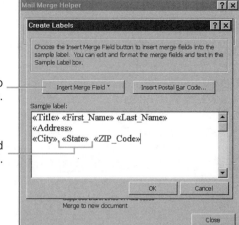

84

CHUNG CHUNG CHUNG

OOPS.

Chapter 9

Everything You've Always Wanted to Know About Printing Documents

In This Chapter

➤ Making a two-page essay run three pages with a few clever margin adjustments

➤ Forcing Word to number your pages for you

➤ Printing a footer on the bottom of every page

➤ Interior decorating with page borders

➤ Sending your document to the printer

Up to this point, you have been micromanaging the document—formatting blocks of text, adding tables and columns, and inserting pictures and other clips. Before you print your document, however, you need to perform a few macromanagement tasks, such as setting the page margins, correcting any funky page breaks, adding page numbers, and perhaps even decorating your page with an attractive border.

This chapter shows you how to perform these preprinting tasks and how to send your completed document off to the printer.

Publishing Electronically?

Although the paperless age hasn't quite arrived, you can publish your document electronically on the World Wide Web. If that's your intent, skip to Chapter 25, "Creating and Publishing Your Own Web Pages."

Setting Up Your Pages for Printing

After typing a document, it's tempting to just click the **Print** button in the Standard toolbar to crank out a paper copy of the document. Avoid the temptation. You usually just end up wasting paper and being sorely disappointed with the results. Before you print, you should first check the Page Setup options.

To display the Page Setup options, open the **File** menu and select **Page Setup**. The Page Setup dialog box appears, presenting four tabs for changing various page and print settings. In the following sections, you learn how to use this dialog box to set margins and control the way Word prints text on the pages.

Setting the Page Margins

The very first time the Page Setup dialog box appears, the Margins tab is up front. If it's hiding, click it to bring it to the front. This tab enables you to change the top, bottom, left, and right margins. Click the up or down arrow to the right of each margin setting to change the setting in increments of .1 inch, or click in a margin setting text box and type a more precise measurement.

The Margins tab offers several additional options for special printing needs:

➤ *Gutter* enables you to add margin space to the inside margin of the pages, in case you plan to insert the pages into a book or binder.

➤ *From Edge* specifies the distance from the top of the page to the top of the header and from the bottom of the page to the bottom of the footer. (For details about headers and footers, see "Head-Banging Headers and Foot-Stomping Footers" later in this chapter.)

➤ *Mirror Margins* is useful if you plan to print on both sides of a page. When this option is on, Word makes the inside margins of facing pages equal.

➤ *2 Pages Per Sheet* shrinks the pages of your document so Word can print two pages on a single sheet of paper.

➤ *Apply To* enables you to apply the margin settings to the entire document, from this point forward in the document, or to only selected text. This is useful for long documents that may require different page layouts for some sections.

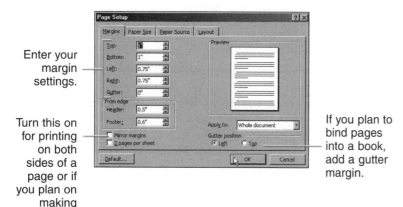

Enter your margin settings.

Turn this on for printing on both sides of a page or if you plan on making two-sided copies.

Set the margins for the entire document.

If you plan to bind pages into a book, add a gutter margin.

Picking a Paper Size and Print Direction

Usually, you print a document right-side-up on 8 1/2-by-11 inch paper. In some cases, however, you may need to print on legal-size paper or print a wide document, such as an announcement or sign, sideways on the page. If that's the case, check out the Paper Size tab. On this tab, you can pick from a list of standard paper sizes or specify a custom size. You can also select a print orientation: **Portrait** (to print normally, as in this book) or **Landscape** (to print sideways on the page). Landscape is especially useful if you choose the 2 Pages Per Sheet option.

Where's Your Paper Coming From?

If you always print on standard 8 1/2-by-11-inch paper, you don't really need to worry about where the paper is coming from. Your printer is set up to use the default paper tray, which is typically loaded with 8 1/2-by-11-inch paper, and all your programs know that. If, however, you need to print envelopes, banners, or any other paper that's not 8 1/2-by-11-inch, check the Paper Source tab before you start printing just to make sure that Word is set up to use the right tray.

Laying Out Your Pages

The last tab in the Page Setup dialog box is the Layout tab. Ignore most of the options on the Layout tab and focus on the following three options:

Vertical Alignment. The Vertical Alignment drop-down list is very useful for making one-page documents (such as a short letter) look good on the page. Open the drop-down list and select **Center** to center the document on the page. This option is especially useful for printing cover pages. To make the document fill the page, select **Justified**.

Line Numbers. The Line Numbers button is useful for legal and literary pieces. These types of documents often contain line numbers so that people can refer to the line numbers when discussing the documents, instead of quoting entire lines and sounding really boring. To insert line numbers, click the button and enter your preferences.

Borders. The Borders button opens the Borders and Shading dialog box, which allows you to add a border around your entire page or at the top, bottom, left, or right margin. For details on how to enter settings in the Borders and Shading dialog box, see "Giving Your Table a Face-Lift with Borders and Shading," in Chapter 5.

Adding Page Numbers

You really have no excuse for not numbering the pages in a multipage document, because Word can do it for you. You can insert a page number code in a header or footer (see "Head-Banging Headers and Foot-Stomping Footers" later in this chapter), or you can use the Insert, Page Numbers command. Follow these steps to use the latter method:

1. Open the **Insert** menu and select **Page Numbers**. The Page Numbers dialog box appears.

2. Open the **Position** drop-down list and specify whether you want the page numbers printed at the top or bottom of the page.

3. Open the **Alignment** drop-down list and select where you want the page number placed in relation to the left and right margins. (The Inside and Outside options are for positioning page numbers on pages that will be bound in a book.)

4. If the first page is a cover page or you just don't want a page number on the first page, make sure that there is no check mark in the **Show Number on First Page** box.

5. Click the **Format** button, enter any additional preferences, and click **OK**. The Page Format dialog box, shown in the following figure, allows you to change the numbering scheme, include chapter numbers, or start with a page number other than 1.

6. Click **OK** to save your changes. The page number is inserted inside a header or footer.

Use these options to include the chapter number.

Select a numbering scheme.

You can start numbering with a different number.

The Page Number Format dialog box offers additional controls.

Viewing Page Numbers

Page numbers do not appear in Normal view. To view page numbers, switch to Print Layout view or Print Preview. You can also view and edit them in the header or footer: Open the **View** menu and select **Header and Footer**. If you're in Print Layout view, simply double-click the header or footer.

Chopping Your Text into Pages

Typing in Word is like working in a sausage factory. As you type, Word stuffs your text and divides it into neat little pages. Word divides the text into pages using *soft page breaks*, which can move automatically as you add or delete text. The trouble is that you might not like where Word divides your text. Word might divide an important list over two pages or perform other similar atrocities. You need a way to control these breaks.

In Print Layout view, you can easily identify a page break by the top or bottom edges of the onscreen pages. In Normal view, a soft page break appears as a dotted horizontal line. If you don't like where Word inserted the page break, insert your own break (a *hard page break*, which stays put). Move the insertion point to the beginning of the paragraph before which you want the break inserted and press **Ctrl+Enter**.

If you insert a break and later decide that it's not working out, you can delete the break or move it. First, change to Normal view (**View**, **Normal**). To select a break, click it. To delete a selected break, press the **Del** key. To move a break, drag it.

Head-Banging Headers and Foot-Stomping Footers

Headers and footers are great tools for stitching together a document and helping your audience find specific pages and information. Headers and footers can include all sorts of useful information, such as the title of the document or of a section inside the document, the date on which the document was created, chapter numbers, page numbers, and the total number of pages in the document. The following figure shows a sample header displayed in Print Layout view.

Header in Print Layout view.

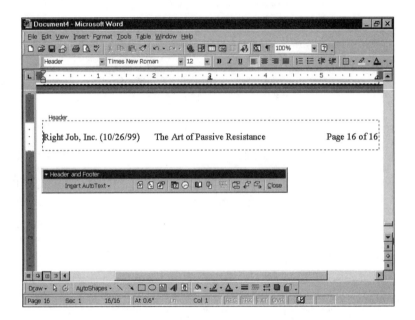

To insert a header or footer, open the **View** menu and select **Header and Footer**. This displays the Header and Footer toolbar and the header of the first page (which should be empty, unless you have gremlins or you inserted page numbers earlier). You can scroll down to see the footer. Before you start typing, familiarize yourself with the Header and Footer toolbar buttons:

 Insert Page Number. Automatically inserts the correct page number on each page. To insert the word "Page," you must type it and then click the Insert Page Number button.

 Insert Number of Pages. Is a new button that inserts the total number of pages in the document. You can use this feature to create headers or footers that say "Page 2 of 27," for example. This feature is very useful for documents that are faxed.

Format Page Number. Displays the Page Number Format dialog box, which enables you to include the chapter number and enter other preferences.

 Insert Date. Inserts a field code that inserts the date from your computer's internal clock.

 Insert Time. Inserts a field code that inserts the current time from your computer's clock.

Automatic Date/Time Changes

When you use the Insert Date or Insert Time button to insert the date or time, Word inserts a field code that pulls the date or time from your computer's clock. The date and time change automatically to reflect the current date and time on your computer. To keep the date from changing, click it and press **Ctrl+Shift+F9**.

 Page Setup. Enables you to create a different header or footer for odd pages and even pages. Use the Show Previous and Show Next buttons to move between the boxes for entering the odd and even page headers or footers.

 Show/Hide Document Text. Turns the document text display on or off. When Hiding, all you see on the screen is the header or footer text box.

 Same as Previous. Enables you to use the same header or footer for this section that you used for the previous section (or a revised version).

 Switch Between Header and Footer. Tells Word to display the footer box if you are currently using the header box and vice versa.

 Show Previous. Moves to the previous header or footer so that you can edit it.

 Show Next. Moves to the next header or footer.

After you are familiar with the buttons, click the **Switch Between Header and Footer** button to display the Header box or the Footer box. Type your text, using the Insert buttons as desired to insert the page number, date, time, or total page count. You can use any of the text formatting options to enhance the appearance of your header or footer. When you're done playing around, click the **Close** button.

Inserting Pictures in a Header or Footer

In addition to enhancing text in the header or footer, consider adding a logo or other graphic, a WordArt object, or a simple line to accent it.

Shrink to Fit

If you have a short document with a few lines of text stranded on the last page, click the Shrink to Fit button in the Print Preview toolbar. Word automatically decreases the font size of all the text to pull the excess text to the bottom of the previous page.

Previewing Pages Before Printing Them

Before you print the document, click the **Print Preview** button in the Standard toolbar. This gives you a bird's-eye view of the page, enables you to quickly flip pages, and provides rulers that you can use to drag the margin settings around. The following figure shows a document in Print Preview.

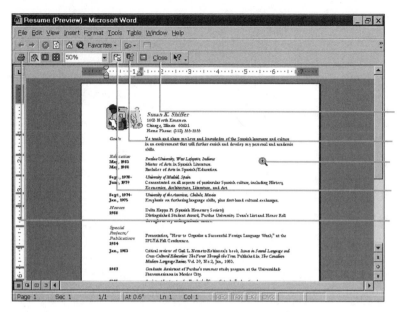

Print Preview enables you to make minor adjustments before you commit the document to paper.

Click here to close Print Preview.

The Shrink to Fit button.

Click to zoom in or out.

Display or hide rulers for changing margins.

Click to start printing.

Ready, Set, Go to the Printer

When you have your printer working successfully with any of your Windows applications, printing is pretty simple. Make sure your printer has plenty of paper and ink or toner, turn on the printer, open your document, and click the **Print** button.

To take more control of the printing—to print extra copies, print sideways on the page (landscape mode), collate copies, select a print quality, or enter other settings—you must display the Print dialog box. To do this, open the **File** menu and select **Print** instead of clicking the Print button. You can then use the Print dialog box to enter your preferences.

Although most of the printing options are straightforward, two might throw you: Page Range and Collate. In most cases, you want to print all the pages in your document. To do this, use the default Page Range setting of All. To print only specified pages, choose **Pages** and type the numbers of the pages you want to print. You might type 1,3,9, for example, to print only pages 1, 3, and 9, or 2-4 to print only pages 2, 3, and 4. If you choose to print more than one copy of the document, the Collate option completely prints one copy of the document before printing the next copy. With this option off, Word prints all copies of the first page, all copies of the second page, and so on, so you have to collate manually.

93

Use the Print dialog box to enter your printing preferences.

Click Properties for additional options specific to your printer.

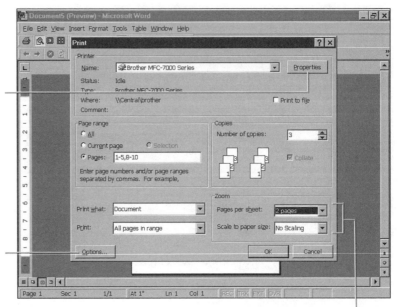

To enter additional settings, click the Options button.

The new Zoom options let you print several pages on a single sheet.

Part 3

Crunching Numbers with Excel Spreadsheets

You know your multiplication tables, and you've mastered long division. Now, you would like to spend a little less time with your calculator and a little more time with your golf clubs.

Well, dust off your clubs because Excel is ready and willing to do your math homework for you. You type some text and values, insert a few formulas, and Excel takes care of the rest—adding, subtracting, multiplying, dividing, and even graphing the results!

Whether you're refinancing your home, analyzing sales figures, or creating a business plan, this part shows you how to automate your calculations with Excel.

Chapter 10

Spreadsheet Orientation Day

In This Chapter

➤ A nickel tour of the Excel screen

➤ The types of data you can put in a spreadsheet

➤ Typing entries in tiny boxes

➤ Automated data entry

➤ Working with multiple worksheets

Contrary to popular belief, you don't have to be a mathematical wizard or a CPA in order to crunch a few numbers. All you need is a good spreadsheet program such as Excel (and a little instruction); and soon, you too will be juggling numbers, entering complex formulas and calculations, balancing budgets, and doing other high-profile tasks to impress your friends and colleagues. You'll probably even impress yourself!

Before you start juggling numbers, however, you have to enter them. In this chapter, you learn how to move around in Excel and enter the raw data Excel needs in order to perform its magic. Along the way, I even show you some quick ways to pour data into your spreadsheets and rearrange the data.

Terminology Check

Microsoft insists on calling its spreadsheets *worksheets*. When you first run Excel, it displays a *workbook* consisting of three worksheets.

Taking Excel on the Open Road

How do you start Excel? First, you have to know where to find the Excelerator. Get it? Excel-erator! Okay, enough of that. Although I told you how to start the Office programs back in the first part of this book, I'll tell you again. To run Excel, choose **Start**, **Programs**, **Microsoft Excel**, or use one of the alternative methods discussed in Chapter 1, "10-Minute Guide to Office 2000 Professional."

After Excel starts, you're left staring at a big blank workbook (shown in the next figure) containing three worksheets.

The Excel window may display some unfamiliar items.

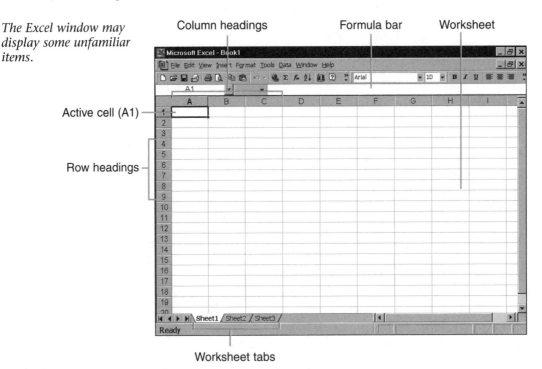

The area surrounding the workbook shows you all the typical application controls, including toolbars, menu bars, and scrollbars. You also see the following less-familiar items:

➤ *Worksheet tabs.* Enables you to flip sheets in your workbook. Click a tab to select it. Right-click a tab for additional options. See "Working with Worksheets," later in this chapter, for instructions.

➤ *Formula bar.* Enables you to enter data into *cells* (the little boxes in the worksheet) and edit entries. You'll learn all about this bar when you start typing entries.

➤ *Column headings.* The gray boxes at the top of the columns. Each column is labeled with a letter of the alphabet (A through Z and then AA through AZ, BA through BZ, and so on to column IV—256 columns in all). To select a column, click its column heading.

➤ *Row headings.* The gray boxes at the left of the rows that indicate the number of the rows (numbered from 1 through 65536). To select a row, click its row heading.

➤ *Active Cell.* The cell with the thick border around it—cell A1 (at first), the cell in the upper-left corner of the worksheet.

What's with the Letters and Numbers?

In a worksheet, rows and columns intersect to form the boxes we fondly refer to as *cells*. Each cell has an *address* made up of its column letter and row number. For example, the address of the cell in the upper-left corner of the worksheet is A1. Addresses are used in formulas to refer to values in particular cells. For instance, the formula =A1+A2+A3 would determine the total of the values in cells A1 through A3. When you click a cell, Excel lights up its row number and column letter and displays its address in the Name Box to the left of the formula bar.

All Data Entries Are Not Created Equal

As with most high-end applications, Excel can accept just about any kind of data that can be digitized. You can insert pictures, sounds, video clips, Web page addresses, email addresses—you name it. But that type of data is merely a decoration for a worksheet. What a worksheet really needs are numbers, formulas, and some labels to indicate what the numbers and formulas stand for:

➤ *Labels.* The text entries that you usually type at the top of a column or the left end of a row to indicate what is in that column or row.

➤ *Numbers (values).* The raw data that Excel needs. You enter this data in rows or columns to keep it all neat and tidy.

➤ *Formulas.* Entries that tell Excel to perform calculations. If you type the formula =A6+C3 into cell D5, for example, Excel adds the value in cell C3 to the value in A6 and inserts the answer in cell D5. When you type a formula and press Enter, the result appears in the cell. You'll learn all about formulas in the next chapter.

➤ *Functions.* Predesigned formulas that perform relatively complex calculations with a single operator. You'll learn more about functions in the next chapter.

You can enter labels, values, formulas, and functions into your worksheet.

Formula in cell D14, as displayed in the Formula bar

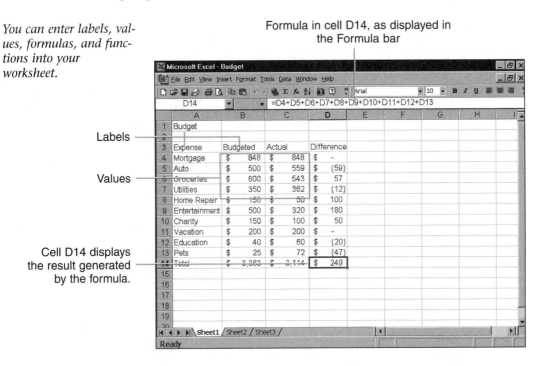

Labels

Values

Cell D14 displays the result generated by the formula.

Entering Data

To enter data, first select a cell; click the cell or use the arrow keys to move to it. A bold box (the *selection box*) appears around the selected cell. When you start typing data into a selected cell, the data immediately appears in that cell and in the formula bar above the worksheet window. Two buttons also appear in the formula bar—a red × and a green check mark. Click the green check mark (or press **Enter**) to accept your entry and insert it into the cell. Click the red × (or press **Esc**) to cancel the entry. (If you press Enter, the selection box automatically moves down so that you can type an entry in the next cell.)

To edit an entry as you type it, use the Backspace and Delete keys as you normally would to delete characters, and then type your correction. If you accept your entry and then decide to change it, you have three options: double-click the cell that contains the entry and edit it right inside the cell; select the cell and edit its entry in the formula bar; or select the cell, press **F2**, and edit the entry right inside the cell.

If you type a relatively long entry in a cell, the entry remains in its own cell, but it may appear to spill over into the cells on the right. If the cell on the right is occupied by another entry, your long entry may appear to be chopped off (if it is a label); or it may appear as a series of pound signs (########) if it is a value. No, Excel isn't trying to drive you crazy; the pound signs alert you to the fact that the entire numerical value cannot be displayed—instead of displaying only a portion of the value (which you might easily overlook), Excel displays the pound signs.

The address of the selected cell

If you type a label that is too wide for the cell, it spills over into adjacent cells.

As you type, your entry appears in the selected cell and in the formula bar.

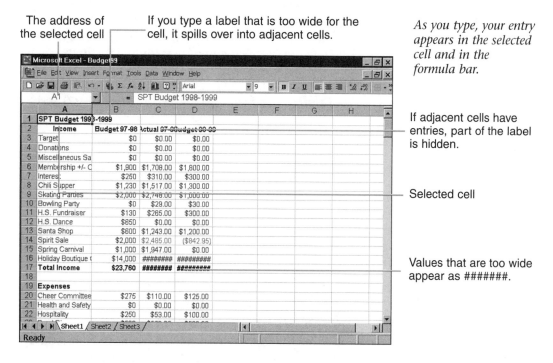

If adjacent cells have entries, part of the label is hidden.

Selected cell

Values that are too wide appear as #######.

In any case, don't panic. Although you can't see your entry, it's still there and is displayed in the formula bar. You just need to widen your column. Click anywhere in the column, open the **Format** menu, choose **Column**, and choose **AutoFit Selection**. This command automatically widens the column so that your text fits. As an alternative, you can place your mouse pointer between the column headings until

101

it becomes a double-headed arrow and then double-click. (For additional control over column width and row height, see "Tweaking Row Heights and Column Widths," in Chapter 12.)

Managing Long Worksheets

To keep your column and row headings onscreen when you scroll your worksheet, freeze a block of cells to prevent them from moving. Click a cell to the right of the column(s) or directly below the row(s) you want to freeze. Open the **Window** menu and choose **Freeze Panes**. A dark line appears below the frozen row(s) or to the right of the frozen column(s). To defrost the panes, choose **Window**, **Unfreeze Panes**.

Another way to fit a long text entry into a cell is to have Excel *wrap* the text from line to line and expand the cell vertically. To turn on text wrap, first highlight the cell(s) in which you want the text to wrap. Open the **Format** menu and choose **Cells.** Click the **Alignment** tab and choose **Wrap Text** to check its box. Click **OK**.

What About Dollar Values and Percents?

Although you can include dollar and percent signs when you enter numeric values, you may not want to. Why? Because you can apply formatting that adds this for you. For example, instead of typing a column of dollar amounts including the dollar signs and decimal points, you can type numbers such as 700 and 19.99, and change the column to Currency format. Excel changes your entries to $700.00 and $19.99, adding your beloved dollar signs where needed. (You learn how to do this in Chapter 12, "Giving Your Spreadsheet a Professional Look.")

Numbers As Text

What if you want your numbers to be treated like text? You know, say you want to use numbers for a ZIP code instead of a value. To do this, precede your entry with a single quotation mark (') as in '90210. The single quotation mark is an alignment prefix that tells Excel to treat the following characters as text and left-align them in the cell.

Numbers As Dates and Times

To use any date or time time values in your spreadsheet, type them in the format that you want them to appear (see the following Table 10.1). When you enter a date using one of the formats shown in the table, Excel converts the date into a number that represents how many days it falls after January 1, 1900. (Excel does this so that it can perform calculations using the dates.) But you never see that mysterious number. Excel always displays a normal date onscreen. And no matter what the news media tells you, you don't have to worry about the year 2000 mucking up your dates. Excel is set up to handle dates up to the year 9999.

Table 10.1   Valid Formats for Dates and Times

Format	Example
MM/DD	9/9
MM/DD/YY	9/9/98 or 09/09/98
MMM-YY	Aug-98 or August-98
DD-MMM-YY	16-Sep-98
DD-MMM	29-Mar
Month, D, YYYY	March 29, 1998
HH:MM	16:50
HH:MM:SS	9:22:55
HH:MM AM/PM	6:45 PM
HH:MM:SS AM/PM	10:15:25 AM
MM/DD/YY HH:MM	11/24/97 12:15

Secrets of the Data Entry Masters

Microsoft realized a long time ago that people don't like to type. In Word, Microsoft built in the AutoCorrect and AutoText features so that people wouldn't have to waste time correcting common typos and typing every character of commonly used words and phrases. In Excel, Microsoft offers these same features and more. The following sections explain how you can use these timesaving features to turbocharge your data entry.

Fill 'Er Up

Let's say you need to insert the same label, date, or value in 20 cells. The mere thought of retyping a date 20 times makes your fingers twitch. You could use the Copy and Paste commands to do it, but that's only slightly less tedious. The solution? Use the *Fill* feature.

To fill neighboring cells with the same entry, drag over the cell that contains the entry and the cells into which you want to copy the entry (up, down, left, right—it doesn't matter). Open the **Edit** menu, point to **Fill**, and click the direction that you want to fill: **Down**, **Right**, **Up**, or **Left**. Excel pours the entry into the selected cells.

We're in the Army Now

Unless you type AM or PM, Excel assumes that you are using a 24–hour military clock; therefore, Excel interprets 8:20 as AM (not PM) unless you type 8:20 PM. In military time, you would have to type 20:20 for 8:20 PM. (After you press Enter, highlight the cell in which you typed the time and check the formula bar to see the 12-hour time.)

A Faster Fill Up

That submenu thing was fun, but there's an easier way. First click the cell that contains the entry that you want to insert into neighboring cells. In the lower-right corner of the cell is a tiny square called the *fill handle*. Move the mouse pointer over the fill handle and it turns into a crosshair. Drag the fill handle over the cells that you want to fill, and then release the mouse button.

You can drag the fill handle for quick fills.

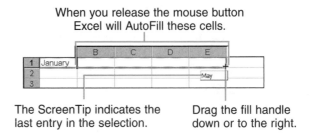

When you release the mouse button Excel will AutoFill these cells.

The ScreenTip indicates the last entry in the selection.

Drag the fill handle down or to the right.

In some cases, this inserts the same entry into all the cells. In other cases, it inserts entries that complete a series. For example, if you use the fill handle to fill January into four neighboring cells, Excel inserts February, March, April, and May. Why? Excel has some built-in *fill series*, which it uses to make AutoFill a more intelligent tool.

Create Your Own AutoFill Series

To create your own AutoFill series, first type the series in a column or row (or open a workbook that already has the series in it). Drag over the entries in the series. Open the **Tools** menu, select **Options**, and click the **Custom Lists** tab. Click **Import**. You can add items to the AutoFill list by typing them in the **List Entries** text box. Click **OK** when you're done.

Fill In the Blanks with AutoComplete

Many spreadsheet users spend a lot of time entering repetitive data or the same labels over and over again in their columns. Excel can help you speed up such entries with AutoComplete. It works like this: Excel keeps track of your entries for each column. Instead of retyping an entry, you right-click an empty cell in the column and select **Pick from List**. A list of entries that you already typed in that column appears below the selected cell. You can then choose from the list, which is a lot faster than typing the word again.

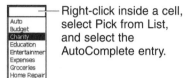 Right-click inside a cell, select Pick from List, and select the AutoComplete entry.

You can quickly insert entries that you have already typed.

You may notice the AutoComplete feature kicking in while you enter text. If you repeat the first few letters of a previous entry, AutoComplete guesses that you're typing repeat information and finishes your word for you. If the word Excel inserts is not the correct word, keep typing and ignore AutoComplete.

AutoComplete also tries to enter values for you, which can become annoying if all the values that you're typing are different. To turn off AutoComplete for values, open the **Tools** menu, select **Options**, click the **Edit** tab, and click **Enable AutoComplete for Cell Values** to remove the check from the box.

Life in the Cell Block: Selecting Cells

So far, we've talked about typing entries into cells. After you have some entries, however, you might need to select the entries to copy, move, delete, format, or perform other operations on a group of cells. To select cells, use the following techniques:

➤ To select a group of cells, drag over them.

➤ To select a column, click the letter at the top of the column. Drag over column letters to select more than one column.

➤ To select a row, click the number to the left of the row. Drag over row numbers to select more than one row.

➤ To select an entire worksheet, click the **Select All** button. (It's that blank button above the row numbers and to the left of the column letters.)

➤ To select multiple neighboring cells, columns, or rows, select the first cell, column, or row. Then press and hold down the **Shift** key and select the last cell, column, or row.

➤ To select multiple non-neighboring cells, columns, or rows, select the first cell or group of cells, columns, and rows. Then press and hold down the **Ctrl** key and click other cells, columns, or rows.

Roaming the Range

After you become accustomed to selecting cells, you might notice that you often need to select the same group of cells to format, copy, print, or refer to in other cells.

Instead of dragging over this group of cells every time you want to perform some operation with it, consider creating a *range*. A range is a rectangular group of cells. You can name the range to make it even easier to select and refer to. (In Chapter 11, "Doing Math with Formulas," I show you how to use ranges in formulas.)

Excel refers to ranges by specific anchor points: the upper-left corner and the lower-right corner. For instance, if you drag over the cells from C3 to E5, you create a range that Excel fondly refers to as C3:E5. (Doesn't this sort of remind you of that game Battleship? You know, A5:D10—Hey! You sunk my battleship!) A range uses a colon to separate the anchor points.

After you have selected a range, you should name it to make it easier to recognize and locate. To name the range, click the **Name** box (at the left end of the formula bar), type the desired name according to the following rules, and press **Enter**.

➤ Start the range name with an underscore or a letter. You can type numbers in a range name, but not at the beginning.

➤ Do not use spaces. You can use an underscore character, a period, or some other weird character to separate words.

➤ You can type as many as 255 characters (but if you type any more than 15, you should be committed).

➤ The name can't be the same as a cell address. (As if you'd want a range name to be as cryptic as those cell addresses.) For example, a range of entries from the fourth quarter of this year can't be named Q4 because Q4 is already the address of a cell in the worksheet. Try FourthQuarter or Qtr4 or something like that.

To select a named range quickly, open the Name box and click the range's name. You can also open the **Edit** menu and select **Go To** (or press **Ctrl+G**). Excel displays a list of named ranges. Click the desired range and click **OK**.

Working with Worksheets

In most cases, a single worksheet is all you need. However, sometimes you might need additional worksheets. If you need to keep track of income and expenses for a small business, you might want to list income categories on one worksheet and expense categories on another. You can then use a third worksheet to summarize income minus expenses.

To change from one worksheet to another, simply click the tab for the desired worksheet. You can take control of your tabs by doing the following:

➤ *Insert a worksheet.* Click the tab before which you want the new worksheet added and then open the **Insert** menu and click **Worksheet**.

➤ *Delete a worksheet.* Right-click the worksheet's tab and click **Delete**. A warning appears, asking you to confirm the deletion. Click **OK**.

➤ *Rename a worksheet.* Right-click the worksheet's tab and choose **Rename** or dou-ble-click the tab. The sheet's current name is highlighted. Type a name for the sheet (up to 31 characters) and press **Enter**. (Keep names short so that the tab doesn't take up the entire tab area.)

➤ *Move or copy worksheets.* To move a worksheet, drag its tab to the left or right. To copy a worksheet, hold down the **Ctrl** key while dragging. To move or copy a worksheet to another workbook, open both workbooks and then right-click the tab and click **Move or Copy**. Enter your preferences to specify the destination of the worksheet and click **OK**.

➤ *Scroll.* If you have more tabs than fit inside the tab area, use the tab scrolling buttons to the left of the tabs to bring hidden tabs into view. The two buttons in the middle scroll one tab at a time back or forward. The button on the left displays the first tab, and the button on the right displays the last tab in the workbook.

➤ *Select multiple worksheets.* **Ctrl**+click the tab of each worksheet that you want to select. Alternatively, click the first tab you want to select, and then **Shift**+click the last tab in the range.

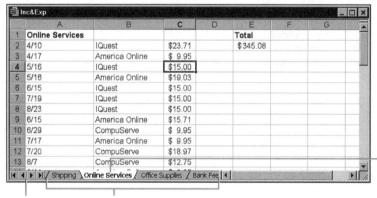

Excel allows you to create an entire workbook full of worksheets.

Click a tab to display the worksheet.

Tab scroll buttons

Worksheet tabs

All This and a Database, Too?

Microsoft Office includes a high-powered database program, Access (which you learn all about in Part 5, "Mastering the Information Age with Access"). Excel, however, provides some great database tools that you might find a little easier to use. If you need a simple database for your address book or to keep track of your video or CD collection, Excel is all the database that you need. You won't have to deal with the complexities of Access.

Start with More Worksheets

You can change the default number of worksheets Excel creates for a new workbook. Open the **Tools** menu, choose **Options**, and click the **General** tab. Use the **Sheets in New Workbook** spin box to enter the desired number of worksheets. Click **OK**.

To create a database in Excel, you type *field names* in the topmost row. You might create a simple address book by typing field names such as Title, FirstName, LastName, Address, and so on in row A. Make the field names bold, or use some other formatting to set them off from the *field entries* (the actual names and addresses of the people in your database). In the remaining rows, type your field entries. Each set of field entries (each row) constitutes a *record* in your database.

When you have entered all the records, you can then use commands on the Data menu to sort, filter, and perform other database management operations. If you need a more full-featured database to manage your records, however, you should consider using Access instead. For example, if you're running your own business and need to keep track of customers, billing, inventory, and employees, you should spend the time learning Access because it saves you time in the long run.

You can create a simple database in Excel.

The Data menu contains commands for sorting and filtering your records.

You can quickly sort records in an Excel database.

Type field names in the topmost row.

Type records in the remaining rows.

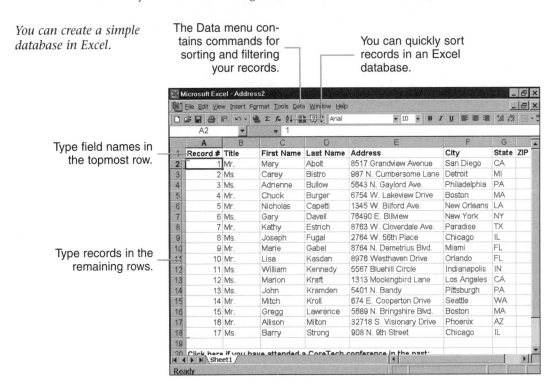

Chapter 11

Doing Math with Formulas

In This Chapter

➤ Transforming your spreadsheet into an automated calculator

➤ Determining quick totals and grand totals with AutoSum

➤ Using functions for those incredibly complex calculations

➤ Special concerns when you move formulas

➤ Playing "What If...?" with sets of values

Although an Excel worksheet is ideal for arranging entries in columns and rows, that's not its main purpose. You can do that with Word's Table feature. What makes a worksheet so powerful is that it can perform calculations using various values from the worksheet. In addition, you can set up unlimited scenarios for your worksheet that supply different numbers in the calculations, enabling you to play "What if...?" with different sets of numbers!

In this chapter, you learn how to unleash the power of Excel's formulas, functions, and other calculation tools.

Understanding Formulas and Concocting Your Own

The term *formula* might conjure up the image of a physicist scrawling abstract mathematical operations on a chalkboard. Excel formulas are much more practical than that. These formulas perform mathematical operations (addition, subtraction, multiplication, and division) on the entries in your worksheet to determine totals, grand totals, percentages, and other practical results. To get you started, here are some helpful facts about formulas:

➤ You type a formula into the cell in which you want the answer to appear.

➤ All formulas start with an equal sign (=). If you start with a letter, Excel thinks you're typing a label.

➤ Formulas use cell addresses to pull values from other cells into the formula. For example, the formula =A1+D3 adds the values in cells A1 and D3.

➤ Formulas use the following symbols:

+	addition
–	subtraction
×	multiplication
/	division
^	raise to the ___ power of
%	percentage

➤ You can include your own numbers in formulas. To determine your annual income, for instance, you would multiply your monthly income by 12. If your monthly income were in cell C5, the formula would be =C5×12.

A simple formula might look something like =A1+B1+C1+D1, which determines the grand total of the values in cells A1 through D1. Formulas can be much more complex, however, using values from two or more worksheets and even values from different workbooks!

Get Your Operators in Order

You're probably dying to start entering formulas to see what happens. Whoa, little filly. First you need a refresher course on a little rule in math that determines the *order of operations*. In any formula, Excel performs the series of operations from left to right in the following order, which gives some operators *precedence* over others:

1st	All operations in parentheses
2nd	Exponential equations or operations
3rd	Multiplication and division
4th	Addition and subtraction

This is important to keep in mind when you are creating equations because the order of operations determines the result. For example, if you want to determine the average of the values in cells A1, B1, and C1, and you enter =A1+B1+C1/3, you probably get the wrong answer. Excel divides the value in C1 by 3 and then adds that result to A1+B1. It calculates this way because division takes precedence over addition. So how do you correctly determine this average? You must group your values in parentheses. In this little example, you want to total A1 through C1 first. To do that, enclose the cell addresses in parentheses: =(A1+B1+C1)/3. This tells Excel to total the values before dividing them.

Tell Me How to Put Them in Already!

You can enter formulas in either of two ways: by *typing* the formula or by *selecting* cell references.

To type a formula, click the cell in which you want the result to appear, type the formula (starting with an equal sign), and press **Enter**. Excel calculates the result and enters it into your selected cell (assuming you have entered some values to calculate).

Error!

If an error message appears in the cell in which you typed your formula, make sure that you did not enter a formula that told Excel to do one of the following: divide by zero or a blank cell, use a value in a blank cell, delete a cell being used in a formula, or use a range name when a single cell address was expected.

To enter a formula by selecting cell references, take the following steps, and don't press Enter until you've entered the entire formula (it's tempting, but don't do it):

1. Select the cell in which you want the formula's result to appear.

2. Type the equal sign (=).

3. Click the cell whose address you want to appear first in the formula. The cell address appears in the Formula bar.

4. Type a mathematical operator (+, –, and so forth) after the value to indicate the next operation that you want to perform.

5. Continue clicking cells and typing operators until you finish entering the formula.

6. When you finish, press **Enter** to accept the formula.

The easiest way to compose formulas is to point and click.

Start with an equal sign.

Type mathematical operators between cell addresses.

Click a cell to insert its address.

	A	B	C	D	E	F	G	H	I
1	Hokey Manufacturing								
2									
3	Income	1st Qtr	2nd Qtr	3rd Qtr	4th Qtr				
4	Wholesale	55000	46000	52000	90900				
5	Retail	45700	56500	42800	57900				
6	Special	23000	54800	87000	45800				
7	Total	123700	157300	161800	=E4+E5+E6				
8									
9	Expenses								
10	Materials	19000	17500	18200	20500				
11	Labor	15000	15050	15500	15400				
12	Rent	1600	1600	1600	1600				
13	Misc.	2500	2500	3000	1500				
14	Total	38100	36850	38300	39000				
15						Total Profit			
16	Profit	85600	120650	123500	155600	485350			
17									
18									
19									
20									

If you make a mistake while entering a formula, simply backspace over it and enter your correction as you would with any other cell entry. If you already accepted the entry (by pressing Enter or clicking the check mark button), double-click the cell (or click it and then click in the Formula bar where you want to make changes).

As you enter formulas, you may notice that Excel automatically performs the calculation. If you change a value in a cell that the formula uses, Excel instantly recalculates the entire worksheet! If you have a long worksheet with a lot of formulas and a slow computer, this can slow down Excel significantly, so you may want to change the recalculation settings. To turn off the Auto Calculation option, open the **Tools** menu, choose **Options**, and click the **Calculation** tab. Select **Manual** and click **OK**. From now on when you want to recalculate the worksheet, press **F9**.

Going Turbo with Functions

Functions are ready-made formulas that you can use to perform a series of operations using two or more values or a range of values. For example, to determine the sum of a series of values in cells A5 through G5, you can enter the function =SUM(A5:G5) instead of entering +A5+B5+C5+D5+E5+F5+G5, which is way too much typing. Functions can save a lot of time. Other functions may perform more complex operations, such as determining the monthly payment on a loan when you supply the values for the principal, interest rate, and number of payment periods.

Every function must have the following three elements:

➤ The *equal sign (=)* indicates that what follows is a formula, not a label.

➤ The *function name* (for example, SUM) indicates the type of operation that you want Excel to perform.

➤ The *argument*, such as (A3:F11), indicates the cell addresses of the values on which the function acts. The argument is often a range of cells, but it can be much more complex.

One other thing to remember is that a function can be part of another formula. For example, =SUM(A3:A9)+B43 uses the SUM function along with the addition operator to add the value in cell B43 to the total of the values in cells A3 through A9.

The Awesome AutoSum Tool

One of the tasks you perform most often is summing up values you've entered in your worksheet cells. Because summing is so popular, Excel provides a tool devoted to summing—AutoSum.

To quickly determine the total of a row or column of values, first click an empty cell to the right of the row or just below the column of values. Then click the **AutoSum** button in the Standard toolbar. AutoSum assumes that you want to add the values in the cells to the left of or above the currently selected cell, so it displays a marching ants box (called a *marquee*) around those cells. If AutoSum selects an incorrect range of cells, you can edit the selection by dragging over the cells whose values you want to add. Once the AutoSum formula is correct, press **Enter** or click another cell.

With a click of a button, AutoSum determines the total.

4 Click the Enter button.　　2 Click AutoSum.

	A	B	C	D	E	F	G
12	Rent	1600	1600	1600	1600		
13	Misc.	2500	2500	3000	1500		
14	Total	38100	36850	38300	39000		
15						Total Profit	
16	Profit	85600	120650	123500	155600	=SUM(B16:E16)	
17							
18							
19							
20							
21							
22							

Microsoft Excel - Profit02

File Edit View Insert Format Tools Data Window Help

SUM   =SUM(B16:E16)

Sheet1 / Sheet2 / Sheet3 /

Point

3 If you want different cells, drag over the cells that contain the desired values.

1 Select the cell where you want the total inserted.

If your worksheet contains two or more cells that contain subtotals, you can also use AutoSum to determine the grand total. Click the cell in which you want to insert the grand total and then click the **AutoSum** button. Click the first subtotal and then **Ctrl**+click any additional subtotals that you want to include in the grand total. Press **Enter**.

AutoCalculate

Drag over a range of values and look in the status bar. You see **Sum=**, followed by the total of the values in the selected cells. This feature, called *AutoCalculate,* can help you determine totals without inserting the total in a cell. Right-click the status bar to display a pop-up menu that enables you to show the average of the selected cells or the count (the number of cell entries).

Demystifying Functions with the Paste Function Feature

The SUM and AVERAGE functions are fairly easy to enter. Some of the other functions, however, such as the financial function that determines the payment on a loan, may contain several values and require you to enter those values in the proper *syntax* (order). To type the function, you must remember its name and know the required syntax, which can be quite difficult. The *Paste Function* feature can make the process much less painful. To paste a function into a cell, take the following steps:

1. Select the cell in which you want to insert the function.

2.  Open the **Insert** menu and choose **Function**, or better yet, click the **Paste Function** button in the Standard toolbar. The Paste Function dialog box appears, displaying a list of available functions.

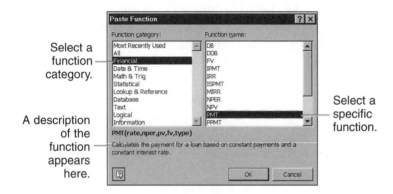

Select a function category.

A description of the function appears here.

Select a specific function.

The Paste Function dialog box enables you to select the function instead of typing it.

3. From the **Function Category** list, select the type of function you want to insert. If you're not sure, select **All** to display the names of all the functions. They are listed alphabetically.

4. Select the function you want to insert from the **Function Name** list and click **OK**. The formula palette appears, prompting you to type the argument. You can type values or cell addresses in the various text boxes. Alternatively, you can click the button to the right of the text box and then click the cell that contains the specified value.

Function Rookie Tip

When you select a function in the Function Name list, Excel displays a description of the function. Read this description to find out the purpose of the function.

Point and Click Function Arguments

If you click a button for one of the items in the function argument, Excel tucks the formula palette out of the way, displaying the address of the currently selected cell and a button for bringing the palette back into view. After you select the desired cell, click the button to the right of the cell address to redisplay the palette. You can also drag the palette out of the way and click cells in the work-sheet as needed.

Enter the values and cell references that make up the argument.

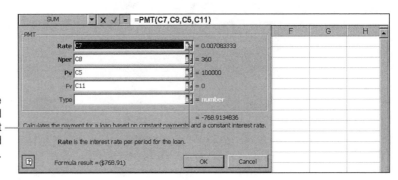

Click this button to hide the formula palette and then click the cell that contains the specified value.

5. Enter the values or cell ranges for the argument. You can type a value or argument, or click the cells that contain the required values. (Some arguments, such as those that start with "If," are optional. Excel must "decide" which action to perform based on entries in your worksheet.)

6. Click **OK** or press **Enter**. Excel inserts the function and argument in the selected cell and displays the result.

When you need to edit a function using the Function Wizard, select the cell that contains the function that you want to edit. (Make sure you're not in Edit mode—that is, the insertion point should not appear in the cell.) Open the **Insert** menu and choose **Function**, or click the **Paste Function** button. This displays the formula palette, which helps you edit your argument.

Seeing a Real Live Investment Function in Action

To get some hands-on experience with functions, check out the FV (*future value*) function. This function allows you to play around with some numbers to determine how much money you'll have socked away when you're ready to retire. Let's say you plan to retire in 20 years, and you invest $200 a month at 8% interest. You would enter the following function:

   =FV(8%/12,240,-200,0,1)

Let's break this down:

   = is an essential element in the function statement, as explained earlier.

   FV is the function name, which stands for "future value."

   8%/12 is the annual percentage paid to you divided by 12 months.

   240 is the number of payments (12 months times 20 years).

   -200 is the amount that you invest each month. Note that this number is negative.

   0 is the amount invested right now. If you already have some money socked away at this same percentage rate, replace 0 with that amount entered as a negative value.

   1 specifies that the monthly investment is made at the beginning of the month. If you invest at the end of the month, use 0 instead or leave a blank.

As you may have already guessed, you can use cell references in place of the values. The following figure shows a sample worksheet used to determine the future value of an investment. Note that each value listed above is in a separate cell.

C9	▼	=	=FV(C4/12,C5,C6,C7,C8)						
	A	B	C	D	E	F	G	H	
1									
2		Investment Worksheet							
3									
4		Annual Interest Rate	0.0800						
5		Payment Periods	240						
6		Payment Amount	($200.00)						
7		Current Investment	0.00						
8		1st of the Month	1						
9		After 20 Years	$118,589.44						
10									

Use cell references instead of values.

Track Down Errors

Excel's worksheet auditors can help you track down errors in formulas and functions. Click the cell that contains the function or formula that is not working properly (or the cell that is referenced by problem formula or function). Then, open the **Tools** menu, point to **Auditing**, and choose the desired auditing tool: **Trace Precedents**, **Trace Dependents**, or **Trace Error**. The auditing tool displays arrows that point to the referenced cells or highlights errors. To remove the arrows, choose **Tools, Auditing, Remove All Arrows**.

Controlling Cell Addresses When You Copy or Move Formulas

When you copy a formula from one place in the worksheet to another, Excel adjusts the cell references in the formulas relative to their new positions in the worksheet. In the following figure, cell B9 contains the formula =B4+B5+B6+B7, which determines the total sales revenue for Fred. If you copy that formula to cell C9 (to determine the total sales revenue for Wilma), Excel automatically changes the formula to =C4+C5+C6+C7.

Excel adjusts cell references when you copy formulas.

Formula in cell B9 calculates Fred's total sales revenue.

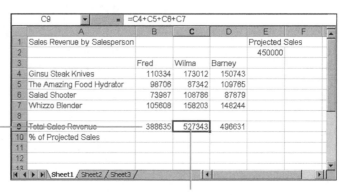

Formula copied into cell C9 to determine Wilma's sales revenue.

118

The preceding example shows a formula in which the cell references are *relative:* Excel changes the cell addresses relative to the position of the formula. In this example, the formula was moved one cell to the right, so all the addresses in the formula are also adjusted one cell to the right.

Sometimes, however, you may not want Excel to adjust the cell references. In order to keep a cell reference from changing when you copy or move the formula, you must mark the cell reference in the formula as an *absolute reference*. To mark a reference as an absolute, press the **F4** key immediately after typing the reference or move the insertion point inside the cell reference and press **F4**. This places a dollar sign before the column letter and the row number (as in E2). You can type the dollar signs yourself, but it's usually easier to let Excel do it.

You may also mark the column letter *or* the row number (but not both) as absolute. This enables the column letter or row number to change when you copy or move the formula. Keep pressing F4 until you have the desired combination of dollar signs.

Playing "What If...?" with Scenarios

After you have some values and formulas in place, let the fun begin! Excel offers a tool that enables you to plug different sets of values into your formulas to determine the effects of different values on the outcome.

Say you're purchasing a home and you need some idea of how much your monthly mortgage payment is going to be for various loan amounts. You have successfully created a worksheet that determines the monthly payment for a $120,000 house at 8.5%; but you want to know what the payment would be for a $110,000, a $130,000, and a $140,000 home. You also want to see the effects of other loan rates. You could create a bunch of separate worksheets, but a better solution is to create several scenarios for the same worksheet. A *scenario* is simply a set of values that you plug into variables in the worksheet.

The Making of a Scenario

Making a scenario is fairly simple. You name the scenario, tell Excel which cells have the values that you want to play with, and then type the values that you want Excel to use for the scenario. The following step-by-step instructions walk you through the process of creating a scenario:

1. Display the worksheet for which you want to create a scenario.
2. Open the **Tools** menu and click **Scenarios**. The Scenario Manager appears, indicating that this worksheet has no current scenarios.
3. Click the **Add** button. The Add Scenario dialog box appears.

4. Type a name for the scenario that describes the specific changes that you're going to make. For example, if you were creating this scenario to determine payments for a $110,000 house at 9.25%, you might type **110K @ 9.25%**.

5. Click the **Changing Cells** text box and click the cell that contains the value you want to change in your scenario. To change values in other cells, hold down the **Ctrl** key and click them. (This inserts the addresses of the changing cells, separating them with commas.)

6. Click **OK**. The Scenario Values dialog box displays the current values in the cells you want to change.

7. Type the values you want to use for this scenario and click **OK**. The Scenario Manager displays the name of the new scenario.

8. To view a scenario, click its name and click the **Show** button. Excel replaces the values in the changing cells with the values you entered for the scenario.

To make a scenario, enter different values for the variables.

This entry replaces the price of the house in cell B2.

This entry replaces the loan rate in cell B5.

Managing Your Scenarios

Whenever you want to play with the various scenarios you've created, open the **Tools** menu and select **Scenarios**. This displays the Scenario Manager, which you met in the previous section. The Scenario Manager offers the following buttons for managing and displaying your scenarios:

➤ *Show*. Displays the results of the selected scenario right inside the worksheet.

➤ *Add*. Enables you to add another scenario.

➤ *Delete*. Removes the selected scenario.

➤ *Edit*. Enables you to select different cells used for the scenario and insert different values for the variables.

➤ *Merge*. Takes scenarios from various worksheets and places them on a single worksheet.

➤ *Summary*. Displays the results of the various worksheets on a single worksheet. As you can see in the following figure, this is great for comparing the different scenarios you've created.

Scenario Summary				
	Current Values:	120K @ 8.25%	110K @ 9.25%	130K @ 9.625%
Changing Cells:				
B2	110,000	120,000	110,000	130,000
B5	9.25%	8.50%	9.25%	9.63%
Result Cells:				
B8	($814.45)	($830.43)	($814.45)	($994.49)
Notes: Current Values column represents values of changing cells at time Scenario Summary Report was created. Changing cells for each scenario are highlighted in gray.				

Scenario Manager can create a summary of the results from different scenarios.

The Scenario Summary creates a new worksheet. When you're done with it, simply click the tab for the worksheet on which you were working before creating your scenarios. To get rid of the sheet altogether, right-click the **Scenario Summary** tab and choose **Delete**.

Chapter 12

Giving Your Worksheet a Professional Look

In This Chapter

➤ Inserting blank rows, columns, and cells

➤ Adding dollar signs, decimals, percent signs, and other valuable ornaments

➤ Spiffing up a worksheet with clip art

➤ Adding borders, shading, and other fancy stuff

➤ Formatting tricks and shortcuts

If you win the lottery or make some savvy investments in the stock market, numbers might grab your attention. In most cases, however, numbers have that ashen Al Gore look to them.

To make your numbers a little more appealing and make the rows and columns easier to follow, you need to format your worksheet. You can format by inserting blank rows and columns to give your values a little elbow room, laying down a few lines around your cells, or even shading individual cells, rows, or columns to make them stand out.

In this chapter, you learn several ways to adorn your worksheets and make your numbers a little more exciting.

Tweaking Row Heights and Column Widths

Worksheet cells are pretty dinky. You can't cram more than about nine characters into a cell without the entry spilling over into the next cell or being lopped off. To accommodate long entries or tall fonts, Excel enables you to adjust the column width and row height.

The easiest way to adjust the column width and row height is to drag the edge of the column or row heading. First select the cell(s) or column(s) you want to resize. Move the mouse pointer over the right edge of the column heading or the bottom edge of the row heading so the mouse pointer appears as a two-headed arrow. Then drag the edge to adjust the column width or row height.

Right-Click for Quick Formatting

As you're working through this chapter, don't forget about your right mouse button. After you select the cells you want to format, right-click a selected cell and choose the desired formatting option.

Quick Alterations with AutoFit

To resize a column or row quickly, double-click the right edge of the column heading or the bottom edge of the row heading. You'll also find this feature on the Format, Row and Format, Column submenu.

The mouse provides an intuitive way to change the row height and column width.

Drag the right edge of the column heading to adjust column width.

ScreenTip shows the new column width as you drag.

Drag the bottom edge of a row heading to adjust row height.

	A	B	C	D	E	F	G	H
1	Sales Revenue by Salesperson				Projected Sales			
2					450000			
3		Fred	Wilma	Barney				
4	Ginsu Steak Knives	110334	173012	150743				
5	The Amazing Food I	98706	87342	109765				
6	Salad Shooter	73987	108786	87879				
7	Whizzo Blender	105608	158203	148244				
8								
9	Total Sales Revenue	$88635	527343	496631				

Width: 18.89 (177 pixels)

For more precise control over the column width and row height, choose **Format**, **Row**, **Height** or **Format**, **Column**, **Width**, and enter the desired settings.

Fission and Fusion: Merging and Splitting Cells

As you enter data, you may need to merge two or more cells to create a single mega-cell that spans two or more rows or columns. In this single merged cell, you can then type a single entry that acts as a row or column heading. For example, you may want to merge the cells at the top of the worksheet to enter a worksheet title that spans the entire worksheet.

The easiest way to merge cells is to use the Merge and Center button in the Formatting toolbar. Drag over the cells that you want to merge (the cells must be *contiguous*, neighboring) and then click the **Merge and Center** button. (You may need to click the **More Buttons** button, on the right end of the toolbar to access the Merge and Center button.) Excel transforms the selected cells into a single cell and centers any text inside the cell. You can click any of the alignment buttons to change the text alignment.

You can also merge cells by changing the cell formatting. Take the following steps:

1. Drag over the cells that you want to merge.
2. Open the **Format** menu and choose **Cells**.
3. Click the **Alignment** tab and check the **Merge Cells** option.
4. Click **OK**.

To return the cells to their original (non-merged) condition, repeat these steps to turn off the Merge Cells option.

Add a Few Rows, Toss in Some Columns

As you are building your worksheet, you may have some need to add a few columns or rows to insert data that you hadn't thought of when you were laying out your worksheet. On the other hand, maybe you need to delete a row or column if your design was a little too ambitious. Whatever the case, adding and deleting cells, rows, and columns is fairly simple.

To insert cells, columns, or rows, first select the number of rows, columns, or cells that you want to insert (drag over the row or column headings to select entire rows or columns).

Check This Out

Look to the Insert Menu

If your right mouse button is broken, you can always use the options on the Insert menu to insert cells, rows, or columns.

After selecting columns, rows, or cells, right-click anywhere inside the selection and click **Insert**. If you selected columns or rows, Excel inserts them immediately. If you selected a block of cells, the Insert dialog box appears, asking which way you want the data in the currently selected cells to be shifted. Select **Shift Cells Right** or **Shift Cells Down** and click **OK**.

When you insert a block of cells, Excel shifts data down or to the right to make room.

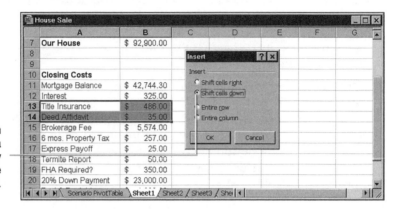

Specify the direction in which you want data from the currently selected cells to be shifted.

Nuking Rows, Columns, and Cells

It's usually easier to destroy than to create. But that's not the case with worksheets because when you delete in a worksheet, all sorts of things can happen. You might destroy only the data in the cells, or you might wipe out the cells or columns entirely, forcing adjacent cells to shift. Therefore, when you set out on any mission of mass destruction, keep the following points in mind:

➤ If you select columns, rows, or cells, and press the **Delete** key, Excel leaves the cells intact, deleting only the contents of the selected cells. This is the same as entering the Edit, Clear, Contents command.

➤ The Edit, Clear command opens a submenu that enables you to clear All (contents, formatting, and comments), Contents (just the cell entries, not the formatting), Formats (the cell formatting, not the contents), or Comments (only the cell comments).

➤ To remove cells, columns, or rows completely, select them, open the **Edit** menu, and select **Delete**. (Alternatively, right-click the selection and select **Delete**.)

➤ When you remove a row, rows below it are pulled up to fill the space. When you delete a column, columns to the right are pulled to the left to fill the void.

➤ If you choose to remove a block of cells (otherwise known as a *range*), Excel displays a dialog box asking you how to shift the surrounding cells.

If you delete cells by mistake, click the **Undo** button right away to get them back. If you make several mistakes, consider closing your workbook *without* saving your changes. You can then reopen the workbook and start over.

Making It Look Great in 10 Minutes or Less

Although the content of your worksheet is more important than its appearance, a little creative formatting can make your worksheet more attractive and functional. For example, you can add shading to rows and columns to make the spreadsheet easier to follow, add lines to set off totals and grand totals, and even have Excel display negative numbers in color to raise a flag when your business is in the red.

The following sections show you how to use the various formatting tools available in Excel to give your worksheets a more professional look.

Web Work!

If you are formatting your worksheet to place it on the Web or on your company's intranet, try to keep the worksheet narrow. If the worksheet is wider than the Web browser window, the people viewing your worksheet have to use the horizontal scroll button to bring columns into view. This may make the worksheet a royal pain to navigate.

Drive-Through Formatting with AutoFormat

Excel offers a formatting feature called *AutoFormat* that makes formatting your worksheet as easy as picking up a bag of burgers at the local drive-through. With AutoFormat, you apply a predesigned format to selected cells. The format controls everything from fonts and alignment to shading and borders.

To use AutoFormat, select the cells you want to format, open the **Format** menu, and select **AutoFormat**. In the AutoFormat dialog box, click the desired format. To turn off any format settings, such as shading or borders, click the **Options** button and select your preferences, as shown in the following figure. Then click **OK**.

You can pick a pre-designed table format for your worksheet.

Click Options to display additional settings.

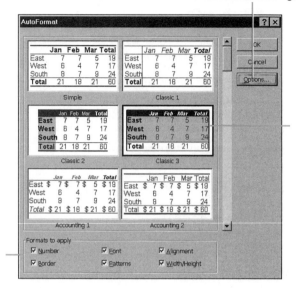

Pick a design.

When you click Options, these options appear.

Conditional Formatting

You can apply *conditional formatting* to a cell to make Excel display a value in a unique way if the value falls within a certain range. For example, you can apply a conditional format telling Excel that if this value falls below zero, it should shade the cell red and place a big, thick border around it to alert you. To apply conditional formatting, select the cell that contains the formula or value you want to format, open the **Format** menu, select **Conditional Formatting**, and enter your preferences.

Don't Forget Your Formatting Toolbar

Overlooking the Formatting toolbar in any of the Microsoft Office applications is like forgetting your laptop when you're going on a business trip. Without it, you have to resort to a system of awkward pull-down menus, dialog boxes, and pop-up menus to get anything done. The Formatting toolbar offers the fastest way for you to change fonts, increase or decrease the type size, align text in cells, change the text color, add borders, and more.

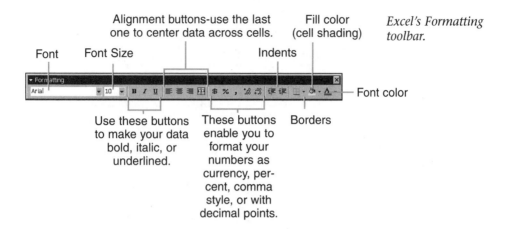

Excel's Formatting toolbar.

More Control with the Format Cells Dialog Box

For additional formatting options, use the Format Cells dialog box. Open the **Format** menu and select **Cells** to open the dialog box. You can easily change many of the formatting features for your data by clicking the appropriate tabs in this dialog box:

➤ *Number* provides various formats to control the appearance of values, including currency, percentages, dates, and times. Choose the desired category and then click the specific format you want to use, as shown in the following figure.

➤ *Alignment* allows you to control the way labels and values are positioned inside cells. You can even rotate text to display it on an angle inside a cell; under Orientation, drag the line next to Text to the desired angle.

➤ *Font* enables you to choose a typeface and size for your text and to add enhancements, such as bold, italic, and color.

➤ *Border* provides options for adding lines between and around cells. (The light gray *gridlines* that Excel uses to mark cell boundaries do not print.) Before you select a border, select a line style from the **Style** list and a color from the **Color** drop-down list. The Presets buttons enable you to add an outline (a line around the outside of the entire selection) and inside lines (between all the cells in the selected area). Click a button to turn the lines on or off. The Border buttons (below the Presets) enable you to add or remove individual lines.

➤ *Patterns* enables you to shade the selected cells. Under Color, click the main color you want to use for the cell shading. To overlay a pattern of a different color, open the **Pattern** drop-down list and click a pattern (from the top of the list). Then open the **Pattern** drop-down list again and click a color (from the bottom of the list). Click **OK**.

➤ *Protection* provides options for locking the cell (to prevent someone from editing it) or hiding the cell's contents. This option does nothing, however, unless you choose to protect the worksheet. To protect your worksheet, choose **Tools**, **Protection**, **Protect Sheet**, enter a password (if desired), and click **OK**.

Use number formatting for currency, dates, and percentages.

Choose a format category.

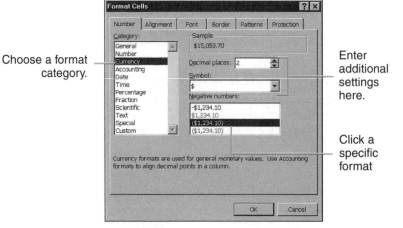

Enter additional settings here.

Click a specific format

Changing the Default Font

To use any font as the normal font for all your worksheets, you can change the default font. Open the **Tools** menu, select **Options**, and click the **General** tab. Open the **Standard Font** drop-down list and click the desired font. Open the **Size** drop-down list and click the font size that you want. Then click **OK**. The change doesn't take effect until you restart Excel.

Applying Formats with a Few Brush Strokes

You can quickly copy the formatting from one cell or a block of cells to other cells by using the Format Painter. Select the cell that contains the formatting you want to copy and click the **Format Painter** button. Drag your pointer (which now has a paintbrush icon next to it) over the cells to which you want to copy the formatting. Format Painter applies the formatting! To paint the format in multiple locations, double-click the Format Painter button to stick it in the on position. Then paint away. When you're done, click the Format Painter button again to turn it off.

Hanging a Few Graphical Ornaments

In the next chapter, "Graphing Data for Fun and Profit," you learn how to add graphs to your worksheets to give your data meaning and to make your worksheets more graphical; however, Excel offers a few additional tools for adding graphics to your worksheets.

The Insert, Picture submenu contains several options for inserting clip art images, graphics stored on your disk, WordArt, AutoShapes, and even scanned images (assuming you have a TWAIN-compatible scanner or digital camera).

These graphics tools are similar (some are even identical) to the tools that Word offers. To learn how to use these tools (Clip Art, WordArt, AutoShapes, drawing, and so on), refer to Chapter 6, "Spicing It Up with Graphics, Sound, and Video."

Web Work!

If you're planning to place your Excel worksheet on the Web, give it a background design. Open the **Format** menu, point to **Sheet**, and select **Background**. In the Sheet Background dialog box, select one of the background designs.

131

Chapter 13

Graphing Data for Fun and Profit

In This Chapter

➤ Graphing without graph paper

➤ In your face with pie charts

➤ Making a chart more understandable with legends

➤ Labeling your chart axes just for fun

During the 1992 presidential race, Ross Perot made charts famous. With his prime time voodoo pointer and his stack of charts, he managed to upset an election and change the political strategies of both parties. At the same time, he proved that a well-designed graph could convey data much more clearly and effectively than could any page full of stodgy numbers.

In this chapter, you learn how to use Excel's charting tools to make your data more graphical and give your numbers context.

Graphs or Charts?

Completely ignoring the fact that most of us grew up calling graphs *graphs*, Excel and most other spreadsheet programs insist on calling them *charts*. They're still graphs, but to make Excel happy and to prevent confusion, I'll try to call graphs charts from now on.

Charting Your Data

To make charting a painless exercise, Excel offers a tool called the Chart Wizard. You select the data you want charted, and then start the Chart Wizard, which leads you step by step through the process of creating a chart. All you have to do is enter your preferences. To use the Chart Wizard, take the following steps:

1. Select the data you want to chart. If you typed names or other labels (Qtr 1, Qtr 2, and so on) and you want them included in the chart (as labels), include them in the selection.

2. Click the **Chart Wizard** button in the Standard Toolbar. The Chart Wizard Step 1 of 4 dialog box appears, asking you to pick the desired chart type. (Ignore the Custom Types tab for now.)

3. Make sure the **Standard Types** tab is up front, and then click the desired chart type in the **Chart Type** list. The Chart Sub-type list displays various renditions of the selected type.

4. In the **Chart Sub-type** list, click the chart design you want to use. (To see how this chart type appears when it charts your data, point to **Press and Hold to View Sample** and hold down the mouse button.)

The Chart Wizard leads you through the process of charting your data.

Pick a chart type.

Pick a chart sub-type.

Hold down the mouse button here to see how your data looks with the selected type.

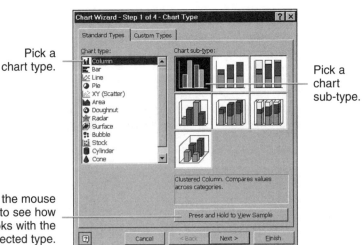

5. Click the **Next** button. The Chart Wizard Step 2 of 4 dialog box appears, asking you to specify the worksheet data you want to chart. (I know, I already told you to select the data; but the Chart Wizard is just making sure you selected the right data. Note that the worksheet name, followed by an exclamation point, appears at the beginning of the range.)

6. If the data you want to graph is already selected, go to step 7. If Chart Wizard is highlighting the wrong data, drag over the correct data in your worksheet. (You can move the Chart Wizard dialog box out of the way by clicking the **Collapse Dialog Box** button just to the right of the Data Range text box.)

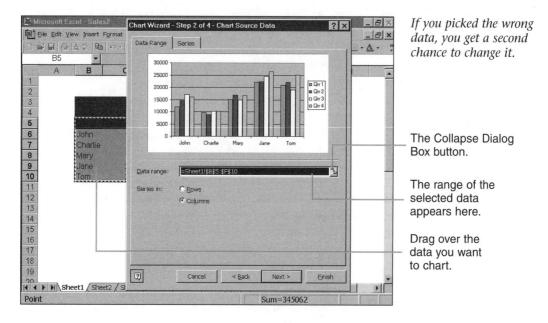

If you picked the wrong data, you get a second chance to change it.

The Collapse Dialog Box button.

The range of the selected data appears here.

Drag over the data you want to chart.

7. Under Series In, click **Rows** or **Columns** to specify how you want the data graphed. Your selection tells Excel which labels to use for the category axis and which ones to use for the legend. This is a tough choice that is best done by trial and error.

8. Click the **Next** button. The Chart Wizard Step 3 of 4 dialog box appears, prompting you to enter additional preferences for your chart.

9. Enter your preferences on the various tabs to give your chart a title, name the X and Y axes, turn on additional gridlines, move the legend, enter data labels, and more. Most of these options are described in "Adding Text, Arrows, and Other Objects," later in this chapter.

10. Click the **Next** button. The Chart Wizard Step 4 of 4 dialog box appears, asking whether you want to insert the chart on the current worksheet or on a new worksheet.

11. If you want the chart to appear alongside your data, select **As Object In**. To have the chart appear on a worksheet of its own, select **As New Sheet** and type a name for the sheet.

12. Click **Finish**. Excel makes the chart and slaps it on a worksheet.

If your chart has only two or three data types to graph, it probably looks okay. If you choose to graph several columns or rows, chances are that all your data labels are scrunched up, your legend is chopped in half, and several other eyesores have popped up. Fortunately, you can fix most of these problems by resizing the chart.

If you inserted the chart as an object, you can move and resize the chart. First click the chart's background to select it. (If you haven't clicked outside the chart since creating it, it is already selected and the Chart toolbar is displayed.) Make sure you click the chart's background and not some object on the chart itself. If you click an object, such as the data area, that object is selected. This can be a bit tricky at first.

Controlled Dragging

When resizing a chart, you can hold down the **Ctrl** key and drag to expand or shrink the chart from the center. Hold down the **Shift** key and drag to ensure that the chart retains its relative dimensions.

Excel displays tiny squares around the chart, called *handles*. To resize the chart, drag one of its handles. To move the chart, position the mouse pointer over the chart (not on a handle), and drag the chart to the desired location. To delete the chart and start over, select the chart and press the **Delete** key. If the chart is on a separate worksheet, delete the worksheet.

So Now You Want to Print It?

After you create a chart, your first impulse is to click the Print button to see what your printer spits out. Resist the urge. Unless you have some great beginner's luck, your chart probably doesn't quite live up to your expectations. It may have some overlapping text, data that's all scrunched together, and a few other minor problems. Work through this chapter to find out how to give your chart an adjustment.

When your chart is ready for the printer or when you think it's ready, click the chart and then click the **Print Preview** button (or choose **File**, **Print Preview**) to check it out. You don't want to waste paper printing a second-rate chart.

No, don't click that Print button just yet. If you want to print a full-page version of a chart that's embedded on a worksheet without printing the cell entries, select the Chart first, and then click the **Print** button. To print the entire worksheet, including the chart, click somewhere in the worksheet, but outside the chart, to deselect the chart, and then click the **Print** button. (For additional instructions on how to use Excel's printing options, see Chapter 14, "Printing Wide Worksheets on Narrow Pages.")

Changing Your Chart with Toolbars, Menus, and Right-Clicks

Before you get your hands dirty tinkering with the many preferences that control the appearance and behavior of your chart, you need to know where you can find these options. The first place to look for options is the Chart menu. If you don't see the Chart menu, you haven't selected a chart yet. Click a chart, and the Chart menu appears. This menu contains options for changing the chart type, selecting different data to chart, adding data, and even moving the chart to its own page.

A quicker way to open these same options is to right-click a blank area of the chart to display a pop-up menu. Why a blank area? Because if you right-click a legend, axis, title, or other element in the chart, the pop-up menu displays options that pertain to that element, not to the entire chart.

The third way to format your chart is to use the Chart toolbar. To display it, right-click any toolbar and click **Chart**. The Chart toolbar offers the following formatting tools:

Chart Objects. Displays a list of the elements inside the chart. Select the item that you want to format from this list, and then click the **Format Selected Object** button. (The name in place of *Selected Object* varies depending on the object. If you selected the legend, the button's name is Format Legend.)

Format Selected Object. Displays a dialog box that contains formatting objects for only the specified chart object, so you don't have to view a bunch of formatting options that you can't apply to it.

Chart Type. Enables you to change the chart type (bar, line, pie, and so on).

Legend. Turns the legend on or off.

Data Table. Turns the data table on or off. A data table displays the charted data in a table right next to (or on top of) the chart, so you can see the data and chart next to each other.

By Row. Charts selected data by row.

By Column. Charts selected data by column.

 Angle Text Downward. Enables you to angle text entries so that they slant down from left to right. Angled text not only looks cool, but it's great for cramming in a bunch of axis labels when you're running out of space.

 Angle Text Upward. Enables you to angle data labels so that they slant up from left to right.

Now that you know the various paths to the chart options, you're ready to tackle some hands-on formatting.

Bar Charts, Pie Charts, and Other Chart Types

Choosing the right chart type for your data is almost as important as choosing the right data. To see how your salespeople are doing relative to each other, a bar chart clearly illustrates the comparisons. To show the percentage of the total sales revenue that each salesperson is contributing, however, a pie chart is better. Excel offers a wide selection of charts, enabling you to find the perfect chart for your data.

To change the chart type, right-click your chart and click **Chart Type**. The Chart Type dialog box appears, providing a list of chart types. Click the **Standard Types** or **Custom Types** tab (the Custom Types tab offers special chart types, most of which are combinations of two chart types, such as a bar chart and a line chart). Select the desired chart type from the **Chart Type** list. On the Standard Types tab, pick the desired chart design from the **Chart Sub-type** list. When you're finished, click **OK** to apply the new settings.

Formatting the Elements That Make Up a Chart

The Chart Wizard is pretty good about prompting you to specify preferences when you first create a chart; but you may have skipped some of the options or chose to omit some objects, such as the legend and chart title. Whatever the case, you can always add and format chart objects later.

The easiest way to add objects to a chart is to use the Chart Options dialog box. To display this dialog box, right-click your chart and click **Chart Options**. You can then add or remove the following items:

➤ *Chart Title.* Click the **Titles** tab and type a title in the **Chart Title** text box. The title appears above the chart, providing a general description of it.

➤ *Axis Titles.* Click the **Titles** tab to type a title for the vertical (Y) axis or horizontal (X) axis. (Axis titles describe the data that's charted along each axis.)

➤ *X and Y Axes.* Bar, column, line, area, and stock charts all have two axes (X and Y). You can hide either or both of these axes by clicking the **Axes** tab and removing the check next to the axis you want to hide. This tab is not available for charts that do not use axes, such as pie charts.

➤ *Gridlines.* Every chart that has X and Y axes displays hash marks along the axes to show major divisions. You can extend these hash marks to run across the chart (sort of like graph paper). Click the **Gridlines** tab and turn on any gridlines you want to use.

➤ *Legend.* This tab enables you to add a legend to your chart. Legends display a color chart matching each color in the chart to the data that the color represents. This chart feature is particularly important if the chart is printed in black and white, using patterns or shades of gray.

➤ *Data Labels.* The Data Labels tab enables you to add text entries from your worksheet above the various bars or lines that graph specific data. These labels usually make the chart more cluttered than it already is.

➤ *Data Table.* This tab enables you turn on a data table to display specific values alongside the graph. This is another option that makes your chart overly cramped.

Run the Chart Wizard Again

If you love the Chart Wizard, you can use it to add items to your chart. Click your chart to select it, and then click the **Chart Wizard** button. This displays the Step 1 through Step 4 dialog boxes that you used to create the chart in the first place.

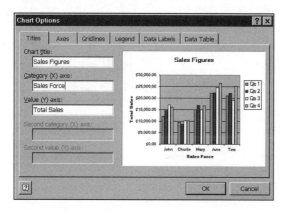

The Chart Options dialog box enables you to add items to your chart.

To dazzle your boss and impress your friends, try the following chart tricks:

➤ If you have a three-dimensional chart, choose **Chart**, **3-D View**, and use the options in the 3-D View dialog box to rotate the chart. You can even provide an aerial view of your chart.

➤ Right-click a series (for example the bars representing the sales for one of your sales people) and click **Format Data Series**. Use the resulting dialog box to change the color and shape used for the series.

➤ Don't like that dingy white chart background? Change it. Right-click the background, choose **Format Chart Area**, and choose the desired color. To give your chart a matching background, right-click the chart, select **Format Plot Area**, and enter your preferences.

Adding Text, Arrows, and Other Objects

You have a chart decorated with all sorts of embellishments, but it's still missing something. Maybe you want to stick a starburst on it that says "Another Record Year!" or point out to your business partner that the new product he developed five years ago is still losing money.

You can add items to your chart by using the Drawing toolbar. Click the **Drawing** button in the Standard toolbar to turn on the Drawing toolbar. (For details on using the Drawing toolbar's tools, see "Sketching Custom Illustrations," in Chapter 6, "Spicing It Up with Graphics, Sound, and Video.")

If you're too lazy to flip back to Chapter 6 (I don't blame you), just rest the mouse pointer on a button to figure out what it does. In most cases, you can draw an object by clicking a button and then dragging the object into existence on your chart. When you release the mouse button, the shape or object appears. You can then drag the object to move it, or drag a handle to resize it. The following figure shows some of the objects you can add to your chart.

You can doodle on top of your chart.

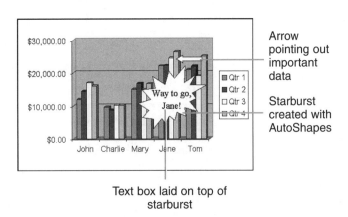

Arrow pointing out important data

Starburst created with AutoShapes

Text box laid on top of starburst

Chapter 14

Printing Wide Worksheets on Narrow Pages

In This Chapter

➤ What to do before you print

➤ Formatting tricks to make your worksheet fit on one page

➤ Repeating column headings on every page

➤ Playing hide-and-seek with columns and rows

➤ Designating print areas

Printing worksheets is Excel's version of two pounds of baloney in a one-pound bag. Worksheets are typically too wide for standard 8.5-by-11-inch paper and often too wide for legal paper, even if you print them sideways on a page. You almost need to print some worksheets on banner paper to get them to fit.

Fortunately, Excel is quite aware of the limitations you face when trying to cram wide worksheets on narrow pieces of paper; and it offers several features that can help. In this chapter, you learn how to use these features.

Preprinting: Laying the Groundwork

Before you even think about clicking that Print button, check your page setup and take a look at how Excel is going to print your worksheets. Nine times out of ten, Excel is going to insert awkward page breaks, omit titles and column headings from some of the pages, and use additional settings that are going to result in an unacceptable printout.

To check your worksheet before printing, click the **Print Preview** button (or choose **File**, **Print Preview**). This displays your worksheet in Print Preview mode, so you can at least see how Excel is going to lay out your worksheet on pages. When you are done previewing your pages, click the **Close** button to return to the main Excel screen.

Preview your worksheet before you print it.

Click the Zoom button to zoom in or out.

With Margins on, you can drag margin and column markers to adjust the margins and column widths.

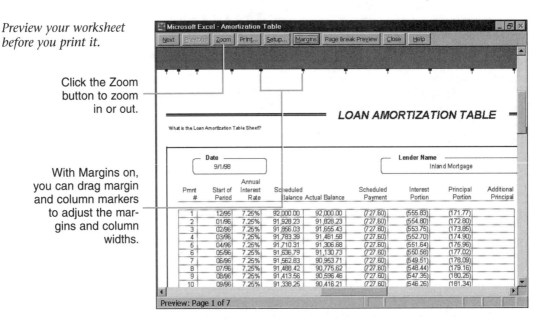

Portrait or Landscape: Setting the Page Orientation

If you have a close fit, you can usually adjust the left and right margins to pull another column or two onto the page. If the worksheet still doesn't fit, your best bet is to change to landscape orientation. This prints the worksheet sideways on the page, giving you about three more inches for your columns. To change the page orientation, take the following steps:

1. Open the **File** menu and choose **Page Setup**.
2. In the Page Setup dialog box, click the **Page** tab and choose **Landscape**.
3. Click **OK**.

Checking and Moving Page Breaks

As you create your worksheet, Excel displays dotted lines to indicate where it is going to divide the pages. You can insert your own page breaks by using the **Insert, Page Break** command. However, Excel has a feature called Page Break Preview that

142

displays page breaks more clearly and enables you to easily move page breaks by dragging them.

To turn on Page Break Preview, open the **View** menu and choose **Page Break Preview** or click the **Page Break Preview** button in Print Preview. Excel displays page breaks as thick blue lines and displays the page number in big gray type on each page. You can then drag the lines with your mouse to move them. Although this does not help you fit the worksheet on a page, it does give you control over how Excel divides the columns and rows that make up your worksheet. When you're done, open the **View** menu and select **Normal**.

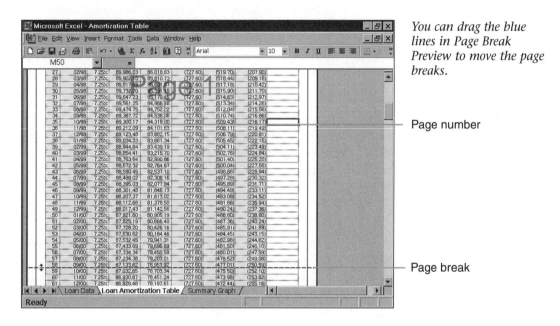

You can drag the blue lines in Page Break Preview to move the page breaks.

Page number

Page break

To insert a new page break, click the cell below and to the right of where you want the new page break inserted. Open the **Insert** menu and choose **Page Break**. Excel inserts a horizontal page break above the selected cell and a vertical page break to the left of the cell. The page breaks appear as dotted lines. (To insert only a horizontal page break, click the cell that's below the point where you want the page break inserted *in column A*. To insert only a vertical page break, click the cell to the right of where you want the page break inserted *in row 1*.)

Resizing Charts

Page Break Preview is excellent for resizing charts to make them fit on a page.

To remove a page break that you inserted, right-click the cell below the horizontal page break or to the right of the vertical page break, open the **Insert** menu, and choose **Remove Page Break**.

Repeating Titles and Column Labels

If your worksheet gets chopped in half by an errant page break, page two omits the row and column labels that indicate the contents of each row or column. This can make it difficult to make sense of any values on page two or subsequent pages. To have Excel repeat the row and column labels on each page, take the following steps:

1. Open the **File** menu and choose **Page Setup**.

2. In the Page Setup dialog box, click the **Sheet** tab.

3. To have column labels repeat, click the button next to the **Rows to Repeat at Top** text box. This hides the dialog box, so you can easily select the rows that contain the desired column labels. A small toolbar appears, displaying a button for redisplaying the dialog box.

4. Drag over the rows that contain the column labels that you want repeated, and then click the button to bring the dialog box back into view.

5. To have row labels repeat, click the button next to the **Columns to Repeat at Left** text box. This hides the dialog box.

6. Drag over the columns that contain the row labels that you want repeated, and then click the button to bring the dialog box back into view.

7. Click **OK**.

You can choose to have row and column labels printed on every page.

Click this button to hide the dialog box so that you can drag over the desired rows.

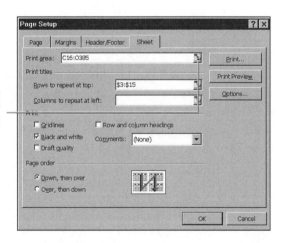

Printing Row Numbers and Column Letters

You might think that the Row and Column Headings option in the Page Setup dialog box would print the labels from your rows and columns. Actually, turning on this option tells Excel to print the row numbers and column letters.

Adding Headers and Footers

Excel can print a footer (on the bottom of each page) or a header (at the top of each page) that automatically numbers the worksheet pages for you and prints the file's name, the worksheet title, the date and time, and other information. To include headers and footers on your worksheets, take the following steps:

1. Open the **View** menu and choose **Header and Footer**. The Page Setup dialog box appears with the Header/Footer tab in front.

2. To use a header, open the **Header** drop-down list and click the desired header.

3. To use a footer, open the **Footer** drop-down list and click the desired footer.

4. Click **OK**.

To create your own header or footer (for example, to include your name or company's name), click one of the **Custom** buttons on the Header/Footer tab. This displays a dialog box that enables you to create a header or footer consisting of three sections. Type the desired text in each section, and use the dialog box buttons to format the text and insert codes for the date, time, file name, worksheet name, and page numbers. To insert "Page 1 of 5," "Page 2 of 5," and so on, type **Page**, press the spacebar, click the **#** button, press the spacebar, and click the **++** button. # inserts the number of the current page, and ++ inserts the total number of pages.

Setting the Page Order

Earlier in this chapter, you saw that Excel divides long, wide worksheets into pages using both horizontal and vertical page breaks. By default, Excel prints pages from top to bottom, printing all pages to the left of the vertical page break and then pages to the right of the vertical page break. In most cases, this is how you want your pages printed, so you can easily read each column from top to bottom. If, however, you typically read the worksheet data from left to right, you want Excel to print the pages from left to right. To change the page order, open the **File** menu, choose **Page Setup**, and click the **Sheet** tab. Under **Page Order**, choose **Over, Then Down**. Click **OK**.

If your worksheet has both horizontal and vertical page breaks, select the desired page order.

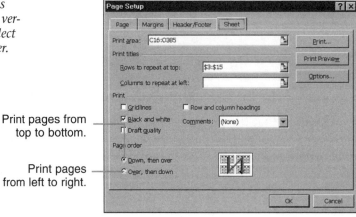

Print pages from top to bottom.

Print pages from left to right.

When It Just Won't Fit

You adjusted the column widths, changed the page orientation, fiddled with the margins, and maybe even cranked down the font settings. Short of selecting a one-point font, you've done everything you could, and the darn thing still doesn't fit on a page. Lucky for you, Excel has a couple more printing tricks tucked up its sleeve. With these tricks, you can have Excel automatically reformat your worksheet to make it fit on a page, hide columns that contain nonessential or confidential data, or even set print areas to selectively print sections of your worksheet.

Stuff It with Print to Fit

To have Excel scale your worksheet to fit on a page, open the **File** menu, choose **Page Setup**, and click the **Page** tab. Under **Scaling**, choose **Fit To**, and then enter the desired number of pages wide and tall. Use the **Wide** spin box if your worksheet has one or more columns that run past the vertical page break, and use the **Tall** spin box if your worksheet runs one or more rows beyond a horizontal page break. Alternatively, choose **Adjust To** and enter the desired scaling percentage to reduce the overall width and height of the worksheet. Click **OK**.

Selective Printing with Print Areas

Worksheets commonly contain much more data than you need to print, so Excel enables you to print selected sections of your worksheets. To print a selection, you mark it as a *print area*. When Excel prints the worksheet, it prints only the area marked as a print area.

To mark a print area quickly, first select the cells that contain the data you want to print. Open the **File** menu, point to **Print Area**, and choose **Set Print Area**. To remove the print area later, open the **File** menu, point to **Print Area**, and choose **Clear Print Area**.

Quick Print Selection

An easier way to quickly print a portion of a worksheet is to select the cells you want to print, open the **File** menu, and choose **Print**. Under **Print What**, choose **Selection** and click **OK**.

Hiding Columns and Rows

Another way to print selectively is to hide columns or rows that contain data not required in the printout. To hide columns or rows and prevent Excel from printing them, take the following steps:

1. Drag over the column or row headers for the columns or rows you want to hide.
2. Open the **Format** menu and choose **Column**, **Hide** or **Row**, **Hide**. (Alternatively, right-click and choose **Hide** from the context menu.) A dark line appears on the worksheet to indicate that rows or columns are hidden.
3. Click the **Print Preview** button. Excel displays the worksheet, omitting the hidden columns or rows.

Bringing hidden rows or columns back into view isn't the most intuitive operation. First, drag over the column or row headings before and after the hidden columns and rows. If columns C, D, and E are hidden, for example, drag over column headings B and F to select them. Open the **Format** menu and choose **Columns**, **Unhide** or **Rows**, **Unhide**.

Finally! Printing Your Worksheets

Your worksheet is looking pretty good in Print Preview, and you're just itching to print it. The quickest way to print is to click the tab for the worksheet you want to print and then click the **Print** button. This sends the worksheet off to the printer, no questions asked. To print more than one worksheet or set additional printing preferences, take the following steps:

1. Click the tab for the worksheet you want to print. **Ctrl**+click tabs to print additional worksheets. (To print all the worksheets in the workbook, you can skip this step.)

2. Open the **File** menu and choose **Print** (or press **Ctrl+P**). The Print dialog box appears.

3. To print all the worksheets in the workbook, choose **Entire Workbook**. Excel prints all worksheets that contain entries.

4. To print one or more pages of the selected worksheets, choose **Page(s)** under **Print Range** and enter the page numbers to specify the range.

5. To print more than one copy, specify the desired number of copies under **Copies**.

6. You can click the **Properties** button to enter additional printer settings, including the print quality. After entering the desired settings, click **OK** to return to the Print dialog box.

7. Click the **OK** button to start printing.

Enter the desired printing preferences and click OK.

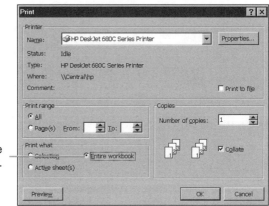

You can print the entire workbook.

Part 4

Snapping Slide Shows in PowerPoint

You probably have seen business presentation programs in action. Some suit stands in front of a group of other suits, usually in a cramped boardroom with a big oak table, and flips through a series of slides to pitch a new product or show how profitable the company is. Each slide is packed with graphs, illustrations, and bulleted lists, carefully designed to drive home the speaker's point.

Now, with PowerPoint and the chapters in this part, you get your chance to play slide show presenter. You learn how to create a professional looking slide show; add graphs, pictures, and lists; and display your slide show on your computer screen or output it on paper, 35mm slides, or even overhead transparencies. You even learn how to make a slide show that runs on any PC, even if it's not running PowerPoint!

Chapter 15

Slapping Together a Basic Slide Show

In This Chapter

➤ Using PowerPoint's ready-made slide shows

➤ Changing the overall design of your slides

➤ The five faces of PowerPoint

➤ Controlling all your slides by changing one master slide

You don't have to be a media expert in order to create the perfect slide show. With PowerPoint, you start with a predesigned slide show, change the background color and design for all your slides, and drop a few objects (pictures, bulleted lists, graphs, sounds, and video clips) on each slide. In this chapter, you learn slide show basics. Later chapters in this part show you the fancy stuff, including how to present your slide show.

Start from Scratch? Nah!

Most applications greet you with a blank screen, daring you to create something. PowerPoint is different. Whenever you start PowerPoint (**Start**, **Programs**, **Microsoft PowerPoint**), a dialog box appears, asking you what you want to do. You have four choices: Use the *AutoContent* Wizard to help you design a slide show based on the content of your presentation, use a PowerPoint template, start with a blank presentation, or open a presentation that you or someone else already created.

Assuming you don't have a presentation and you don't want to start from scratch, create your presentation using the AutoContent Wizard or a template. The following sections provide instructions for each method.

*When you start
PowerPoint, it asks how
you want to proceed.*

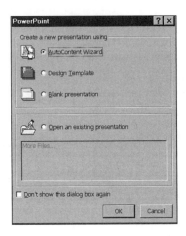

Using the AutoContent Wizard

Do you need to pitch a marketing strategy? Sell a product? Train new employees?
Advertise your company on the World Wide Web? Whatever you need to do, just tell
the AutoContent Wizard and let it lead you through the process of creating your slide
show. The wizard picks the template you need, enables you to specify the desired output type (35mm slides, overhead transparencies, and so on), and creates a standard
presentation, which you can customize.

To use the AutoContent Wizard, start PowerPoint, make sure **AutoContent Wizard**
is selected, and click **OK**. The first wizard dialog box appears on your screen. (If the
startup dialog box is no longer on the screen, choose **File**, **New**, and double-click the
AutoContent Wizard icon.)

Follow the wizard's onscreen instructions, entering preferences for your presentation.
Click the **Next** button to advance from one dialog box to the next. You can display
the previous dialog box at any time during this process by clicking the **Back** button.
The only tricky question is the desired type of output:

➤ *Onscreen presentation* designs the presentation to be played on a computer.
Choose this option if you plan on having your audience play the presentation
on a computer or you plan on giving the presentation using special equipment
connected to a computer (such as a projector and speakers).

➤ *Web presentation* converts the slides into Web pages that your audience can view
using a standard Web browser, such as Internet Explorer or Netscape Navigator.
Choose this option to create a presentation to be stored on a Web server.

➤ *Black and white overheads* provides slide designs that are optimized for black-and-
white output on overhead transparencies. Choose this option if you don't have
a color printer or if you want to cut costs by printing in black and white.

➤ *Color overheads* optimizes the slide show design for color output. If you have a
color printer, choose this option.

➤ *35mm slides* transfers your presentation to 35mm slides to create a slide show such as those used in the old days. If you don't have the proper equipment, you can send your slide show on disk or via modem to a company that has the required equipment. (See Chapter 17, "Shuffling and Presenting Your Slide Show," for details.)

When you reach the final dialog box, click the **Finish** button. The wizard creates the slide show and displays it in Normal view. (Each slide contains instructions that you must replace with your own text.)

Outline of the entire presentation

PowerPoint displays your presentation in Normal view.

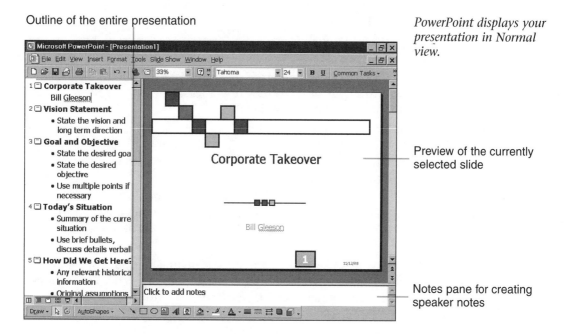

Preview of the currently selected slide

Notes pane for creating speaker notes

Starting with a Template

No wizardry is involved in creating a presentation from a template. After you start PowerPoint, click the **Design Template** option and click **OK**. Alternatively, open PowerPoint's **File** menu, choose **New** and click the **Design Templates** tab. Either way you do it, PowerPoint displays the New Presentation dialog box, offering you a collection of templates for various types of presentations.

Click the desired template and click **OK**. When PowerPoint prompts you to choose a layout for the slide (to indicate the desired objects you want placed on the slide), click the desired layout and click **OK**. PowerPoint displays the first slide of the presentation.

Changing Views to Edit and Sort Your Slides

Assuming that all has gone as planned, you now have a slide show (or at least one slide) on your screen. PowerPoint enables you to display your slide show in six different views so that you can work more easily on different aspects of your presentation. Before you start modifying your slide show, familiarize yourself with these different views:

➤ *Normal.* A combination of Slide, Outline, and Notes views, Normal view displays your presentation outline in the left pane, the selected slide in the right pane, and a notes area in the lower right pane. This is the default view, as shown in the previous figure. The notes area is useful for creating speaker notes.

➤ *Slide.* The best view for adding objects such as titles, lists, graphs, and pictures to individual slides. (See the following section, "Working on Slides," for details.)

➤ *Outline.* Best for working on the content of your presentation. Outline view enables you to organize your slides so they flow logically. (See "Organizing Your Presentation," later in this chapter, for details.)

➤ *Slide Sorter.* Great for rearranging the slides in your presentation. Slide Sorter view displays a thumbnail sketch of each slide, which you can drag to move the slide. (Slide Sorter view is explained in greater detail in Chapter 17, "Shuffling and Presenting Your Slide Show.")

➤ *Notes Page.* Displays speaker notes pages, should you choose to create them. A copy of the slide appears at the top of the page, and your notes appear at the bottom. (To view the Notes page, open the **View** menu and choose **Notes Page**.)

➤ *Slide Show.* Displays your slides as they will appear in an actual slide show. It enables you to check the transitions from one slide to another and test any animation effects that you may have added. (See Chapter 17 for details.)

The easiest way to change from one view to another is to click the button for the desired view in the lower-left corner of the window (see the following picture). You can also choose the desired view from the View menu.

Use the view buttons to change quickly from one view to another.

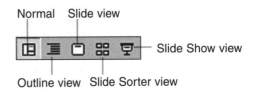

Normal   Slide view

Outline view   Slide Sorter view   Slide Show view

Working on Slides

If you created a slide using the AutoContent Wizard, you probably have at least one slide that has a box telling you to "double click" to add something. Simply double-click where PowerPoint prompts you to double-click and follow the onscreen instructions. (Chapter 16, "Adding Text, Graphics, and Sounds to a Slide," tells you how to place additional text boxes and other objects on your slides.)

To edit text directly on a slide, click the text. When you click a text object, a box appears around it with several selection handles (small squares). To work with these text boxes, use any of the following techniques:

➤ To move a text box, position the mouse pointer over an edge of the box until it turns into a four-headed arrow, and then drag the box. (When the box is selected, you can use the arrow keys to position it more precisely.)

➤ To resize a box, position the mouse pointer over one of the handles (the mouse pointer turns into a two-headed arrow). Drag the handle.

➤ To edit text inside a box, drag over the text and type new text.

Black and White View

If you're planning to print your slide show using a black-and-white printer, it's a good idea to change to Black and White view. Open the **View** menu and choose **Black and White**, or click the **Grayscale Preview** button in the Standard toolbar. (You may need to click the **More Buttons** icon on the right end of the Standard toolbar to display the Grayscale Preview button.)

Organizing Your Presentation

To rearrange your presentation using the outline, display the Outlining toolbar by right-clicking any toolbar and choosing **Outlining**. You can then use the following buttons to restructure your presentation:

Promote. Raises the selected items one level in the outline. If you select a bullet that's directly below a slide title and click Promote, for example, the bullet becomes the title of a new slide.

Demote. Lowers the selected items one level in the outline. If you click an item in a bulleted list and click Demote, the bullet becomes part of a bulleted sublist.

Move Up. Moves any items you select up in the outline. You can use this button to rearrange items on a slide or move items from one slide to another. (Before using the Move Up or Move Down button to move slides, click the Collapse All button as explained later in this list.)

Move Down. The same as the Move Up button, but in the other direction. You can also move items up or down by selecting them and then dragging their icons or bullets up or down.

 Collapse. Displays less detail on a slide. Select the slide's title before clicking this button to hide any bulleted items or other subtext.

 Expand. Redisplays the detail on a slide that you hid using the Collapse button.

 Collapse All. Hides all the bulleted text in your slide show so that only slide titles are displayed.

 Expand All. Redisplays bulleted text that you hid by clicking Collapse All.

 Summary Slide. Inserts a slide that pulls titles from other slides in the show to create an overview of the presentation. You can then transform these titles into hyperlinks and use the summary slide to jump to different slides or slide show sequences.

 Show Formatting. Turns the character formatting for the slide show text on or off. (Sometimes you can focus more effectively on the content if you don't have to look at the formatting.)

Inserting and Deleting Slides

PowerPoint's prefab presentations are great, but they either stick you with a bunch of slides you don't need or they leave you short, providing you with one solitary slide. In other words, you're going to have to either delete slides or insert them. Deleting slides is easy. In the outline or in Slide Sorter view, click the slide you want to nuke and press **Delete**. In Normal or Slide view, display the slide, open the **Edit** menu, and choose **Delete Slide**.

 Crisis Management with Undo

If you mistakenly delete a slide that you just spent the last half hour creating, click the **Undo** button to get it back.

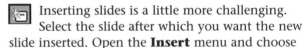 Inserting slides is a little more challenging. Select the slide after which you want the new slide inserted. Open the **Insert** menu and choose **New Slide**, or click the **New Slide** button in the Standard toolbar. Don't confuse the New Slide button with the New button. The New button (at the far left of the toolbar) creates a new presentation. The New Slide button (about nine buttons to the right) creates a new slide in the current presentation.

The New Slide dialog box appears, asking you to pick an overall layout for the slide. These predesigned layouts contain text boxes for titles and bulleted lists, graphic boxes for inserting clip art or charts, and additional objects that you must alter to create your slide. Click the desired layout and click **OK**. PowerPoint inserts the slide, giving it the same background and color as all the other slides in the presentation.

Changing the Background, Color Scheme, and Layout

When you use a wizard or a template to create your presentation, PowerPoint gives all the slides in the presentation the same overall appearance, which is usually what you want; however, the color scheme and background design are not carved in stone. You can easily change them for one slide or for all the slides in the presentation.

To change the background, color scheme, or layout for a *single* slide, first select the slide. (You don't have to select a slide if you're changing the background or color scheme for the whole show.) After you select a slide (or choose not to select a slide), read the following sections to learn how to change the background, color scheme, and layout for the slide(s).

Applying a Different Design to the Entire Presentation

When you first created your slide show, you picked an overall design for your presentation. If you have since changed your mind, open the **Format** menu and choose **Apply Design Template**, or open the Common Tasks drop-down list and click **Apply Design Template**. The Apply Design Template dialog box appears, displaying a long list of templates. Click the name of the desired template and click the **Apply** button.

Changing the Background

Behind every slide is a color background. You can change the background color and pattern and even use a picture as the background. To change the background, open the **Format** menu and choose **Background** to display the Background dialog box. Open the **Background Fill** drop-down list and choose

Lifting a Design from a Presentation

If you or someone else has already created a custom design for a presentation, you can apply that design to the current presentation. In the Apply Design Template dialog box, change to the drive and folder where the presentation is stored. From the **Files of Type** drop-down list, choose **Presentations and Shows**. Click the desired presentation and then click the **Apply** button.

the desired color swatch. To use a custom color, click **More Colors**, and then use the Colors dialog box to pick a color or create your own custom color.

Think Ahead

When choosing colored or textured backgrounds, think about how you are outputting your slides. A textured background may look great on 35mm slides, but awful in print or on transparencies. If you're planning to publish your presentation electronically on the Web, keep in mind that the background may look fine in PowerPoint but terrible when displayed in a Web browser.

Colors are swell, but if you want to jazz up a slide show, you need to give your slides a background pattern or texture. To do this, display the Background dialog box, open the **Background Fill** drop-down list, and choose **Fill Effects**. The Fill Effects dialog box appears, offering four tabs packed with options for adding shading styles, textures, patterns, or a background picture to your presentation. The best way to get a feel for these options is to experiment while keeping an eye on the Sample area.

Experiment with the background fill effects to give your background a unique look.

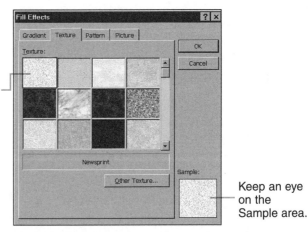

Textures provide a sort of bathroom Formica look.

Keep an eye on the Sample area.

Picking a Different Color Scheme

Every template is set up to display the various elements on a slide in a different color. Slide titles are one color, bulleted items are another color, and fills are another color. You can change the colors used for the various elements. Open the **Format** menu and choose **Slide Color Scheme**.

158

The Color Scheme dialog box enables you to choose a predesigned color scheme or create your own custom color scheme. To stay on the safe side, choose one of the prefab color schemes to ensure that you won't have clashing colors or a weird text/background mix. If you're feeling a little daring, click the **Custom** tab and choose a color for each element on the slides. When you're done, choose **Apply to All** (to apply the new color scheme to all the slides) or **Apply** (to apply the scheme to only the selected slide).

Taking Control with the Master Slide

Behind every good slide show is a Master slide, which acts as the puppet master, pulling the strings that make the other slides behave the way they do. The Master slide controls the font style and size for the slide titles and bulleted lists, and it contains any graphics that appear on all the slides. In addition, it inserts the date, slide number, and any other information that you want to display on *all* slides in the presentation.

To display the Master slide, open the **View** menu, point to **Master**, and click **Slide Master**. This displays the Title Master, so delete it—see the next page. Then make any of the following changes to the Master slide that you want to affect all the slides in the presentation:

Restructuring Your Slides

To quickly rearrange objects on your slide, select the slide and then open the Common Tasks drop-down list (on the Formatting tool-bar) and click **Slide Layout.** Choose the desired layout and click the **Apply** button.

➤ To change the appearance of the slide titles, drag over the slide title on the Master slide, and then use the **Font** and **Font Size** drop-down lists in the Formatting toolbar to change the font and font size. For additional font options, open the **Format** menu and choose **Font**.

➤ To change the appearance of the text in bulleted lists, drag over the bullet level, and then use the **Font** and **Font Size** drop-down lists to change the font. Right-click a bullet level that you'd like to change, select **Bullets and Numbering** from the context menu, and change the bullet style to something you like better—for instance, little plants, hearts, or big orange diamonds.

➤ You can place additional text or graphics on the Master slide just as if you were placing them on any slide in the show. (See Chapter 16, "Adding Text, Graphics, and Sounds to a Slide.") The picture will then appear in the same location on all slides.

➤ If the Master slide has a text box that inserts the date or slide number on every slide, you can edit the text in the box or change its font and alignment.

159

Format the Master slide to control the appearance of all slides in the presentation.

Change the format of the title to change the appearance of every slide title.

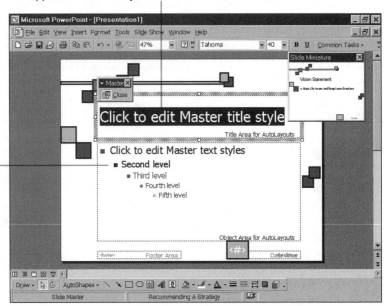

Change the format of a bullet to change its appearance on all slides.

When you're done fooling around with the Master slide, click the **Close** button in the Master toolbar (to return to Slide View) or click the desired view button in the lower-left corner of the PowerPoint window.

The Masters Tour

PowerPoint offers additional Master views, including Title Master, Handouts Master, and Notes Master, which are all listed on the **View**, **Master** submenu. Title Master enables you to control the formatting for all titles and subtitles on your slides. To quickly view the Title Master, Shift + click the **Slide View** button in the lower left corner of the window.

Although the Master slide initially controls all aspects of every slide in your slide show, any changes you make to an individual slide override the formatting of the Master slide. You can, for example, change the font used for the title on one slide. If you decide later that you want to use the formatting from the Master slide, select the slide that contains the special formatting, open the **Common Tasks** drop-down list, click **Slide Layout**, and click **Reapply** in the Slide Layout dialog box.

If you add a graphic such as a company logo to the Master slide, it appears on all slides in the presentation. To prevent any image (including images that are part of the original template) from appearing on a particular slide, select the slide, open the **Format** menu, choose **Background**, click **Omit Background Graphics from Master**, and click **Apply**.

Chapter 16

Adding Text, Graphics, and Sounds to a Slide

In This Chapter

➤ Adding boxes for titles, lists, and other text

➤ Presenting data graphically with charts

➤ Spicing up your presentation with clip art and line drawings

➤ Exploring the third dimension with sound and video

Managing Existing Objects

Throughout this chapter, you're going to be placing new objects on your slides, which may obstruct existing objects. To learn the basics of working with layered objects, see "Working with Layers of Objects" and "Working with Two or More Objects as a Group," in Chapter 6, "Spicing It Up with Graphics, Sound, and Video."

Starting a presentation with a template or even with the AutoContent Wizard doesn't give you much to work with. These tools provide you with a background design and color scheme, and they may give you some direction on what to include in your presentation; but overall they're pretty drab. If you decide to go with this arrangement, your audience will be nodding off long before the grand finale.

To hook your audience and to keep your presentation lively, you need to spice it up with graphics, sound, video and any other media that reduce the time you have to speak and cut down on the amount of reading required from your audience. In this chapter, you learn how to add various media objects to your slides.

As If You Didn't Have Enough Text

I know. I just said that your slides probably have *too* much text, and now I'm going to tell you how to add even more text. The problem is that the text boxes on your slides might not be the text boxes you want to use.

To insert a text box on a slide, display the slide and then open the **Insert** menu and select **Text Box**. Drag the mouse pointer over the slide where you want the text box positioned, and then release the mouse button. Type your text. If you type more text than the text box can hold, the box automatically expands.

The Amazing Shrinking Text

The Slide Master has text boxes that display *text placeholders* on the slides in your presentation. If you type more text than fits in a placeholder box, PowerPoint automatically bumps down the type size to make it fit! (This doesn't work with the text boxes you draw on your slides.) If you don't like this feature, you can turn it off via the **Tools**, **Options** command.

Jazzing Up Your Slides with Clip Art and Other Pictures

Office comes with a ClipArt gallery that works for all the Office applications. You may have met the gallery in Chapter 6, "Spicing It Up with Graphics, Sound, and Video." You can insert clip art from the gallery into your slides. Take the following steps to do just that:

1. Display the slide on which you want to insert the clip art.
2. Open the **Insert** menu, point to **Picture**, and click **Clip Art**. The Insert ClipArt dialog box appears.
3. Click the category of clip art from which you want to choose.
4. Click the image that you want to insert and click the **Insert Clip** button.
5. Click the ClipArt dialog box's **Close** button. The Clip Gallery pastes the image on the current slide and displays the Picture toolbar, which contains tools that you can use to edit the picture.
6. You can drag one of the handles that surround the image to resize it, and drag the box that surrounds the image to move it to the desired location.

Click the image you want to insert.

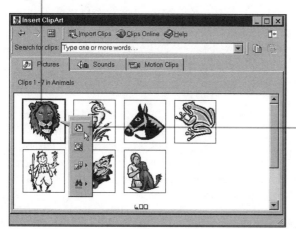

You can decorate your slides with predrawn art from the ClipArt gallery.

Click the Insert Clip button.

The Insert, Picture submenu also enables you to insert graphics files that you may have on your hard drive. Open the **Insert** menu, point to **Picture**, and select **From File**. In the Insert Picture dialog box, pick the graphics file that you want to insert.

Backing Up Your Claims with Charts (Graphs)

The staple of most effective presentations is the graph (or *chart*, as Microsoft likes to call it). Charts provide a great way of conveying numerical information visually so that your audience doesn't have to think about the numbers in order to grasp their significance.

Check This Out

Adding Shapes, Lines, and WordArt

If none of the predrawn images works for you, you can use the Drawing toolbar to create your own drawings, insert AutoShapes, add lines and arrows, and do much more. This is the same Drawing toolbar that you saw in Word. (To learn more about using this toolbar, see Chapter 6, "Spicing It Up with Graphics, Sound, and Video." To insert a WordArt object, see "Inserting WordArt Objects" in Chapter 4.)

Inserting Excel Charts

If you've already created a chart in Excel, there's no sense wasting your time re-creating it in PowerPoint. Simply copy the chart in Excel, and then paste it on a slide in PowerPoint.

If you created slides with the AutoContent Wizard or with the Slide Layout dialog box, the slide may already have a space for the chart. You should see something like **Double-click to add chart**. Double-click the chart icon. If there is no designated space for the chart, click the **Insert Chart** button on the Standard toolbar.

Either way you do it, the Datasheet window appears, displaying some sample data. To enter the data you want to graph, click inside the cell (the box) where you want to insert the data, type your entry, and press **Enter** or use one of the arrow keys to move to the next box.

Initially, data is graphed by rows, so the column headings appear below the horizontal (X) axis in the chart. To graph by column (so the row headings appear below the axis), click the **By Column** button in the Standard toolbar. (If the By Column button is not on the toolbar, click the **More Buttons** button on the right end of the toolbar and click **By Column**.) To learn more about customizing your chart, see Chapter 13, "Graphing Data for Fun and Profit." When you're done playing around with your chart, click anywhere outside the Datasheet window and outside the chart area.

The Datasheet window prompts you to enter the data that you want to chart.

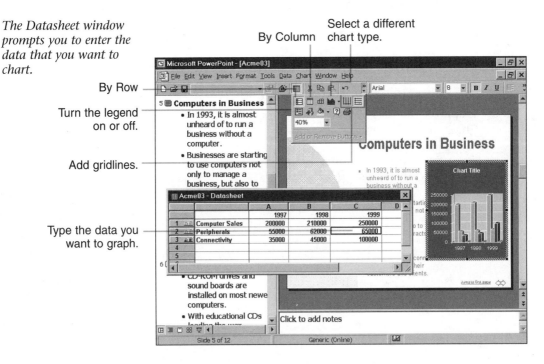

Adding Sounds to Your Slides

Does your voice shake when you speak in front of a group? Does your mouth go dry? Do you have a bad case of Tourette's syndrome? Instead of dealing with the cause of the problem, just avoid public speaking altogether! You can do it in PowerPoint by attaching sounds and recordings to your slides—assuming, of course, that you are creating an onscreen presentation and that your system is equipped with a sound card and speakers. The following is a list of the types of sounds PowerPoint enables you to use:

➤ Sounds from the Microsoft Clip gallery.

➤ Sounds recorded and saved in files on your disk.

➤ CD audio tracks. You can tell PowerPoint to play a specific track from an audio CD in the background while the slide show is playing. Just make sure you have the right CD in the drive when you're presenting your slide show.

➤ Microphone input. PowerPoint can record your voice or whatever else you want to input and display an icon for it on the slide. You can make PowerPoint play the sound automatically during the slide show or whenever you click the icon for the sound.

To insert a sound, first display the slide on which you want the sound to play. Open the **Insert** menu, point to **Movies and Sounds**, and click the desired sound option: **Sound from Gallery**, **Sound from File**, **Play CD Audio Track**, or **Record Sound**.

What you do next depends on the option that you selected. The Sound from Gallery and Sound from File options are fairly straightforward: You choose the audio clip or sound file you want to use and then confirm the action. If you choose Play CD Audio Track, use the Play Options dialog box to select the track which you want PowerPoint to start playing and the track on which PowerPoint should stop playing. If you choose **Record Sound**, the process is a bit more complicated (see the following section for details).

Attaching a Recorded Sound to a Slide

If you choose the Record Sound option, you now have the Record Sound dialog box on your screen. First, make sure your microphone is connected to your sound card and is turned on. Drag over the entry in the **Name** text box and type a name for the recording. When you are ready to speak, click the **Record** button and start speaking into the microphone (or making whatever sound you want to record). When you're done recording, click the **Stop** button and click **OK**. PowerPoint inserts a little speaker icon on the slide. Drag it to the position where you want it to appear. You can double-click the speaker icon to play the recorded sound.

Assuming that you present your slide show onscreen (instead of with 35mm slides, overhead transparencies, or handouts), whenever you advance to a slide on which you have placed a sound, the speaker icon appears. To play the sound, double-click the icon.

You can make PowerPoint play your sound automatically whenever you advance to the slide. You do this by adding animation effects (explained in Chapter 17, "Shuffling and Presenting Your Slide Show").

Narrating an Entire Slide Show

You can use the Record Sound option as described in the previous section to narrate your slide show. Just add a separate recorded sound to each slide. An easier way to narrate an entire slide show is to use the Narration feature. You advance through the slide show while speaking into your microphone. PowerPoint records your voice and attaches your narrative to the correct slides. Turn on your microphone and follow these steps to get started:

1. Go to the first slide in your presentation. (You can start recording on any slide, but it's easier to start at the beginning.)

2. Open the **Slide Show** menu and click **Record Narration**. The Record Narration dialog box appears, showing how many minutes of recording time you have based on the free space on your hard drive.

3. Click **OK**. PowerPoint changes to Slide Show view.

4. Start narrating your slide show by speaking into your microphone. Click anywhere on the slide to advance to the next slide. Keep talking. Although it looks as though PowerPoint is doing nothing, it is actually recording your voice. At the end of the show, a message appears, asking whether you want to save the timing of the slide show along with your narration.

5. To save the slide timing along with the narration, click **Yes**. To save the narration without the timing, click **No**. PowerPoint changes to Slide Sorter view; the amount of time each slide appears during the presentation is displayed below each slide.

When you run the slide show, the narration automatically plays with the show. To run the slide show without narration, open the **Slide Show** menu and click **Set Up Show**. Select **Show Without Narration** and click **OK**.

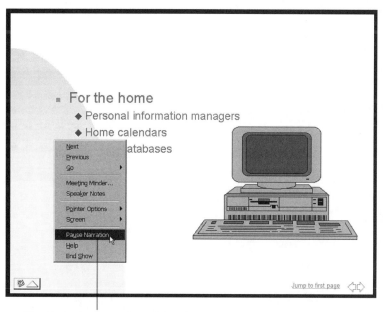

Flip through the slides and keep talking.

To pause the recording, right-click and select Pause Narration.

Going Multimedia with Video Clips

Even though the computer offers about the worst video quality imaginable, everyone seems to think that no presentation or Web page is complete without a video clip. PowerPoint has followed this lead by making it possible for you to insert video clips into your slide show.

To insert a video clip, display the slide into which you want to insert the clip. Then open the **Insert** menu, point to **Movies and Sound**, and click one of the following options: **Movie from Gallery** (you need to insert the Microsoft Office CD-ROM) or **Movie from File**. If you selected the Movie from Gallery option, the Insert Movie dialog box appears, presenting you with a list of categories. Click the desired category, click the desired clip, and click the **Insert Clip** button. If you select the File option, use the Insert Movie dialog box to pick a flick from your disk. PowerPoint supports most movie clip formats, including AVI, MPG, MPE, and VDO; so anything you lift off the Web (with permission, of course) should work.

Chapter 17

Shuffling and Presenting Your Slide Show

In This Chapter

➤ Shuffle your slides in Slide Sorter view

➤ Animate an onscreen slide show with special effects

➤ Make your own interactive presentations

➤ Rehearse and give onscreen presentations

Before you unveil your presentation, leave it for a day or two, and then come back and try to look at it from the perspective of your audience. Maybe you need to tweak one or two slides, move a bulleted list, fix a chart, or perform some other minor maintenance.

You also might need to make some more substantial changes, such as rearranging your slides and animating your slides to make your presentation more active. Before you take the stage, you also might want to draw up some speaker notes, prepare handouts for your audience, and even rehearse. This time spent in preparation will help you perfect your slide show and become more comfortable presenting it. In this chapter, you'll learn how to use PowerPoint's powerful presentation tools to do all this and more.

Rearranging Your Slides

When creating a slide show, you usually focus on individual slides, making each slide the best it can be. When you step back, however, you notice less of what's on each slide, and more of how the slides are arranged in your presentation. From this bird's eye perspective, you might notice that you need to rearrange the slides in your presentation.

The best view for arranging slides is Slide Sorter view, which displays a small version of each slide. To change to Slide Sorter view, click the **Slide Sorter View** button. To move a slide, drag the slide to the desired location. As you drag, a vertical line appears, showing where PowerPoint will insert the slide. When you release the button, the slide moves to the new position. To copy a slide instead of moving it, hold down the **Ctrl** key and drag.

In Slide Sorter view, you can move slides by dragging them.

Drag a slide to move it.

This line shows where the slide will be placed.

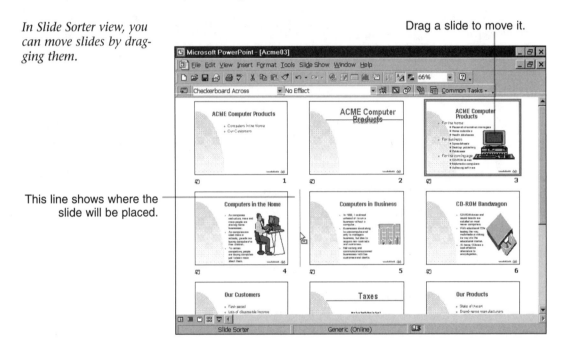

Although Slide Sorter view offers the most graphical way to shuffle your slides, the presentation outline provides a better view for evaluating the content and flow of your presentation. To move a slide in the outline, simply drag the slide icon up or down to the desired position.

Adding Special Effects

Adding special effects to your presentation can really jazz up the message and keep your audience awake. For example, if you plan to present your slide show using a computer, you can animate the transitions from one slide to the next. Perhaps you want one slide to fade out while the next fades in. The following sections show you how to add these special effects.

Special Effects on the Slide Sorter Toolbar

First, let's finish looking at all the details found in Slide Sorter view. Switch to Slide Sorter view by clicking the **Slide Sorter View** button at the bottom of your screen. Each slide in your presentation appears onscreen, as shown in the previous figure. PowerPoint also displays the Slide Sorter toolbar. As you begin working with slide effects in the following sections, you'll have occasion to use the Slide Sorter toolbar to assign special effects. Table 17.1 provides a brief description of each button.

Table 17.1   Slide Sorter Toolbar Buttons

Toolbar Button	Name	Description
	Slide Transition	Opens the Slide Transition dialog box, which offers options for animating the transition from one slide to the next.
No Transition	Slide Transition Effects	Displays a list of animation effects for slide transitions.
No Effect	Preset Animation	Enables you to animate the movement of bulleted lists and other text on the screen.
	Animation Preview	Displays the animation effects in action.
	Hide Slide	Hides the currently selected slide so it will not appear in the show. This is us ful when you want to present different versions of one show to different aud ences or keep backup material at hand.
	Rehearse Timings	Switches to Slide Show view and pro-vides a dialog box that lets you set the amount of time each slide remains on the screen.
	Summary Slide	Pulls titles from other slides in the pre entation to create a new slide. You can transform the slide titles into hype links, so you can click the titles of the other slides to quickly jump to them.
	Speaker Notes	Displays a dialog box that lets you type notes you can refer to during your presentation.

Animating Transitions from Slide to Slide

If you're using a computer to display your slide show on a monitor or using a special projector connected to your computer, you can time the transitions and add interesting animation effects. Here's what you do:

Consistency and Conformity

In most cases, you should apply the same transition effect to all slides in the presentation. However, you can apply a transition to a single slide or to a group of slides. To select several slides, click one and then **Ctrl+click** the others.

Automatic Pilot Isn't Always the Best

If you plan on presenting your slide show to a live audience, make sure On Mouse Click is selected. You never know when a question is going to pop up, and you don't want your slide show running automatically while you field questions.

1. Click the slide to which you want to apply an animated transition. (To use the same transition for all of your slides, click any slide in the presentation. You can choose to apply the transition effect to all of the slides in the last step.)

2. In Slide Sorter view, click the **Slide Transition** button.

3. Open the **Effect** drop-down list and pick a transition option. Look in the preview area (above the list) to see a demonstration of the transition.

4. Under the Effect drop-down list, click **Slow**, **Medium**, or **Fast** to set a speed for the transition.

5. Under Advance, select **On Mouse Click** to advance slides whenever you click the mouse, or select **Automatically, After ___** to have PowerPoint automatically display the next slide for you after the specified time period.

6. To add a sound to the transition, open the **Sound** drop-down list and choose the desired sound. (If you want to use a sound not found on the list, select **Other Sound** at the bottom of the list and locate the sound file you want to use.) To have the sound continue to play until the next sound starts, click **Loop Until Next Sound**.

7. When you finish with the dialog box, click **Apply** to apply the transition effect to the selected slide(s) or click **Apply to All** to use the same transition for all slides in the presentation.

Click here to preview the
selected animation effect.

*The Slide Transition
dialog box.*

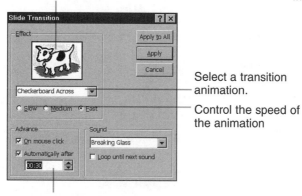

Select a transition
animation.

Control the speed of
the animation

Specify the amount of time the
slide should remain onscreen.

Using Animated Builds

Slide transitions are cool, but you can use
them only on entire slides. PowerPoint also
offers animation effects for objects on the
slide. For example, you can make your slide
text appear onscreen as if it is being typed
and even accompany the animation with the
clicking sounds of a keyboard.

PowerPoint offers these options via the
Animation Effects toolbar. To display
this toolbar, first change to Normal or Slide
view, and then click the **Animation Effects**
button in the Formatting toolbar. Table 17.2
lists and describes the buttons you'll find on
this toolbar. (You may need to click the **More
Buttons** button on the right end of the
Formatting toolbar to access the Animation
Effects button.)

Build It!

The effect of having your slide
items appear at different times and
in different ways onscreen is called
a *build*. PowerPoint includes a wide
selection of builds, such as bulleted
items appearing one bullet at a
time when you click the slide or a
graphic flying in from the side of
the screen.

Table 17.2   The Animation Effects Toolbar

Button	Name	Description
	Animate Title	Turns on the animation effect for the slide title.
	Animate Slide Text	Turns on animation effects for other text on the slide.
	Drive-In	"Drives" the object onto the slide and plays the sound of a speeding car.
	Flying	Flies the selected object onto the slide.
	Camera	Inserts object into slide with the sound of a camera click.
	Flash Once	Flashes object onto slide and then off again.
	Laser Text	Writes text onto slide with a laser-like effect and sound.
	Typewriter Text	Inserts slide text one character at a time, as if it is being typed on your screen.
	Reverse Text Order	Builds your text block from bottom up, Dave Letterman style.
	Drop In Text	Drops in each word one at a time, as if the words are falling from the top of the slide.
	Animation Order	Lets you specify the order in which items should appear on the slide.
	Custom Animation	Displays the Custom Animation dialog box, which offers additional options for controlling build animations.
	Animation Preview	Displays the animation effects in action.

To apply an animation effect, first click the object to which you want to apply the effect and then click the desired effect. Open the **Animation Order** drop-down list and select the order in which this object should appear on the slide. (If this is the first item you are choosing to animate, you have only one Animation Order option, 1.) You can select the animation order at any time.

When you're ready to run your slide show (which I'll tell you how to do shortly,) the assigned slide effects appear on your screen on command.

Animating Your Charts

PowerPoint also offers animation effects for your charts. For example, if you have a bar chart showing company profits for 1997, 1998, and 1999, you can have the bar showing each year's net profit fly onto the chart separately.

To add animation effects to a chart, right-click the chart you want to animate and click **Custom Animation**. The Custom Animation dialog box appears, with the Chart Effects tab on top. Enter your preferences for introducing the various chart elements and then click **OK**.

Making an Interactive Presentation with Action Buttons

If you are creating an online presentation to train individual workers or an information kiosk for online users, you can give your audience control over the presentation by adding *action buttons* to your slides. A simple action button might allow the user to click it to advance to the next slide. Another button might prompt the user to click it to play a video.

To add an action button to a slide, open the **Slide Show** menu, point to **Action Buttons**, and click the desired button. The mouse pointer transforms into crosshairs. Drag the mouse pointer to create a box where you want the button to appear. When you release the mouse button, the action button appears on the slide, and the Action Settings dialog box appears and prompts you to assign some action to the button. Enter your preferences and click **OK**.

This feature is particularly useful for creating slides that jump directly to other slides. For example, you can add an action button to jump directly to a slide containing backup figures for a chart. The user can jump to that slide if desired, or just ignore the button.

It's Show Time!

This is it—the moment you finally get to see how your presentation looks and runs. I'll tell you how to show your presentation electronically, give you tips for stopping and adding notes, and even show you how to write on your slides during the presentation. Places, everyone! Cue monitor...lights, camera, action!

Display the first slide in your presentation and then click the **Slide Show** view button or choose **View**, **Slide Show**. Your first slide appears in full-screen view. You can now do the following:

➤ To progress to the next slide or advance the animation, click anywhere on the screen, or press the right arrow or down arrow key on the keyboard.

➤ If you set up a specific transition time (as described earlier in this chapter), it kicks in automatically.

➤ If you selected a build effect for your slide or any slide elements, click your screen to "build" each effect (unless, of course, you timed the builds).

➤ If you've inserted any sound clips, movie clips, or other special effects, you can click their icons to start them during the presentation.

➤ To quit the show at any time, press **Esc**.

Ready for dress rehearsal? You can rehearse your slide show while specifying the amount of time each slide is to appear onscreen. Open the **Slide Show** menu and select **Rehearse Timings**. PowerPoint displays the Rehearsal dialog box, showing the number of seconds that the slide has been onscreen. When you are ready to advance to the next slide, click the **Next** button (the one with the right-pointing arrow on it). If someone bursts into your office during rehearsal, you can click the **Pause** button (the one with the double vertical lines). To change the timing for a slide, edit the numbers displayed in the time text box. When you reach the end of the show, PowerPoint asks if you want to save your slide show timings. Click **Yes**.

The New Projector Wizard

If you have a special projector that connects to your computer, you can use PowerPoint's new Projector Wizard to set it up. Open the **Slide Show** menu and choose **Set Up Show**, click the **Projector Wizard** button, and follow the wizard's lead.

Take a gander at PowerPoint's slide show controls by clicking the control button in the lower-left corner of the screen or right-clicking anywhere on the screen. This opens a menu from which you can select controls for moving to the next slide, turning the arrow pointer into a pen that writes onscreen, and even ending the show.

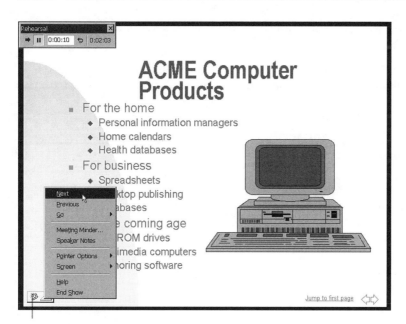

A slide during the course of the slide show.

Click here to view a menu of slide show controls.

Here's what each menu item controls:

Next takes you to the next slide or the next build effect. (It's easier to use the arrow keys or just click a slide.)

Previous takes you back to the previous slide or build effect.

Go opens a submenu that lets you select the name of a specific slide you want to view.

Meeting Minder lets you stop your slide show and compose notes, comments, and other observations made by your

Flipping Slides with the P and N Keys

To flip back a slide, press the P (previous) key. To forge ahead, press N (next).

audience. Meeting Minder even lets you type the meeting minutes during the presentation, so you can quickly review the meeting at a later date.

Speaker Notes enables you to add notes about a specific slide or to view notes you've already typed.

Pointer Options displays a submenu with options for hiding the mouse pointer, displaying the pointer as an arrow, or turning the pointer into a pen that you can use to scribble on the slides during the presentation. (The scribbles are not saved as part of your presentation.)

Screen opens a submenu for blacking out your current slide, pausing the show, or erasing your pen scribbles.

End Show puts a stop to your slide show.

Part 5

Mastering the Information Age with Access

Information is power; however, too much information, if not managed properly, can cripple your intelligence and derail any train of thought. Fortunately, we people of the late twentieth century have computerized databases that can manage the information for us. We type in the data (in the proper form), and the database does the rest: sorting it, summarizing it in reports, and helping us pull it into our other documents.

Although databases can be complicated beasts, Access provides a complete, yet simple, set of tools designed to make it easy to work with databases. In this section, you learn how to use these tools to create and manage your own databases.

Making Your First Database

Our society thrives on information. Magazines and TV news shows broadcast results of the latest polls. Telemarketers and junk mailers pay for lists of names, addresses, and phone numbers of prospective customers. People call and show up at our doors asking survey questions. And television networks use the Nielsen Ratings to figure out which shows to create (or kill).

We collect this data and pour it into computers, but then what? Someone (or something) has to tally the results and arrange the data in some meaningful format so we can use it. This something is a *database*. In this chapter, you'll learn how to create your own database so you can start dumping data into it and generating reports that make your data meaningful.

What Is a Database, Anyway?

A database is a collection of data. A phone book is a database. Your collection of cooking recipes is a database. Even your summer reading list is a database.

You can create databases in Excel by typing entries in worksheet cells and in Word by creating a table. In fact, if you need a simple database to create a mailing list or keep track of your worldly possessions, Excel can handle the job.

So why use Access? Because it provides superior reporting tools and lets you create a *relational database* that can pull entries from several tables. For example, if you need a complex database for keeping track of products, customers, and suppliers, you can create a single database consisting of several tables. When you need an invoice, you then create an invoice report that pulls entries from the customers and products tables. This lets you organize the data in smaller units and gives you more flexibility with using that data. But let's slow down and approach this relational database thing with the fear and trepidation it deserves.

Database Lingo You Can't Live Without

Before you dive in and start creating a database, there's some terminology you should know. Of course, you can proceed in ignorance; but then you wouldn't know what I was talking about when I told you to "create a field" or "select a record." Here's a quick rundown of the terms you should know and their definitions:

➤ *Form.* A fill-in-the-blanks document you use to type entries into your database. This is just like a form you would fill out to apply for a new credit card.

➤ *Field.* On a fill-in-the-blanks form, fields are the blanks. You type a unique piece of data (such as last name, first name, middle initial) into each field.

➤ *Record.* A completed form. Each record contains data for a specific person, thing, or other being or nonbeing. In a recipe database, for example, each recipe is a record.

➤ *Table.* Another way to display records in a database. Instead of displaying data on separate forms, you can have Access display the data in a table. Each row displays a record. Each column represents a separate field. A teacher's grade book, for example, would be stored as a table.

➤ *Query.* To pull data from one or more databases. If you have one database that contains customer names and addresses, and another database that contains a record of bills you have sent out, you can use a query to pull information from both databases and create a list of customers who owe you money. You'll learn more about queries in Chapter 20, "Finding, Sorting, and Selecting Records."

➤ *Report.* A document that pulls data from one or more databases and arranges it in various ways to present the data in a meaningful context and help you analyze it.

Cranking Out a Database with the Database Wizard

Now that you know all the hip database lingo, you're ready to create your own database. If you need to create a standard database, such as an inventory list, address book, or a membership directory, your job is going to be easy. The Access Database Wizard can lead you step by step through the process:

1. Start Access. (Click **Start**, point to **Programs**, and click **Microsoft Access**.) The Microsoft Access dialog box appears, asking if you want to create a new database or open an existing database.

2. Click **Access Database Wizards, Pages, and Projects** and click **OK**. The New dialog box appears, prompting you to specify the desired type of database.

3. Click the **Databases** tab, and click the wizard icon for the type of database you want to create. The preview area shows a graphic representation of what you can do with the selected type of database.

4. Click **OK**. The File New Database dialog box appears, prompting you to name your database file.

Running the Database Wizard

If the Microsoft Access dialog box is not displayed when you start Access, open the **File** menu, select **New**, click the **Databases** tab, and double-click the icon for the type of database you want to create. This runs the Database Wizard.

5. Type a name for your new database file in the **File Name** text box and select the drive and folder in which you want to store the file. Click the **Create** button. As Access creates the database file, it displays a Database dialog box and then the first Database Wizard dialog box.

6. Read the information in the first Database Wizard dialog box to find out what the wizard is going to do. Click the **Next** button. The Database Wizard displays a list of tables it will create for your database and a list of fields on each table.

7. In the **Tables in the Database** list, click the table whose fields you want to change (if any). The Fields in the Table list box shows the available fields; optional fields appear in italics.

8. Click a field name to turn it on or off. A check mark next to a field name indicates that the field will be included in the table. Repeat steps 7 and 8 to specify which fields you want included in each table.

*The Database Wizard
helps you create the
tables into which you
type your data entries.*

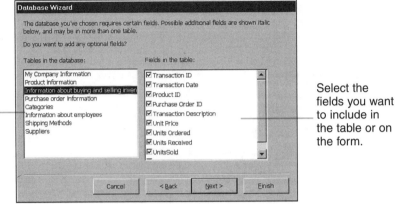

Most databases
include more than
one table.

Select the
fields you want
to include in
the table or on
the form.

9. Follow the wizard's remaining instructions to complete the process, clicking **Next** to move from one dialog box to the next.

10. When the wizard displays the final dialog box, click the **Finish** button. Access makes the database and then displays the *Database* window, which contains icons for the various elements that make up your database: Tables, Queries, Forms, Reports, Macros, Pages, and Modules.

Access may display a window called the Main Switchboard, which provides buttons for performing the most common tasks related to this database. To work on your database, you can click a button in the Switchboard or minimize the Switchboard and restore the Database window (which is minimized and in the lower left corner of the screen). The instructions in this chapter assume you are working with the Database window.

*The Database window
offers access to forms,
tables, and reports.*

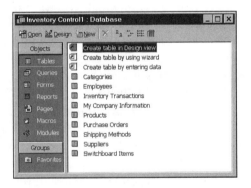

The toolbar near the top of the Database window contains buttons for adding and controlling objects in the selected category. To open a form so you can start entering data, click the **Forms** icon (in the bar at the left), click the form you want to use, and click the **Open** button. You can click the **Design** button to customize the form, table, report, or other object. The **New** button lets you create a new object, such as a table or form.

Creating and Customizing Tables

The central element in any database is the *table*. This is the structure that stores all the data you enter and supplies that data when you create a query or report, or choose to flip through your records using a form. Before you start entering data into your tables, make sure you have all the tables you need and that each table contains fields for the required data entries. The following sections show you how to take control of existing tables and create new tables from scratch.

Configuring Tables: Pick a View

You can display tables in either of two views to configure them: Datasheet view or Design view. Datasheet view displays the table as if it were an Excel worksheet. Design view displays a list of all the fields in the table and specifies the data type of each field. To open a table, click the **Tables** icon on the left side of the Database window and double-click the name of the table you want to open. To switch views, open the **View** menu and select **Design View** or **Datasheet View**.

In either view, you can move or delete fields or insert new fields. To select a field in Datasheet view, click the field name at the top of the column. You can then perform the following tasks:

➤ To move a field, drag it to the left or right.

➤ To widen a field, drag the line on the right side of the field name to the right. To make the field more narrow, drag the line to the left.

➤ To delete a field, right-click it and choose **Delete Column**.

➤ To insert a field, select the column to the left of which you want the new column (field) inserted, open the **Insert** menu, and click **Column**.

➤ To rename a field, double-click the column name and type a new field name.

As you're doing all this editing, keep in mind that the Undo feature is a little less reliable in a database program. Because Access saves your data automatically as you enter it, the database has a little trouble recovering from mishaps.

Click the field name to select the column.

In Datasheet view, a table looks and acts like an Excel worksheet.

185

You can perform the same actions in Design view, but the layout is a little different. Design view does not show the data in the table. Instead, it shows the field names and the settings that control each field. The following figure shows you how to move and delete fields in Design view. To insert a new row (add a new field), choose the **Insert**, **Rows** command.

Design view displays a list of field names and their types.

Select a field and press the Delete key to remove it.

Click the button next to a row to select it.

Drag a button up or down to move a row.

Type or change field names in this column.

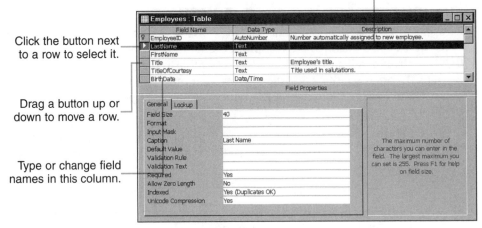

Inserting Fields That Take Data from Other Tables

To insert a field that can copy data from another table in your database, you should create a *Lookup field*. Instead of choosing **Insert**, **Rows**, choose **Insert**, **Lookup Field**. This runs the Lookup Wizard, which leads you through the process of connecting this field to the corresponding field in the other table.

Changing the Field Properties

Whenever you create a new field, you must type two entries for the field: the *field name* and the *data type*. The field name appears at the top of the column in the table and tells you what is stored in that field. The *data type* specifies the type of data you can enter into the field. For example, if you set a field's data type as Number, you can't type a regular text entry in that field.

To change the data type for a field, change to Design view. Click the **Data Type** box for the field whose data type you want to change. A button appears inside the box; click the button to open the **Data Type** drop-down list. Select the desired data type from those described in the Table 18.1.

Table 18.1   Access Data Types and What They're Good For

Data Type	What It's Good For
Text	Text entries or combinations of text and numbers: names, addresses, phone numbers, zip codes, Social Security numbers, and any other text or number that doesn't have to be sorted numerically or included in a calculation. (Text fields hold up to 255 characters.)
Memo	Lengthy descriptions over 65,000 characters.
Number	Any number except a dollar amount. Use the Number data type for numbers you might include in calculations or for numbers you want to sort, such as record numbers or part numbers. Don't use this data type for numbers you want to treat as text, such as addresses and phone numbers.
Date/Time	A calendar date or a time.
Currency	Dollar amounts.
AutoNumber	A field that automatically inserts a number for you. Excellent for numbering records sequentially.
Yes/No	True/False or Yes/No entries. As in: Did we get a Christmas card from them last year? Yes/No.
OLE Object	A picture, sound, spreadsheet, document, or other file created using some other application. (You can insert an object as large as 1 gigabyte!)
Hyperlink	A link to another file on your hard drive or the network, or to a Web page.
Lookup Wizard	Entries from other tables in the database. Choosing this data type runs the Lookup Wizard, which prompts you to pick the table from which you want to insert data. If you create a combo box (a text box with an arrow button that opens a drop-down list), you can then choose entries from a drop-down list instead of typing them into the table.

187

At the bottom of the Design view window are additional options for changing the properties of fields. For the Currency data type, for instance, you can specify that you want no decimal places used so that amounts are shown only in dollars, or you can specify that this field is required (so Access won't accept the record unless you type an entry in the required field). When you click a field name in the upper half of the window, the options in the lower half show the settings for that field. You can then change the settings. When you click a setting, some options display an arrow button to access a drop-down list. In any case, watch the big box to the right for details and suggestions on using the setting.

As you work in Design view, save your changes every five minutes or so, using the standard File, Save command. You don't want to spend your entire day fiddling with field properties and then lose it all if your system locks up.

In Design view, you can change the data types and enter additional field properties.

Select the desired data type.

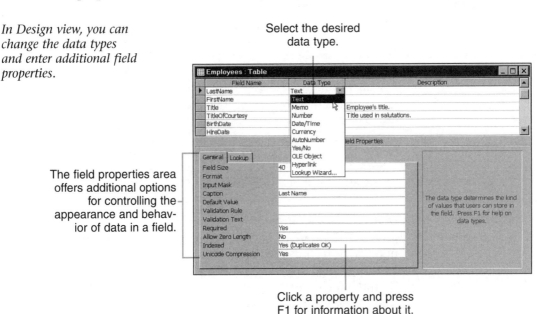

The field properties area offers additional options for controlling the appearance and behavior of data in a field.

Click a property and press F1 for information about it.

Creating New Tables

So far, you've been rearranging the fields and changing field data types in *existing* tables. But what if your database needs another table? How do you create one? First, return to the Database window, and click the **Tables** icon. The right pane in the Database window provides three options for creating a new table:

➤ *Create Table in Design View* displays a blank table in Design view, so you have to start from scratch—not the best option for a rank beginner.

➤ *Create Table by Using Wizard* runs the Table Wizard, which leads you step by step through the process of creating a new table using fields from existing tables.

➤ *Create Table by Entering Data* displays a blank table in Datasheet view, so you can immediately start typing entries. Before you start entering data, consider renaming the column headings (field names), as explained previously in this chapter.

Creating and Customizing Data Entry Forms

If you created a database using the wizard, you already have some forms you can start using. If, however, you changed your table in the previous section or created a new table, you might need to customize your data entry forms or create a new form. The following sections provide the instructions you need to get started.

Restructuring a Form

If you open a form and find that it does not contain the fields you want or that the fields are not in the correct order, you can restructure the form in Design view. In the Database window, click the **Forms** icon and click the name of the form you want to restructure. Click the **Design** button. The form appears in Design view, displaying the various controls that make up the form. When you click a control, handles appear around it, indicating that it is selected. You can then perform the following tasks:

➤ To move a control, drag it.

➤ To resize a control, drag one of the control's handles.

➤ To change the appearance of the text inside the control, select the control and then select a font, font size, or attribute (bold, italic, underline) from the toolbar.

➤ To delete a control, select the control and press the **Delete** key. (Be careful about deleting controls. Controls link the form to your table. If you delete a control, you won't be able to use the form to enter that piece of data into the table.)

➤ To change a label, drag over the existing text in the label box, and type new text. (This label should match the field name in the table or at least resemble it.)

➤ To change the Control Source (the field into which you type your entries), see the next section, cleverly titled "Changing the Control Source and Other Control Properties."

➤ To add a field or control, see "Adding Controls to a Form," later in this chapter. (You can also change the control type.)

➤ You can change the overall appearance of the form by using AutoFormat. Open the **Format** menu and select **AutoFormat**, or click the **AutoFormat** button in the Form Design toolbar.

189

In Form Design view, you can change the appearance and arrangement of the controls.

Drag the control to move it.

Drag a handle to resize the control.

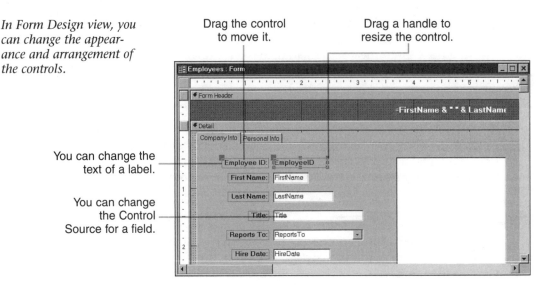

You can change the text of a label.

You can change the Control Source for a field.

Changing the Control Source and Other Control Properties

The *Control Source* links the field into which you type your entries to the table in which the entries are inserted. Say your form has text boxes into which you type a contact's last name and first name. The Control Sources for these text boxes are the LastName and FirstName fields in the table. If you created your database using the Database Wizard, you probably don't want to mess with the Control Source settings. If you're creating a new form, however, you may need to specify the Control Source for a field.

To change a Control Source, first right-click the field whose Control Source you want to change and click **Properties** (or double-click the field). Click the **Data** tab, open the **Control Source** drop-down list, and click the name of the field into which you want the data from this control inserted.

Adding Controls to a Form

If you added any fields to a table earlier in this chapter, you must add controls to the corresponding form. You do this by using the Toolbox toolbar and by "drawing" the controls on the form in Design view. You can add controls such as Text Boxes, Check Boxes, Option Buttons, Drop-Down Lists, and Images Boxes to your form.

To draw a control, click the button in the Toolbox toolbar for the desired control. (If the Toolbox is not displayed, click the Toolbox button.) Position the mouse pointer over the form and drag the mouse pointer to draw a box where you want the control to appear. When you release the mouse button, the control appears, and you can change its properties as explained in the previous section. With some controls, a dialog box appears after you create the control, asking you for more information.

190

In most cases, the control is accompanied by a box that enables you to type a label describing the control. If a label text box does not appear next to the control, you can use the **Label** button to add a Label control to the form.

Click the button for the type of control you want to add.

The Toolbox button

You can add controls to your form that correspond to fields in the table.

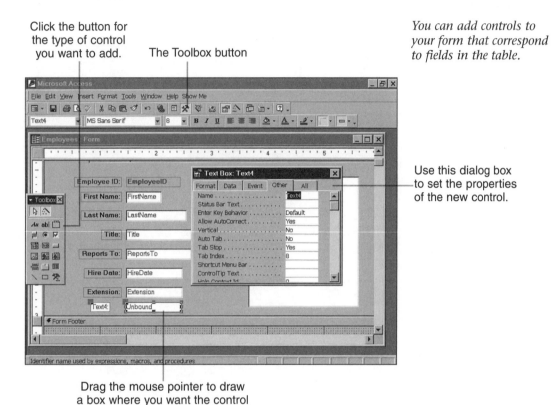

Use this dialog box to set the properties of the new control.

Drag the mouse pointer to draw a box where you want the control to appear on the form.

Creating a New Form

After you have all the tables you need for your database, creating forms for entering data into those tables is easy. The Form Wizard can lead you step by step through the process. All you have to do is tell the wizard which table fields you want included on your form and the order in which you want the fields placed.

To run the Form Wizard, click the **Forms** icon in the Database window and double-click **Create Form by Using Wizard**. The first Form Wizard dialog box asks you to pick all the fields you want included on the form from the various tables in your database. You can select fields from more than one table. Try to insert the fields in the order in which you want them to appear on the form; you can change the order later, but it's easier to do it right the first time.

After you select the fields, click the **Next** button and follow the wizard's instructions to select the layout and style for the form and to give the form a title. Click the **Finish** button when you reach the last dialog box. Congratulations, you're the proud parent of a new form!

Chapter 19

Entering Data: For the Record

In This Chapter

➤ Filling out forms when you can't find a data-entry clerk

➤ Entering data in a table

➤ Understanding a little more about the relationships between tables

➤ Selecting data entries from drop-down lists

Now that you have all your tables and forms in place, you're ready to start typing data and entering the records that make up your database. This is the boring work behind database creation, the kind of job that can give you a bad case of carpal tunnel syndrome and make you wish you had stayed in school.

You can enter data in three ways: by filling out pages full of forms, by typing entries in a table, or by entering the data in a query. This chapter shows you how to enter data using a form and a table. In Chapter 20, "Finding, Sorting, and Selecting Records," you'll learn more about queries.

How Forms, Tables, and Datasheets Differ

Before you start entering data into your database, you should understand the differences between Datasheet view, forms, and tables so you can make an educated decision about how to enter data. The following list will help you decide.

➤ If you create a form that matches one table blank for blank, you can use either the form or the table to enter data. You are filling in the same blanks, so it really doesn't matter.

➤ A form can have blanks that correspond to fields in more than one table. In such a case, it makes a big difference whether you type the data on a form or use a table.

➤ Datasheet is a *view* that is available for both tables and forms. A table in Datasheet view is very similar to a form displayed in Datasheet view, but the function of a form differs from that of a table. Even though a form in Datasheet view *looks* like a table, remember that you're still working with a form.

Filling Out Forms

We are all accustomed to filling out forms. You do it in your checkbook, at the license bureau, when you apply for a job, and even when you fill out an application for a credit card. Because you know how to fill out forms, the most intuitive way to enter data in your database is to use a fill-in-the-blanks form.

To complete a form, first display the form you want to fill out. In the Database window, click the **Forms** icon and double-click the name of the form you want to use. Either way you do it, the form pops up on your screen.

If you have any records in the database, the form displays the data that makes up the first record. To display a blank form for entering a new record, click the button that has the asterisk (*) on it.

The Form window displays records and lets you edit them or create new records.

Move ahead one record.

Display the last record.

Create a new record

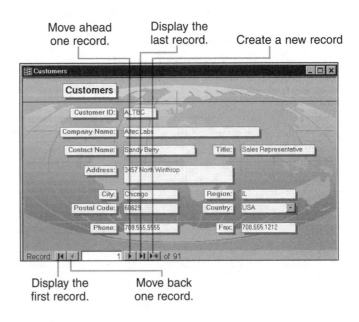

Display the first record.

Move back one record.

If you choose to create a new record, a blank form appears, prompting you to fill in the blanks. How you fill in the blanks depends on the blanks you're filling. Some blanks are drop-down lists that contain entries from other tables. To enter data, you open the drop-down list and select the desired entry. Other blanks are text boxes; type an entry in the text box. Still other blanks might require that you insert a picture. In such a case, right-click the blank, select **Insert Object**, and use the Insert Object dialog box to select the picture (or other object) you want to insert.

To move from one blank to the next, press the **Tab** or **Enter** key, or point and click with the mouse. To move back one blank, press **Shift+Tab**. (If a blank is too short for the entry you're typing, you can display the Zoom dialog box by pressing **Shift+F2** and then type entire paragraphs.) Some blanks scroll to the left on their own. If the form has another page, you can view the page by scrolling down or by clicking the desired page button at the bottom of the form.

After you have entered all the data for a record, click the **New Record** button (the one with the asterisk). This transfers all the data you entered into the corresponding table(s) and displays a new blank record for you to fill out. You can also create a new record by pressing **Ctrl** and the plus sign (**Ctrl++**).

Editing Records

You perform the same steps to edit your records. However, when you press Tab, Enter, or an arrow key to move from one blank to the next, Access highlights the entire entry in that blank. If you want to replace the entry, go ahead and start typing. To edit the entry, click the entry to move the insertion point to the position where you want to type your change. Once you have clicked in the text to edit it, you can use the left and right arrow keys to move the insertion point.

Entering Data in a Table

Although forms provide a more intuitive way to enter records into your database, a table might be more efficient. A table also enables you to focus on a single set of data, whereas a form might contain data fields for several tables.

To enter records in a table, click the **Tables** icon in the Database window, and then double-click the name of the table in which you want to add records. Scroll down to the bottom of the table, where you'll find a blank row, just waiting for you to create a new record. Just start typing; press the **Tab** key to move from one field to the next. After you type an entry in the last field in the row and press the **Tab** key, Access creates a new row into which you can type entries for the next record.

You can also create a new record by clicking the **New Record** button or choosing **Insert**, **New Record**. Access always creates a new record as a new row at the bottom of the table. After you enter the record, Access automatically rearranges the records according to the key field. To move to the first record, press **Ctrl+Home**. To move to the last record, press **Ctrl+End**.

Datasheet view lets you type records in a table.

Each row represents a record.

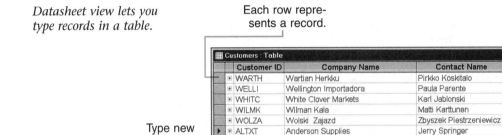

Type new records in the bottom row.

Type your field entries.

What Are These Drop-Down Lists For?

Check This Out

Creating Relationships Between Tables

The easiest way to create relationships between tables is to use the Database Wizard to set up your tables. If you need another table, use the Table Wizard to create the new table.

As you enter data in tables and forms, you'll start to notice that some of the blanks are actually drop-down lists from which you can choose an entry. You might also notice that you can't type any entries into these blanks unless they're on the list. Why? Because these fields, called *foreign keys*, are linked to fields called *primary keys* in other tables.

The following figure shows a home inventory database form for entering a record of each item you own for insurance purposes. The Categories field lets you categorize your prized possessions as furniture, collectible, appliance, and so on. The entries in this field come from another table, the Categories table. If you want to enter some other category in the Home Inventory table, you should first enter it into the Categories table so you can keep track of all the categories in your database.

Key field sup-
plies data to the
foreign field.

*Access relates data in two
or more tables by using
matching fields.*

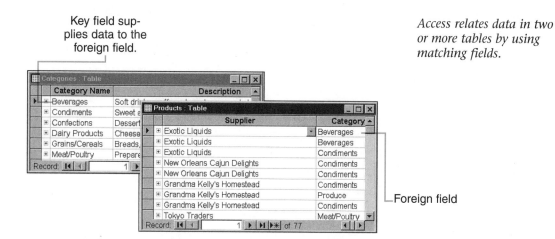

Foreign field

There is one exception to these drop-down lists. If you created a Lookup Data table (using the Lookup wizard), the second wizard dialog box lets you create the table on your own (by choosing **I will type in the values**). If you choose that option, you can type any entry; you're not locked into the entries on the list. If you choose **I want the Lookup column to look up the values in another table or query**, then another table restricts your entries.

Chapter 20

Finding, Sorting, and Selecting Records

> ## In This Chapter
>
> ➤ Taking control of your records
>
> ➤ Sorting records by name, date, and other criteria
>
> ➤ Pulling selected records out of the database with queries
>
> ➤ Making it easy with the Query Wizard

Now that you have this oversized filing cabinet sitting in your computer, how do you go about getting at those records? You didn't enter all that information just to give your computer something to do. Now you can answer the pressing questions of your business life: "How many kerflibbles did we sell last year and to which customers? Did we sell more after the Christmas promotion, or was that pretty much just another tax write-off?"

You have at least three options: You can browse through the records one at a time (which you already did in the previous chapter), list the information in every record according to field name, or create a query that pulls records that match certain criteria out of the database. In this chapter, you'll learn how to use the latter method to take control of your records.

Sorting Your Records by Number, Name, or Date

Access can sort records based on any field entry in the records. For example, you could sort a list of invoices by date, company name, the amount of the order, the payment overdue date, or even by the zip codes. Access offers two sort options: Sort Ascending and Sort Descending, which you can find on the Records, Sort submenu or as buttons in the toolbar. Sort Ascending sorts from A to Z or 1 to 10. Sort Descending sorts from Z to A or 10 to 1.

You can sort records in either Datasheet view or Form view, although Datasheet view displays the results of the sorting operation more clearly. Take one of the following steps:

➤ In Form view, click inside the field you want to use to sort the records, and then click the **Sort Ascending** or **Sort Descending** button.

➤ In Datasheet view, click the column whose entries you want to use to sort the records. Click the **Sort Ascending** or **Sort Descending** button.

Filtering Records to Lighten the Load

Sometimes you want to look at a distinct group of records. Maybe you work for a collection agency and you need to prioritize a list of people who owe money to one of your clients, and you need to know who has owed the most money for the longest period of time. To extract a select group of records you can *filter* the records, as explained in the following sections.

Filtering the Easy Way

The easiest way to filter records in Access is to use a technique called *Filter By Selection*. To use this technique, select the entry on a form that you want to use as the filter. For example, open a record that has "New York" in the City field (in Form or Datasheet view) and click in the **City** field. Then click the **Filter By Selection** button. Access displays only those records that have the specified entry in the selected field (in the example, only those records that have New York in the City field). Filter By Selection is case-sensitive, so when you're typing entries, keep this in mind.

If the list of records is still too long, you can filter the list again using another field entry. Repeat the steps using an entry in another field. To remove the filter and return a complete list of records, click the **Remove Filter** button.

When Your Filtering Needs Become More Complex

Filtering by selection is great if you have a specific entry in your record that you can use for the filter and it's easy to find. However, sometimes you need to specify a range of records. You might want a list of clients whom you haven't called for over a month or a list of records for people whose last name begins with A through K. Filter By Selection can't handle anything this complicated.

To create a more complex filter, use the *Filter By Form* technique. With this technique, you type filter criteria into various fields on a blank form to tell Access which records to pull up. In a billing database, for example, you might type <=#10/25/98# (less than or equal to 10/25/98) in the Date field to find all bills dated 10/25/98 or earlier. Table 20.1 shows some sample expressions.

Table 20.1   Filter Criteria Expressions in Action

Field	Sample Expression	Filter Displays
City	"Chicago"	Only those records that have Chicago in the City field
City	"Chicago" or "New York"	Records that have Chicago or New York in the City field
DueDate	Between #10/1/97# and #7/10/98#	Records that have an entry in the Date Due field between the dates listed
LastName	>="K"	All records with a last name entry starting with K or a letter after K in the alphabet
LastName	<="J"	All records with a last name entry starting with J or a letter before J in the alphabet
LastName	"K*"	All records with a last name entry starting with K
LastName	"*K"	All records with a last name entry ending with K
State	Not "IN"	Only records that have a State entry other than IN
Customer	Like "L*"	Records for companies whose names start with L

Access is a pretty smart database. You can omit the quotes, and Access will filter the records just as if you had typed the quotes. In addition, whenever you use the asterisk as in the last example, Access supplies "Like" for you. For example, if you type R*, Access filters the records as if you had typed Like "R*".

To filter by form, open the table that contains the records you want to filter, and then click the **Filter By Form** button. A single-row datasheet appears, displaying the names of all the fields in the table or form. Type a filter criteria expression in each field you want to use to filter the records. (The arrow next to each field displays a list of data, which allows you to perform a quick Filter By Selection operation.)

You can type a criteria expression in more than one field to further limit the group of records that the filter will display. In essence, you are telling Access to show only those records that meet the first condition *and* the second condition. To broaden the filter, you can click one or more **Or** tabs and enter expressions in the fields. For example, you might want a list of customers who owe you money *or* customers to whom you owe money.

After you've typed your filter criteria expressions, click the **Apply Filter** button. Access filters the records and displays a list of only those records that match the specified criteria. To cancel the filter and show all records, open the **Records** menu and choose **Remove Filter/Sort**.

Filter By Form gives you greater control over the filter operation.

Type a criteria expression in one or more fields.

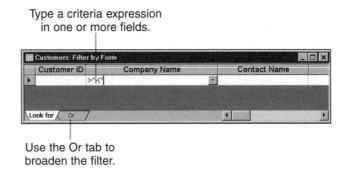

Use the Or tab to broaden the filter.

Using Queries to Sort, Select, and Calculate

Although filters are powerful tools for extracting records from individual tables, they are somewhat limited. Filters don't really do anything with the records; they don't let you combine information from different tables; and they can't extract only selected fields—they display entire records.

Access provides a more powerful data management tool called a *query*, which can do everything a filter can do and much more. The following sections explain two ways to create and use queries in your database.

Using the Query Wizards

Like all wizards, the Query Wizards are designed to simplify your life. Instead of designing your own query from scratch, you can use the Query Wizards to step you through the process of creating the following four types of queries:

➤ *Simple* queries pull data from fields in various tables, place it in a query table, and (optionally) sort the records. (This is the most common type of query.)

➤ *Crosstab* queries pull data from fields, assemble it in a table that's structured like an Excel worksheet, and (optionally) perform calculations using the data. The Crosstab query is excellent for determining totals and subtotals.

➤ *Find Duplicates* queries select all records that have the same entry in a specified field. In the Home Inventory database, for example, you could use a find duplicates query to find all possessions located in the living room.

➤ *Find Unmatched* queries select all records that have no related records in another table. This type of query is useful for finding records with missing entries. After the query is done, you can enter the missing data.

The following steps lead you through the process of creating a simple query. The steps for creating other types of queries may differ.

1. In the Database window, click the **Queries** icon.

2. Double-click **Create Query by Using Wizard.** The New Query dialog box appears, listing the Query Wizards. The first Simple Query Wizard dialog box appears, prompting you to select the fields you want included in the query.

3. Open the **Tables/Queries** drop-down list and select one of the tables whose field you want to include in the query. The Available Fields list displays the names of all the fields in the selected table.

4. In the Available Fields list, double-click a field name to move it to the Selected Fields list to include the field in the query. (You can move all the fields from the Available Fields list to the Selected Fields list by clicking the double-headed arrow.)

5. Repeat steps 3 and 4 to add more fields to the query. (You can add fields from more than one table.) When you're done adding fields, click the **Next** button. If you clicked the double-headed arrow in Step 4 to include *all* fields, skip to Step 8. If you chose fields individually, the next dialog box asks if you want a detailed query or a summary—move on to Step 6.

6. Select **Detail** to display the complete information for each field. (If you want only summary information, such as an average or sum, click **Summary** and enter your summary preferences.)

7. Click the **Next** button. The next dialog box asks you to type a title for the query or accept the suggested title and gives you the option of opening the query or modifying the query design.

8. If desired, type a title for the query.

9. To display the results of the query, choose **Open the Query to View Information**. To change the Query design, click **Modify the Query Design**.

10. Click the **Finish** button. The Simple Query Wizard creates the query and displays it in its own window.

If you chose to view the information (the results of the query), the query appears in Datasheet view. You can click a column heading to select a column and then drag the column to move it. You can also sort the query or filter it as explained earlier in this chapter. (Any changes you make to columns in the Query table do not affect the original tables.)

If you chose to modify the query design, the query appears in Design View, where you can enter additional instructions for sorting and filtering the data. When you're done entering your instructions, change to Datasheet view to display the results.

Sorting a Query in Design View

Instead of using the Sort Ascending or Sort Descending buttons to sort the records in a query, change to Design view. This view gives you more control over filtering and sorting your records. In some large databases a single level sort creates huge subgroups that are as unmanageable as when the records were unsorted. Those subgroups need to be sorted further. So you sort by State, then by County, then by City.

Creating a Query Without a Wizard

Although the Query Wizards are helpful, they may not create the type of query you need. To make a custom query, take the following steps:

1. In the Database window, click the **Queries** icon.

2. Double-click **Create Query in Design View**. The Show Table dialog box appears, prompting you to select the tables from which you want to extract data.

Drag and Drop

You can Shift+click a list of fields and drag and drop them on the fields row to add them as a group. You can Ctrl+click to select non-contiguous fields.

3. Double-click the name of each table from which you want to extract data. When you double-click the name of a table, the table is added to the **Query#: Select Query** window.

4. Click the **Close** button. The Query window shows the names of all the tables you added, as well as a list of fields in each table.

5. For each field you want to add to your query, click inside the Field box at the bottom of the window and double-click the field name in one of the tables at the top of the window. The field names are added to the Field boxes. Table names appear directly below the field names. (Or you can open the drop-down list and select the field name. Each field name starts with its table name and a colon.)

2. Double-click a
field name.

4. Click here to
run the query.

3. These fields
will appear in
the query.

*Add the fields from the
tables to your query.*

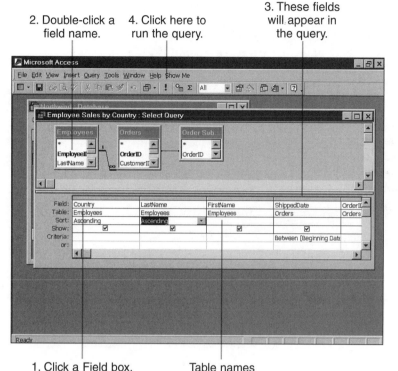

1. Click a Field box.

Table names

6. To sort the records in the query based on the entries in one of the fields, click in the **Sort** box for that field, open the drop-down list, and select **Ascending** or **Descending**.

7. To filter the records based on the entries in one field, click inside the **Criteria** box in that field and type a filter criteria expression. See "Filtering Records to Lighten the Load" earlier in this chapter for details.

8. The **Show** check boxes let you hide or display a field in a query. Remove the check from the box to hide the field if desired.

9. To run the query, click the **Run** button (the button with the exclamation point) in the toolbar. Access runs the query and displays the results in Datasheet view.

Saving, Opening, and Editing Queries

Access does not automatically save queries. To save your query, open the **File** menu and select **Save**. Type a name for the query and click **OK**. Queries are saved with the database. To open a query you saved, first open the database file. In the Database window, click the **Queries** icon and double-click the name of the query you want to open.

Totally Cool

You can add a Total row to your query to help group records and include sums, averages, and other operations in your query. To add the Total row, right-click in the query table in Design View and click **Totals**.

Whenever you open a query, Access displays it in Datasheet view. To edit it, you must change to Design view. Open the **View** menu and select **Design View**, or open the **View** drop-down list (on the left end of the toolbar) and click **Design View**. Then you can add or delete fields, hide fields, move fields, or sort and filter your records.

Chapter 21

Giving Data Meaning with Reports

In This Chapter

➤ Understanding the purpose of reports

➤ Creating reports with the Report Wizard

➤ Changing the overall structure and appearance of a report

➤ Printing your reports

Data is like money: If you don't do something with it, it's useless. Reports do something with your data. You can use a report to transform a membership directory into sheets of mailing labels or a phone list. You might also use a report to pull together a list of contributors, the amount each person contributed to the annual fund drive, and the total amount that the fund drive pulled in. Reports can even pull data from one or more tables and graph it.

In this chapter, you learn various ways to create and customize reports; and you learn how to print reports after you've created them.

The Report You Need May Already Exist!

You can save yourself some time and effort by checking to see if your database already has the report you need. If you used one of the Database Wizards to create your database, you might be in luck. The wizard makes several reports you can use immediately.

In the Database window, click the **Reports** icon to view a list of reports. Double-click the name of the report you want to view.

The Database Wizard may have already created a report for you.

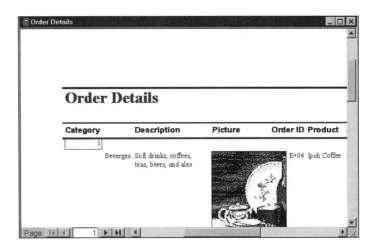

Customize an Existing Report

Even if an existing report doesn't have all the data you need arranged just the way you want it, you might be able to save time by customizing one of the existing reports instead of starting from scratch. See "Customizing the Appearance and Content of Your Report" later in this chapter for details.

Making Reports with the Report Wizard

No matter which task you want to perform in Access, you can be certain that there's some philanthropic wizard waiting in the wings to lend a hand. This is true with reports as well. The following steps walk you through the process of creating a report with the wizard:

1. Open the database file that has the data you want to include in the report.

2. In the Database window, click the **Reports** icon.

3. Double-click **Create Report by Using Wizard**. The first Report Wizard dialog box appears and prompts you to select the fields you want included in the query.

4. Open the **Tables/Queries** drop-down list and select one of the tables or queries that contain a field you want to include in the report. The Available Fields list displays the names of all the fields in the selected table. (You can select fields from more than one table.)

5. In the **Available Fields** list, double-click a field name to include the field in the report. The field moves to the Selected Fields list. (You can move all the fields from the Available Fields list to the Selected Fields list by clicking the double-headed arrow button.)

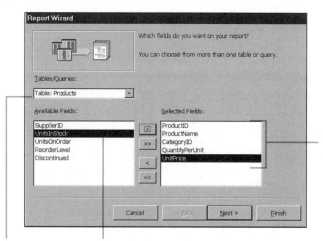

Select the fields you want to include in the report.

These fields will appear in the report.

Select a table or query.   Double-click a field to add it to the report.

6. Repeat steps 4 and 5 to add more fields to the report. When you finish adding fields, click the **Next** button. If you included fields from more than one table, proceed to step 7; otherwise, skip to step 8.

7. Click the desired table to use its fields to structure your report. Click the **Next** button. The next dialog box asks if you want to use any fields to group the data in your report.

8. Double-click a field if you want to use it to group records. If you're creating an inventory of your possessions, for example, you might want to group them by rooms. (You can insert additional fields as group headings by double-clicking their names.) Click **Next**. The next dialog box asks whether you want to sort records using any of the fields.

9. Use the drop-down lists as shown in the following figure to select the fields that contain the entries you want to use to sort the records. (For example, you might sort by LastName.) Click the sort button to the right of the drop-down list to change from ascending to descending or vice versa. Click the **Next** button. The wizard now asks you to pick a layout for the report.

You can sort the records using one or more fields.

Select the field you want to use to sort the records.

Click this button to set the sort order.

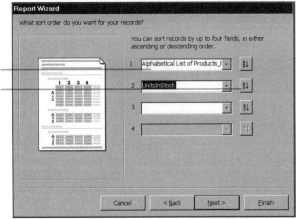

10. Click the desired layout and print orientation. Click the **Next** button. The wizard asks you to pick a font style for the report.

11. Click the desired style and click **Next**. The final dialog box lets you give the report a title or change its design.

12. Type a title for the report.

13. Choose **Preview the Report** (to display it) or **Modify the Report's Design** (to view it in Design View and modify it). Click **Finish**. The wizard creates the report and displays it.

Customizing the Appearance and Content of Your Report

If the Report Wizard just dropped the perfect report in your lap (fat chance), click the **Print** button in the toolbar—and you're done. It's more likely, however, that your report needs a little tweaking before it's ready to present to the general public. The report might need something minor, such as a font change, or some major reconstruction that requires you to move columns or perform some other heavy-duty restructuring.

To make any of these changes, display the report (in the Database window, click the Reports icon and double-click the report), and then open the **View** menu and select **Design View**. Access displays the structure behind the report. In the next few sections, you'll learn how to work in Design view to modify the report.

Working with a Report in Design View

In Design view, your report looks nothing like the report you just created. For one thing, your report doesn't have those gray bars separating it into sections. The

210

following list explains the various sections in your report and what you'll find in each section:

➤ *Headers* print on every page of the report. The report header appears only at the top of the first page. The page header and any additional headers appear at the top of every page. In addition, most reports use a header that contains the field names from one or more tables as column headings. This helps your audience figure out which information goes with which column.

➤ *Detail* is used for the data you pull from the various tables in your database. The controls in the Detail section are usually fields that pull data from one or more tables and list it under the column headings.

➤ *Footers* appear at the bottom of every page. The Report footer appears on the last page of the report; you can use it to calculate grand totals. The Page footer is useful for including a date or page number on every page. The footer just below the Detail section is useful for subtotals.

The Report Selector button

The Report header contains the title.

A report in Design view.

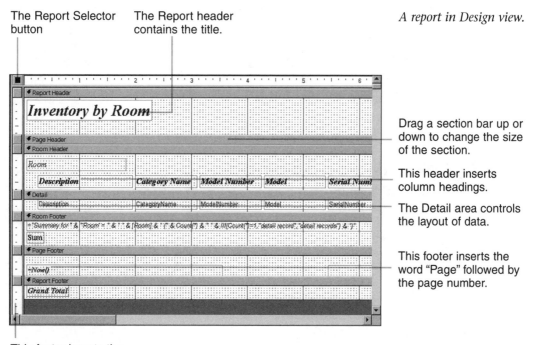

Drag a section bar up or down to change the size of the section.

This header inserts column headings.

The Detail area controls the layout of data.

This footer inserts the word "Page" followed by the page number.

This footer inserts the total number of products.

You can increase the space used for a particular section of the report by dragging the top of the bar for that section up or down. (Keep in mind that this *will* affect the page breaks in your report.) If there is no space below a section bar, double-click the bar, click the **Format** tab, and type a measurement in the **Height** box (for instance, type 1 to give the section 1 inch of space).

211

You can change the properties of a section by double-clicking the bar and then entering your preferences. To enter settings that control the entire report, double-click the **Report Selector** button, which appears at the intersection of the two rulers.

AutoFormatting Individual Objects

You can use AutoFormat to change the appearance of individual objects (controls) on the form by selecting the object before running AutoFormat. However, this might give your report an undesirable ransom note effect.

Changing the Overall Appearance of the Report

The easiest way to change the overall appearance of a report is to use AutoFormat. Click the **Report Selector** button in the upper-left corner of the window (where the horizontal and vertical rulers intersect). A black square appears on the button indicating that it is active. You can also select the entire report (or specific objects on the report) by selecting Report (or the object's name) from the Object list on the left end of the Formatting toolbar.

Open the **Format** menu and select **AutoFormat**. The AutoFormat dialog box appears, prompting you to select a style for your report. Click the desired style and click **OK**. The selected style doesn't appear in Design View. To view the report with the new design, open the **View** menu and choose **Print Preview**.

Selecting, Moving, and Aligning Controls

Design view reveals that your report is no more than a collection of text boxes and other controls. Working with these controls is very much like working with objects in a drawing program. To select a control, click it. **Shift**+click additional controls to work on more than one at a time. When you click a control, a box and a set of handles appear around the control. You can then move, resize, or delete the control:

➤ To move a control, rest the mouse pointer on the outline of the box that defines the control. When the mouse pointer turns into a hand, drag the box.

➤ To change the size of the control, drag one of its handles.

➤ To delete the selected control, press the **Delete** key.

When moving controls, you might want to align one control with another. Access can do this for you. First, select the controls you want to align; you can Shift+click controls or drag a selection box around the desired controls. Then open the **Format** menu, point to **Align**, and select the desired alignment option: **Left**, **Right**, **Top**, **Bottom**, or **To Grid** (which aligns one edge of the control with an invisible gridline).

Changing Font Styles and Sizes

You learned earlier how to change font styles for the entire report. You can also change font styles and sizes for individual controls. To do so, first select the controls that have the text you want to format. Then use the tools in the Formatting toolbar to set the desired font and font size, add attributes such as bold and italic, and change the text and background color. You can also add a border, drop shadow, or other special effect to give the control another dimension.

Adding Controls to the Report

In Design view, Access displays a toolbox containing buttons for adding controls, such as Labels, Text Boxes, Check Boxes, and Lines to your report. If this toolbox is not displayed, choose **View**, **Toolbox** or click the **Toolbox** button. The easiest way to add a control is to use a Control Wizard. These steps show you how:

1. Click the **Control Wizards** button to turn it on, if desired. (You don't have to use the Control Wizards; you can create controls without using the wizards.)

2. Click the button for the control you want to create.

3. Move the mouse pointer over the report where you want to insert the control. Drag the mouse to create a box that defines the size and location of the control. When you release the mouse button, the control appears, and the Control Wizard dialog box appears, providing instructions on how to proceed, if the control has a wizard.

4. If a wizard appears, follow the Control Wizard's instructions to create the control. In most cases, you need to supply a name for the control and tell the wizard which field to link the control to. If a wizard does not appear, simply complete the control (the Label control does not have a wizard; simply type in the label).

> *Check This Out*
>
> ### Inserting Fields
>
> If you want to insert a field in your report, there's an easier way to do it than by using the Toolbox. Open the **View** menu and select **Field List**. This displays a list of the available fields. Drag a field from the field list to the desired location on the report; Access then inserts a label box and a text box for the field. Click in the box and change the label, if desired.

Calculating Totals, Subtotals, and Averages

Some reports simply present data in an easily digestible format, such as a phone list or address list. Other reports are designed to help you draw conclusions or determine final results. You might have a report that lists income and expenses to determine profit. If the report simply lists the numbers, it won't do you much good. You need to know a final number—the profit or loss.

To perform such a task, enter a formula into your report. The formula performs calculations using the data that the report extracts from various tables. You typically enter a formula inside a text box in a section below the section that contains the numbers you want to total (in other words, below the Detail section). Before you start typing formulas, figure out which section you want the formula to appear in:

➤ To insert a calculation at the end of a row, type the formula at the end of the row that contains the numbers the formula will use in its calculations. For example, a record might include the number of items ordered and the price of each item. You could insert a formula at the end of the row that multiplies the number of items times the price to determine the total cost.

➤ If the report has more than one Detail section, you can enter formulas to perform subtotals on a column of numbers in the section just below the Detail section.

➤ To determine a grand total that appears at the bottom of the last page of the report, add the formula to the Report Footer section.

To enter a formula in a text box, click the **Text Box** button in the Toolbox and drag the box where you want to insert the formula. In the Text box, type the name of the result (for example, Total, Grand Total, or Average). Then click inside the **Unbound** text box and type your formula. For example, type **=SUM ([Income])** to total all the values from the Income fields. The following are some other examples of formulas you might use:

=SUM ([Income])–SUM ([Expenses]) determines the total profit.

=[Quantity]*[Price] determines the total cost of a number of items times the price of each item.

=AVG ([Grades]) determines the average of a series of grades.

=[Qtr1]+[Qtr2]+[Qtr3]+[Qtr4] calculates the total profit over the last four quarters.

=[Subtotal]*.05 multiplies the subtotal by .05 to determine a 5% tax on an order.

=*[Subtotal]+[Tax]* determines the total due by adding the subtotal of the order and the amount of tax due.

The formulas you see here are very similar to formulas you might use in Excel worksheets (except for the funky brackets). The main difference is that instead of using cell addresses in the formulas, you use field names to specify values. For details on using formulas in Excel worksheets, see Chapter 11, "Doing Math with Formulas."

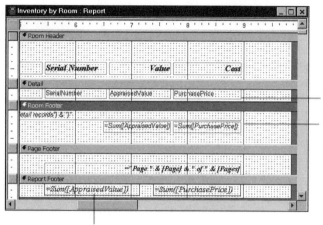

Sample formulas in Design view.

Enter formulas here to insert results at the end of a row.

Enter formulas here to insert results at the bottom of each column.

Enter a formula here to place its result on the last page of the report.

After you enter a formula in a text box, you should format the text box. If the formula enters a dollar amount, for example, you should change the **Format** property of the text box to **Currency**. To change the property of a control on a report, double-click the control, and then enter your preferences in the Format dialog box.

Saving and Printing Reports

After you've spent a good part of your day designing a report, you don't want to lose it when you shut down, so be sure to save it. In fact, you should save the report regularly as you're designing it to prevent losing any of your work. One little mistake can wipe out your report before you've had a chance to use it. Open the **File** menu and select **Save**, or click the **Save** button in the toolbar. Type a name for the report and click **OK**.

To print one copy of the report quickly, make sure your printer is turned on, and then click the **Print** button. If you want to print more than one copy of the report, or if you want to change other printer settings, open the **File** menu and select **Print**. Enter your preferences and click **OK**.

Web Work!

You might want to place your report on the Web so you can boast about your company's profits and try to attract investors. To save your report as an HTML (Web) document, choose **File**, **Export** and then open the **Save as Type** drop-down list and choose **HTML Documents**. Click the **Save** button.

Part 6

Looking After Your Life with Outlook

You've always wanted your own personal secretary to inform you of upcoming meetings, remind you of important dates (such as Secretary's Day), prioritize your list of things to do, filter your mail and memos, and basically run the office while you're out playing golf with prospective clients. Office 2000 provides you with your own tireless secretary called Microsoft Outlook.

No, Outlook can't arrange a business trip, drive deposits to the bank, or tuck you into bed when your spouse is out of town, but it can help you keep track of appointments and dates, organize your email, and even remind you of the brilliant ideas that popped into your head during the course of a day. In this section, you learn how to use Outlook to do all this and more!

Chapter 22

Keeping Track of Dates, Mates, and Things To Do

In This Chapter

➤ Get up and running with the Outlook Bar

➤ Schedule appointments

➤ Have Outlook notify you in advance of upcoming appointments

➤ Never again forget a birthday or anniversary

➤ Create and use an electronic Address Book

A handful of overachievers are ruling our lives. There's the mother who takes her lunch break to help with craft time at school. The father who comes home from a full day's work to organize the neighborhood soccer league. The retired lady, down the street, who starts a membership drive for her philanthropic organization. They quietly force us to pack our calendars with appointments, sell coupon books and candy, and do more than any generation has ever done before, driving us to early graves with hypertension.

To control this madness and preserve your sanity, let Outlook help you manage your life. In this chapter, you'll learn how to use Outlook to keep track of your appointments, contacts, and all the activities you can't seem to avoid.

Getting Started with Outlook

Before you can take advantage of Outlook, you have to run it. Open the **Start** menu, point to **Programs**, and click **Microsoft Outlook** (or click the **Microsoft**

Outlook button on the Windows desktop). The first time you start Outlook, the Startup Wizard runs and leads you through the process of setting up Outlook to access email. Follow the Wizard's instructions to complete the setup. Outlook Setup provides you with the following installation options:

➤ *Internet Only.* If you plan on using Outlook only for Internet email, choose this option. If you choose this option, the first time you run Outlook, the Internet Connection Wizard appears and leads you through the process of entering the settings required to set up your email account.

➤ *Corporate or Workgroup.* If you're on a network and use a central email server to access your company's email system, choose this option. If you choose this option and are not on a network, you may run into problems running Outlook and using its email features. To use an email service, you must set it up as explained in "Adding Email Accounts," in Chapter 23, "Managing Your Email."

➤ *No E-mail.* Who doesn't use email?!

When the setup is complete, the Microsoft Outlook window appears, as shown below. The Outlook Bar (on the left) is your key to the various features of Outlook. Here you can switch to your Inbox, Calendar, Contacts, Tasks, Journal, Notes, or list of items you deleted. Just click the icon for the desired folder in the Outlook Bar. The Information Viewer (on the right) displays the contents of the folder. You can change the relative dimensions of the Outlook Bar and Information Viewer by dragging the bar that separates them.

Outlook makes it easy to access information.

Drag these bars to change the relative dimensions of the panels.

The Information Viewer displays the contents of the folder.

Click to display a list of folders.

Click a shortcut to activate it.

Click a group bar to view its shortcuts.

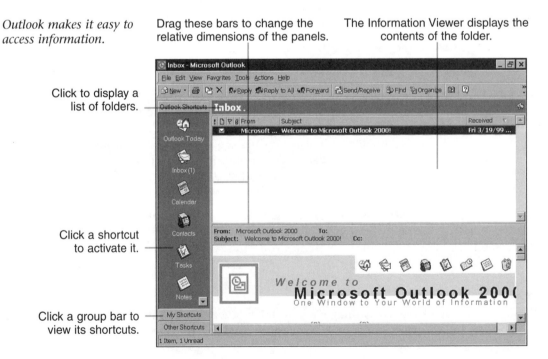

At the bottom of the Outlook Bar are short gray bars that represent other (hidden) shortcut groups. To see the shortcut icons in any of these groups, click the group (such as My Shortcuts or Other Shortcuts). Also notice that just above the Information Viewer is a folder banner that displays the name of the current folder. Click that name to display a list of folders. You can then select a folder from the list instead of from the Outlook Bar to view its contents.

Using the Standard Toolbar

Like every other Windows application, Outlook has a toolbar you can use to bypass the menu system for commands you frequently enter. Although the toolbar changes depending on what you're currently doing (setting appointments, checking email, entering journal entries), you can count on a couple of things. First, as with all toolbars, Outlook's Standard toolbar displays a ScreenTip when you rest the mouse pointer on a button. The ScreenTip shows the name of the button so you have some idea of what it does. Second, the following buttons are usually on the toolbar, no matter what you're doing:

Outlook Today

The Outlook Today icon provides a quick overview of how bad your day is going to be. When you click Outlook Today, the Information Viewer displays a list of your appointments, the number of email messages you've received, and your to-do list. To have Outlook Today appear when you start Outlook, click the **Outlook Today** icon and click **Customize Outlook Today** in the viewing area. Click the check box next to **When Starting, Go Directly to Outlook Today**, and then click **Save Changes** in the upper right of the viewing area.

New enables you to create a new mail message, new note, new appointment, or some other new item depending on the current view. In the Inbox, for example, this button lets you create a new email message.

Print prints the currently displayed item. If you're working with your calendar and you click the Print button, for example, Outlook prints the calendar.

Move to Folder displays a dialog box that contains a list of the Outlook folders, allowing you to move selected items from one folder to another.

Delete lets you quickly delete a message, note, or other item.

Find displays a new pane at the top of the Information Viewer that can help you find specific messages.

Organize displays a new pane at the top of the Information Viewer that contains tools for moving messages from one folder to another and for having Outlook automatically filter incoming messages and place them in a specific folder.

Configuring the Outlook Bar

Outlook is designed to offer you an alternative to the Windows desktop. In addition to keeping track of appointments, dates, and email, Outlook can help you organize your files and run applications. If you click the **Other Shortcuts** group in the Outlook bar, Outlook displays an icon for My Computer. Click the **My Computer** icon to display a list of icons for disk drives and folders. You can use the Outlook window just like the Windows Explorer window to copy, delete, move, and open files.

The Outlook Bar contains various folders for organizing your work.

Click Other Shortcuts to view file-management icons.

My Computer as displayed in Outlook

Click My Computer to view disk, folder, and file icons.

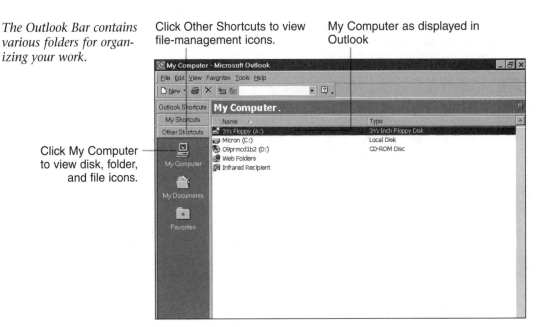

You can add folders to the Outlook Bar, in existing groups or in new groups, to give yourself quick access to other resources on your computer or on the network. You can also delete or rename existing groups:

➤ To create a new group in the Outlook Bar, right-click a blank area of the bar, select **Add New Group** and type a name for the group.

➤ To remove a group, right-click it and click **Remove Group**.

➤ To rename a group, right-click it, select **Rename Group**, and type a new name for the group.

➤ To add a folder to a group on the Outlook Bar, click the group's bar. Right-click a blank area inside the group's bar and click **Outlook Bar Shortcut**. Open the **Look In** drop-down list and select **Outlook** (to add an Outlook folder to the group) or **File System** (to add a folder from your hard drive or network). Use the folder name list to select the desired folder, and then click **OK**.

➤ To remove a folder from a group, right-click it and select **Remove from Outlook Bar**. Don't worry, you're just deleting a shortcut—not the stuff it refers to on the hard disk or in Outlook.

➤ To rename a folder, right-click it and select **Rename Shortcut**. Then type a new name for the folder.

Keeping Appointments with the Calendar

Outlook offers a Calendar that enables you to keep track of appointments and plan your days and weeks. Outlook's Calendar can even notify you of upcoming appointments ahead of time so you won't be late. In the following sections, you'll learn how to work with the Calendar in various views (by day, week, or month), how to add and delete appointments, and how to set advanced appointment options.

Daily, Weekly, and Monthly View

 To open the Calendar, click the **Outlook Shortcuts** group in the Outlook Bar and click the **Calendar** shortcut. When you first open the Calendar, it displays three items: a daily schedule, showing the hours of the day; two months, the current month and next month; and the TaskPad, displaying the names of any tasks you need to accomplish (assuming you've typed them in).

> **Techno Talk**
>
> ### Appointments, Meetings, and Events
>
> Outlook draws a distinction between appointments, meetings, and events. An *appointment* is something you do on your time, which does not demand the time of another person, such as getting your teeth cleaned. A *meeting* is something you do with other people; it requires that you coordinate a time block. An *event* is an activity that takes one or more days as opposed to a block of time during one day. An *annual event*, such as a birthday or anniversary, recurs each year.

You can change views in Outlook to display different Calendar objects or to display another arrangement. Use the following controls in the Standard toolbar to change the display:

Go to Today   *Go To Today* activates today's date as reported by the clock inside your computer.

      Day is the default setting. This option displays an hourly rundown of the current day on the left side of the Calendar window.

223

Work Week displays a five day breakdown of your schedule (Monday through Friday). It doesn't leave much room for the hourly breakdown of your days, but it does show just how hectic your schedule will be for the current week.

 Week replaces the day list with a list showing the seven days of the current week. This gives you a quick look at what's going on during a given week.

 Month displays a full-screen view of the currently selected month, showing the names of all appointments scheduled for each day. This is like the monthly calendar you have hanging in your home or office.

Setting Appointment Dates and Times

You can quickly enter an appointment in the Calendar so the Calendar displays the name of the appointment and sounds an alarm to remind you of the appointment 15 minutes ahead of time. To do this, take the following steps:

1. Click the **Day** button to switch to Day view (if you selected a different view earlier).

2. Drag over the scheduled appointment time. For example, if you have a one-hour appointment that starts at 10:00 a.m., drag over the time blocks for 10:00 and 10:30.

3. Type a description of the appointment. (For example, you might type "Meet with Ned about building plans.")

4. Press **Enter**. The appointment description appears on the Day list, and a blue box shows the time blocks that the appointment will take up.

When you set an appointment, it appears on the daily, weekly, or monthly calendar.

Bell indicates that alarm will sound prior to the appointment time.

This line shows the time you will be at the appointment.

Scheduled appointments

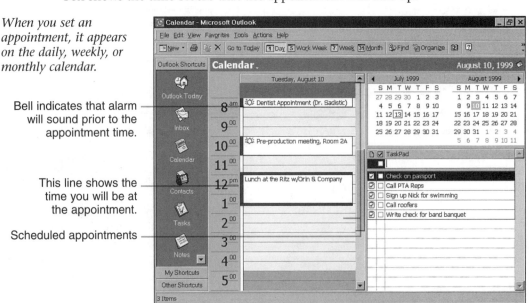

Setting an appointment by dragging and typing is quick, but it does not enable you to enter special settings, such as whether you want the reminder alarm on or off (it's off by default). To enter additional settings, use the Appointment dialog box to schedule a new appointment. To display the Appointment dialog box, double-click a time block on the daily schedule, or click the **New Appointment** button (at the left end of the Standard toolbar). Use the New Appointment dialog box, as shown in the following figure, to enter settings for the appointment.

Two Places at the Same Time?

Outlook will let you set overlapping appointments, but shoves one appointment box off to the right to provide a visual cue that your schedule might be a little tight. Darn, I guess I can't make it to that quarterly meeting after all.

Enter a name for the appointment.

Type a location, if desired.

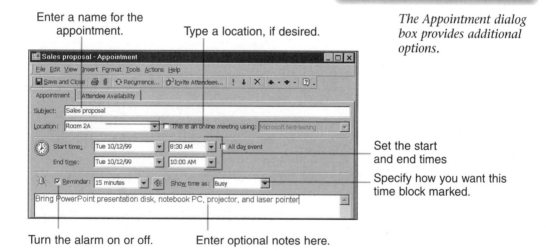

The Appointment dialog box provides additional options.

Set the start and end times

Specify how you want this time block marked.

Turn the alarm on or off.

Enter optional notes here.

When you are done entering the appointment, click the **Save and Close** button. The appointment then appears on the daily schedule. If you click the Close (X) button instead of Save and Close, don't worry. Like a good secretary, Outlook reminds you to save the appointment.

If you turned on the alarm, you might be a little surprised the first time it pops up on your screen and starts beeping. If you dozed off, you might instinctively try to hit the snooze button. Well, there is a snooze button! Click **Snooze** to be reminded again in 15 minutes (or whatever number of minutes you specify). Or you can click **Dismiss** to turn off the reminder altogether.

Divide Your Day into Shorter Intervals

You can change the default settings for the Calendar to change the times that your day starts and ends and change the days that comprise your work week. Open the **Tools** menu, select **Options**, and click the **Calendar Options** button. Enter your preferences and click **OK**. To divide your day into different intervals, right–click inside the area that displays the time intervals and click the desired interval: **60 Minutes, 30 Minutes, 15 Minutes**, and so on.

Editing, Moving, and Deleting Appointments

Unless you have a regularly scheduled appointment, you can count on the fact that your appointment will be rescheduled two or three times before the scheduled date. That's why you need some way to rearrange appointments, delete canceled appointments, and edit the appointment information. The following list provides you with all the instructions you need to perform these tasks:

➤ Double-click the appointment to display its settings in the Appointment dialog box and then enter your changes.

➤ If the appointment is rescheduled for a time on the same day, drag the appointment up or down on the daily schedule to the new time.

➤ To move an appointment to a different day, change to Week or Month view and drag the appointment to the desired day. The time will stay the same, so you might have to adjust that after moving it to the correct day.

➤ You can increase or decrease the scheduled time for the appointment. Drag the top or bottom line of the time block up or down.

➤ If your computer is on a network and you don't want other people on the network to know about your appointment, right-click the appointment and select **Private**. A key appears on the appointment, indicating that it is hidden from public view. For example, you might want to keep that appointment with the special prosecutor to yourself.

➤ You can drag an item from the Task List to the Calendar to place it on your schedule. When you release the mouse button, the Appointment dialog box appears, prompting you to enter additional details.

➤ If someone cancels the appointment altogether, you can delete it by right-clicking the appointment and selecting **Delete**.

Scheduling a Recurring Weekly or Monthly Appointment

If you have the same appointment at the same time every week or every month, you don't have to enter the appointment into the calendar for each week or month. Have Outlook do it for you by marking the appointment as a *recurring appointment*.

First, double-click the appointment to display the Appointment dialog box. Then click the **Recurrence** button. The Appointment Recurrence dialog box appears. Use it to set the frequency of the appointment, its duration, and the number of times you want Outlook to place it on the calendar. Click **OK** after entering your preferences and then click the **Save and Close** button to set the appointment.

Planning a Meeting

If you're on a network, you can set up a meeting with your colleagues using Outlook's meeting planner. Open the **Actions** menu and click **Plan a Meeting**. Click the **Invite Others** button, choose the names of the people who must attend the meeting, and click **OK**. Outlook displays the blocks of free time available for all the attendees. Drag the vertical lines to mark the start and end times for the meeting and then click the **Make Meeting** button to send your invitations.

Keeping Track of Birthdays, Anniversaries, and Other Big Events

Do you have a big family? Have they nearly disowned you because you forget to send out birthday and anniversary cards on time? Does your spouse make jokes about how you always forget your wedding anniversary? Well, the Event schedule can help remind you of these big events to help you avoid embarrassment, save your marriage, and reestablish your family ties.

Scheduling an event is no different than scheduling an appointment. First display the Calendar, and then open the **Actions** menu and select **New All Day Event**. The Event dialog box appears, looking like the Appointment dialog box's evil twin. In the Subject text box, type a brief description of the event. To have Outlook remind you before the big day, click the Reminder check box. To have Outlook remind you a few days in advance so you have time to buy a present and a card, drag over the entry in the Reminder drop-down list, and type the number of days in advance you want to be warned (for example, 5 days).

If you want Outlook to mark this as an annual event (so Outlook will remind you every year), click the **Recurrence** button. Click **Yearly** and click **OK**. This returns you to the Event dialog box. Click **Save and Close**.

Check This Out

Removing the Annual Event

You finally record your wedding anniversary in the calendar so you'll never again miss it. You're so proud of yourself. Two months later your wife informs you that you are the one thing in her life getting in the way of her happiness. Now, you *want* to forget. To remove the recurrences, click the entry for the joyous event, click the **Delete** button, choose **Delete All Occurrences**, and click **OK**. Now, add recurring entries for alimony and child-support payments.

There's a Rolodex on Your Screen!

Electronic address books used to be only slightly better than their corresponding paper versions. They enabled you to edit entries easily without erasing, and they typically provided search tools to help you find people. The current breed of electronic address books enables you to do much more. For instance, if you have an email connection, you can quickly address email messages from the Address Book. If you have a modem, the Address Book can dial phone numbers for you.

In the following sections, you'll learn how to add names, addresses, phone numbers, and other information to your Address Book and use that information to simplify your life.

Adding Address Cards to the Contacts List

Before you can use the Contacts List, you must display it. In the Outlook Bar, click **Contacts**. To add a person's name and contact information to your Address Book, click the **New Contact** button in Outlook's toolbar (all the way on the left). The New Contact dialog box appears. Use the New Contact dialog box to enter the person's name, address, phone number, email address, and other contact information. Click the **Save and New** button to save the address card and display a new blank card, or click Save and Close to close the window.

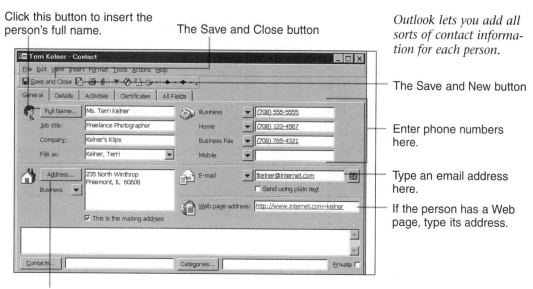

Click this button to insert the person's full name.

The Save and Close button

Outlook lets you add all sorts of contact information for each person.

The Save and New button

Enter phone numbers here.

Type an email address here.

If the person has a Web page, type its address.

Click here to insert the person's address.

When you switch back to the main Outlook screen, Outlook displays a tiny address card for each contact, arranged alphabetically by last name. If you have gobs of cards, you can click a button on the right side of the screen to display an alphabetical grouping of cards. (This is like using the lettered tabs in a paper address book.) To select a card, click it. To display all the information a card contains or edit the information on the card, double-click it.

Making Your Modem Dial Phone Numbers

If your computer has a modem, you can use Outlook to transform your three-thousand-dollar computer into a hundred-dollar programmable phone. Your modem should have two phone jacks: one that connects it to the incoming phone line (so it can dial out and talk to other modems), and another one that lets you plug in your phone. First, connect your modem to the phone jack, and then plug your phone into the modem; make sure you have the right wires plugged into the right jacks. Now you're ready to roll.

To dial out, click the address card for the person you want to call. Then open the **AutoDialer** drop-down list in the toolbar and click the number you want to dial. (If you didn't enter a phone number on the person's address card, it won't appear on the Dial drop-down list.) The New Call dialog box appears. Click the **Start Call** button. Outlook dials the phone number (with the help of your modem). Pick up the phone and start talking.

Using the Speed Dialer

The AutoDialer drop-down list contains a Speed Dial submenu on which you can list the phone numbers of the people you call most often (or emergency numbers). To add a number to the Speed Dial submenu, click the person's card, click the **AutoDialer** button, click **Dialing Options**, enter the person's name and phone number, and click **Add**. When you're done adding speed dial numbers, click **OK**. To dial a number quickly, click the down-arrow next to the **AutoDialer** button and select the number from the Speed Dial submenu.

Web Work!

If you typed a Web page address for your contact's personal or business Web page, you can quickly pull up the page (assuming you have a Web browser installed) by double-clicking the person's address card and clicking the Web page address you entered.

Sending Email Messages to Your Contacts

If you entered an email address for one of your contacts, you can quickly send the person an email message. Click the person's address card and then click the **New Message to Contact** button in the toolbar. This opens a Message dialog box with a new message addressed to the selected contact. Type a description of the message in the **Subject** text box; type the full message in the large message area at the bottom of the dialog box, and click the **Send** button. For more information about sending email messages, see Chapter 23, "Managing Your Email."

What Do You Have to Do Today?

If you like to be constantly reminded of what you have to do, get married. Short of that, you can use Outlook's TaskPad. Click the **Tasks** shortcut in the Outlook Bar. In the Task List, you can type the various tasks you need to perform. Just click the **Click Here to Add a New Task** text box, type a brief description of the task, and press **Enter**.

To enter additional information about the task, double-click it. This displays a Task dialog box, which enables you to change the name of the task, specify a starting date and due date, and turn on an alarm that sounds when the due date arrives. You can also enter billing information and other notes that provide useful information about the task.

After you've completed a task, click the check box next to the name of the task. A check mark appears inside the box, and Outlook draws a line through the task title to indicate that you've completed it. This is for management types who need to reward themselves for their minor accomplishments. For the rest of us, there's a **Delete** button. Click it to remove the task from the list.

Chapter 23

Managing Your Email

In This Chapter

➤ Creating your own email messages

➤ Incoming! Checking the mailbox

➤ Firing off replies

➤ Tidying up your messages with folders

➤ Faxing without a fancy fax machine

When you are scheduling appointments, keeping track of contacts, and honing your other life management skills, you don't want to have to switch to some other program to manage your email. You need something more convenient. You need Outlook's Inbox.

In this chapter, you learn how to use the Inbox to check for incoming mail and manage the messages in the Inbox. You also learn how to reply to messages and create and send your own electronic missives and faxes.

Nickel Tour of the Inbox

To view the Inbox, click the **Inbox** shortcut in the Outlook Bar. Two panes appear. The top pane displays a list of messages. Initially, the top pane contains a single message from Microsoft, welcoming you to Outlook. The bottom pane displays the contents of the selected message (the message itself). If two-pane view is not on, open the **View** menu and click **Preview Pane**. Just above the message list, Outlook displays the following Sort By column headings:

➤ *Importance*. Displays an icon that shows whether the sender marked the message as high importance or low importance.

➤ *Icon*. Shows a picture of a sealed envelope. After you double-click a message to read it, the envelope appears opened.

➤ *Flag Status*. Displays a flag if you choose to flag a message. You can use flags to mark messages that you might want to reread or respond to later.

➤ *Attachment*. Shows whether the sender attached a file to the message. If a file is attached, you can open it or save it to your disk.

➤ *From*. Displays the name of the sender.

➤ *Subject*. Displays a brief description of the message.

➤ *Received*. Shows the date and time the message was received.

To sort the messages by the entries in one of the columns, click that column's heading. For example, you can sort the messages by the date and time they were received by clicking **Received**. Clicking the same button again uses the same sort category, but reverses the order.

Customizing Your Columns

You can rearrange or resize the columns in the Inbox by dragging them. Drag the column bar to the left or right to rearrange. To resize a column, point between the buttons until the pointer shows a double-headed arrow, and then drag left or right. To further customize the Inbox, choose **View, Current View, Customize Current View** and enter your preferences.

When you display the Inbox, notice that the toolbar changes to provide email buttons and controls. You can use these buttons to reply to messages, display the address book, or send and receive messages, as shown in the following figure.

Compose a new message.

Reply to the selected message.

Search for messages.

Display email addresses for your contacts.

The toolbar enables you to quickly enter common email commands.

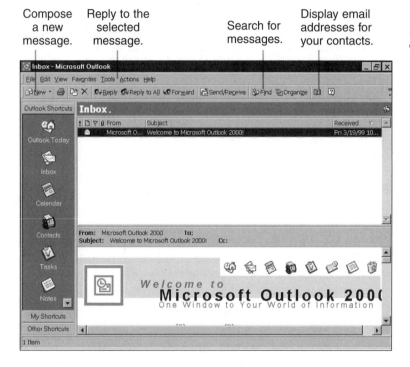

For additional email folders and options, click the **My Shortcuts** group on the Outlook Bar. The Outlook Bar changes to display shortcuts for Drafts (messages you are working on and have saved as drafts), Sent Items (messages you have already sent), Outbox (messages that you will send in the future), and Deleted Items (only if you deleted an item).

Adding Email Accounts

To check for mail and send mail, Outlook needs to know which types of email accounts you are using. The steps you take to set up an email account vary depending on the option you selected when you first ran Outlook:

➤ If you chose Internet Only, you can add an email account by opening the **Tools** menu and choosing **Accounts**. Click the **Add** button, choose **Mail**, and follow the Internet Connection Wizard's instructions to set up your email account. Your Internet Service provider should have given you the information for filling in the blanks.

➤ If you chose Corporate or Workgroup, you add *services* in Outlook that specify the type of email system you need to access, such as Microsoft Exchange or Internet email. To add an account, open the **Tools** menu, choose **Services**, and click the **Add** button. Select the desired service, click **OK**, and follow the onscreen instructions to enter the required settings.

If you chose the wrong option when you installed Outlook, open the **Tools** menu, select **Options**, and click the **Mail Delivery** tab. Click the **Reconfigure Mail Support** button near the bottom of the Options dialog box and follow the onscreen instructions.

Creating a New Email Message

After you've set up your email accounts, sending messages is fairly simple. Click the **New Mail Message** button (at the left end of the toolbar) to display the Message dialog box. In the **To** text box, type the email address of the person to whom you want to send the message. If you entered the email address on the Address card in Contacts, click the **To** button to select the person's name from a list instead of typing it. You can send a copy of the message to other people by entering their email addresses in the **Cc** (carbon copy) text box. If you type more than one address in a text box, separate the addresses with semicolons.

Click the **Subject** text box and type a brief description of the message. Then click the message area at the bottom of the window and type your message. If you want to send only a text message, you're finished; click the **Send** button. If you want to attach a file, set the importance of the message, or do some other fancy feat, use the appropriate technique described here:

➤ To attach a file to the message, open the **Insert** menu and choose **File.** Change to the disk and folder in which the file is stored and double-click the file's name.

➤ You can add fancy formatting to the message. Open the **Format** menu and choose **Rich Text** or **HTML**. Drag over the text that you want to format, and use the toolbar buttons to select a font, font size, and add attributes such as bold and italic.

➤ To use Outlook's stationery to create a fancier email message, open the **Actions** menu (on Outlook's main screen), point to **New Mail Message Using**, and click **More Stationery**. Choose the desired stationery, click **OK**, and then compose your message.

Attach a file.

Although sending a message is fairly easy, Outlook offers several options for customizing the message.

With Rich Text or HTML on, you can format text.

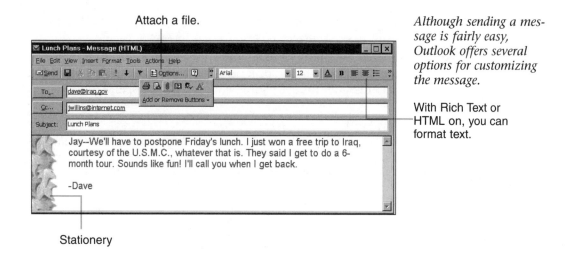

Stationery

Retrieving and Reading Incoming Messages

Whenever someone sends you an email message, it sits in a special area on the mail server waiting for you to fetch it. To retrieve your messages, click the **Send/Receive** button. Outlook connects to each mail server you set up earlier, retrieves the messages (assuming you have some), and displays a list of the messages in the Inbox. Click the message in the top pane to view a few lines of the message in the bottom pane.

You can then scroll down in the bottom pane to read the rest of the message and click the **Forward** or **Reply** button in the Outlook toolbar to forward the message or send a reply.

To display the message in its own window, double-click the message. Outlook displays the message in a special Message window, where you can use the following toolbar buttons:

➤ The **Reply** button enables you to reply to the person who sent you the message. If you click this button, a Message window appears, addressing your reply to the sender. Outlook inserts the text of the original message, with a right angle bracket (>) before each quoted line, to remind the sender what your reply is referring to. There is also a header above the original message—Original Message—so the receiver knows when your message ends.

➤ Click **Reply to All** to send a reply to the sender and to any people other than yourself listed in the To or Cc or Bcc boxes of the original message.

➤ Click **Forward** to send the message on to someone else, without necessarily adding a reply. You don't need to retype a message when you can just forward it. Besides, this is a great tool for delegating work so you can spend more time at the driving range.

➤ Click the **Previous Item** or **Next Item** button to view the previous message or the next one. These buttons double as drop-down lists providing additional options; for example, you can view the next or previous message sent by the same person, or view the next or previous message concerning this topic.

The Message window enables you to flip through the new messages and reply to them.

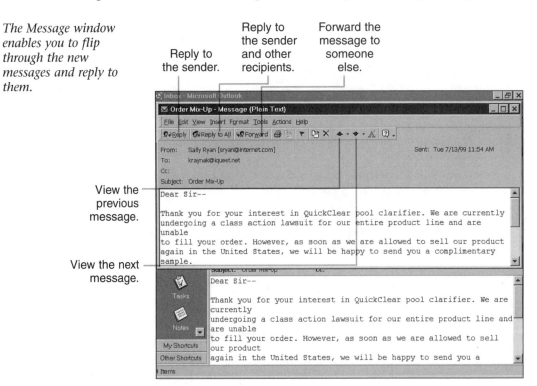

Organizing Messages in Folders

One email box is enough for most people, but if it gets cluttered and your personal mail gets all mixed up with your business correspondence, you may need additional mailboxes (or folders) to keep your mail organized. You could, of course, simply do a little manic housecleaning and delete everything from the previous nine months, but can you afford to lose those messages? By creating folders and organizing your mail, you have a comprehensive yet manageable message diary.

To create a new folder, take the following steps:

1. Open the **File** menu, point to **New**, and click **Folder** (or press **Ctrl+Shift+E**). The Create New Folder dialog box appears, prompting you to name the folder.
2. Type a name for the folder in the **Name** text box.
3. Open the **Folder Contains** drop-down list and click **Mail Items**.
4. Under **Select Where to Place the Folder**, select the folder below which you want the new subfolder created (select **Personal Folders** to place the new folder on the same level as the Inbox and Outbox folders).
5. Click **OK**. The **Add Shortcut to Outlook Bar?** dialog box appears, asking if you want the folder added to the Outlook Bar.
6. Click **Yes**. Outlook creates the new folder and displays a shortcut icon for it in the My Shortcuts group of the Outlook Bar.

You can move messages to the new folder by dragging them from one folder (probably the Inbox folder) to your new folder in the folder list. Another way to regroup your messages is to click the **Organize** button in Outlook's toolbar. This displays a pane at the top of the screen with controls for reorganizing folders and messages.

Sending Faxes

Windows 95 came with a fax program that worked all right, and you could access it through Outlook. Everything was hunky-dory. Then, Windows 98 came along, and the fax software disappeared. Microsoft gave up and struck a deal with Symantec to include its WinFax Starter Edition software in the latest version of Outlook.

To use the fax features, you must have Outlook set up for the Internet Only configuration, as explained earlier in this chapter. In addition, you must install Symantec WinFax Starter Edition from the Office CD. To run the installation, open Outlook's **Actions** menu and choose **New Fax Message**. Follow the onscreen instructions to complete the installation. (If you chose the Corporate or Workgroup configuration, you can use Microsoft At Work Fax, but you must download and install it from Microsoft's Web site; choose **Help**, **Office on the Web**.)

Rules Wizard

To have Outlook automatically move messages from a specific person or messages that contain unique content to a folder when you receive them, use the Rules Wizard. Click the Rules Wizard link near the top of the Organize pane, click **New**, and enter the requested settings to create a rule that tells Outlook how to handle incoming messages.

Once you have installed Symantec WinFax Starter Edition, sending a fax is as easy as sending an email message. Take the following steps:

1. If you are connected to the Internet, disconnect. (Outlook cannot dial the fax number if your modem is currently connected.)

2. Open the **Actions** menu and choose **New Fax Message**. The fax window appears, looking suspiciously like the email message window. (If necessary, follow the onscreen instructions to install and configure WinFax Starter Edition.)

3. If you created an entry for the recipient in your Address book and entered the person's fax number, click the **To** button and choose the person's name.

   To enter a fax number manually, type **fax@555-555-5555**, replacing the 5s with the fax number you want to dial. If you're dialing a local fax number (not long distance), omit the first three digits. For example, type **fax@555-5555**.

   If you need to dial a number to get an outside line, type **fax@9w555-555-5555**, where 9 is the number you must dial to access an outside line.

4. Type the fax message as you normally would in the message area.

5. Click the **Send** button. If you are sending the fax to a contact who has both an email address and fax number, click the arrow to the right of the **Send** button and choose **Symantec Fax Starter Edition**. Otherwise, Outlook may send the fax as an email message using your Internet account. (Try choosing **Symantec Fax Starter Edition** if you have trouble sending any fax.)

Outlook keeps a copy of the fax in the Sent Items folder, so you have a record of it. If you're sending out your résumé from your office, you might want to delete that copy.

Sending Faxes from Other Office Applications

There's an easier way to fax a document that you created in Word or Excel. Open the document that you want to fax, and then open the File menu, point to Send To, and click Fax Recipient. This starts the Fax Wizard, which leads you through the process of faxing the document. By using this method, you don't have to worry about attaching files to the fax.

Part 7

Getting Productive with Office 2000

After you've mastered the Office 2000 basics, you might start to wonder how you can use advanced features to make the most of your investment, save time, and become more productive.

In this part, you use the Office applications together and on the Web to get the most out of Office. You learn how to share data dynamically between documents created in different applications, create your own Web pages and online presentations, publish your documents electronically on the World Wide Web, and create your own shortcut keys and buttons to automate tasks.

Sharing Data Between Applications

In This Chapter

➤ Swapping data between two documents in different applications

➤ Inserting pieces of Excel worksheets into Word documents

➤ Transforming a Word document into a slide show

➤ Printing an Access database from Word

Your Office applications actually *like* to share and help one another. Excel nearly jumps out of its seat when a Word document asks to share some worksheet data or a graph. When your Access report looks as dull as Ted Koppel sounds, Word enthusiastically lends a hand, transforming that bland collection of Access data into a beautifully formatted document.

After all, Microsoft Office is a *suite* of applications. Although they take initiative and work independently, they're also designed to work as a unit—all for one and one for all! This chapter shows you various techniques for using the Office applications together in this way to create more dynamic documents and save yourself some time.

Dynamic Data Sharing with OLE

You can usually share data simply by copying it from a document you've created in one application to a document you've created in another. But just how is the data between the two documents related? If you change the data in one document, is it automatically changed in the other? The answer is: That depends. It depends on how the two applications are set up to share data, and it depends on how you inserted the copied data. You can share data in any of the following three ways:

➤ *Link*. If you're using Office applications or any other applications that support OLE (pronounced "Oh-lay," and short for Object Linking and Embedding), you can share data by creating a *link*. With a link, the pasted data retains a connection with the source document (the document from which it was copied). Whenever you edit the data in the source document, any changes you make to it appear in the destination document (the document that contains the pasted data). For example, suppose you insert an Excel graph into a Word document as a link. Whenever you change the graph in Excel, those changes appear in the Word document.

➤ *Embed*. With OLE, you can also embed data from one file in another file. With embedding, the pasted data becomes a part of the file into which you pasted it. If you edit the source document, your changes do not appear inside the document that contains the pasted data. The pasted data does, however, retain a connection with the program that you used to create it. So if you double-click the embedded data, Windows automatically runs the application, and you can edit the data.

➤ *Paste*. You can paste data in any number of ways, including as an embedded or linked object; however, not all applications support OLE. For those applications that do not support OLE, you can still share data between programs by copying and pasting the data. The pasted data, however, has no connection with the source document or the application that you used to create it.

Sharing Data with Scraps

When you're working with the Office applications, don't forget one of the great data-sharing features built right into Windows— *scraps*. If you select data in a document and then drag it to a blank area on the Windows desktop, Windows creates a shortcut for the data and marks it as a scrap. You can then drag this scrap into another document to insert it.

Embedding an Object with Copy and Paste Special

Think of embedding as using a photocopier to make a copy. With a photocopy, the original remains intact in the original location, and you have the copy. You can manipulate the copy in any way you want. You can edit it, delete part of it, highlight it, and so on, all without affecting the original. To embed data in a document, take the following steps:

1. Select and copy the data you want to use.

2. Change to the document in which you want to embed the copied data and position the insertion point where you want the data pasted.

3. Open the **Edit** menu and choose **Paste Special**.

4. To retain a connection between the pasted data and the program used to create it, choose the option with "Object" in its name. If you are pasting data copied from Excel, for example, choose **Microsoft Excel Worksheet Object**.

5. Click **OK**. The copied data is inserted as an object, and handles appear around it. Word automatically switches to Print Layout view when you insert an object, because the object does not appear in Normal view.

Choose the "Object" option.

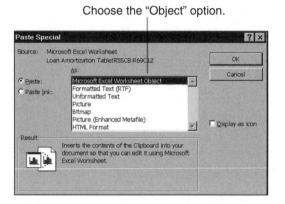

You can paste copied data so that the data retains a connection with the program used to create it.

To edit an embedded object, double-click it. The toolbars and menus change to provide options for editing and manipulating the object. If you double-click an Excel chart that's embedded in a Word document, for example, the Excel toolbar and menus appear inside the Word window. Keep in mind that you're not editing the original object in its original document—just a copy. The advantage of this method versus static sharing (described in the following note) is that the copy comes with its own editing tools. Isn't that convenient?

Creating a Link Between Two Files

In many cases, you are creating a document with data from several sources. You can wait

Static Sharing

If you need to insert data from one document into another, without retaining a connection between the pasted data and the program used to create it, choose Edit, Paste to paste the data in the destination document. You can also drag selected data from one document to the other.

until each document is absolutely, completely finished and then copy the appropriate data from the source documents; but things can—and usually do—seem to change up to the last minute. To avoid including outdated information in your final document, you can create a *link* between the two documents. Then, when copied data in the original document (called the *source* document) is changed, the pasted data in the other document (called the *destination* document) is updated too. The following are the key points to remember about linking data:

➤ You can link data between Excel, Word, PowerPoint, and any other application that supports OLE by using the **Paste Special** command on the **Edit** menu. If a program does not support OLE, the Paste Special command is not available.

➤ When you link data, you have two separate documents stored in two separate files. If you send someone a file that contains a link, you must also send the linked file.

➤ Linking works only one way. If you edit data from the source document in the destination document, the source document is not changed. (In most cases, Office does not allow you to edit source data in the destination document, but if you paste the link as HTML or RTF data, you may be able to edit the source data right inside the destination document.)

➤ Linking works best when you use the same data in several documents. You can maintain the one source document without having to worry about updating the documents that use information from the source.

Creating a link is almost as easy as embedding. If you remember the words from the preceding section, feel free to sing along:

1. Copy the data.
2. Change to the target document and choose **Edit**, **Paste Special**.
3. Click the **Paste Link** option button.
4. Pick the format that has "Object" in its name.
5. Click **OK**. Olé!

To create a link, you must specify how you want the data pasted.

Choose the desired format.

Choose Paste link.

You can have the link displayed as an icon.

If you decide later to break the link between the pasted data and its original file, or if you want to change the way the links are updated, open the **Edit** menu and select **Links**. This displays the Links dialog box that lists all the links in the document. By default, Update is set to **Automatic**. You can change the setting to Manual; but then, whenever you want your links updated, you have to display this dialog box again, click the desired link, and click **Update Now** (not the most efficient method). To break the links, click the desired link and click **Break Link**.

Be Careful when Moving Files

Because a link points to another file in a folder on your hard drive or on the network, you must be careful when moving, deleting, or renaming your files or folders. If you shuffle around your files and folders, your Office applications are unable to find them.

Embedding a New Object with Insert Object

You can also link or embed with the Insert Object command. You use this command when you know that you want to link or embed something, but you have not yet created the object in the source application. Say you're writing a letter to order some plants and you need a worksheet that lists the items that you're ordering, quantities, prices, and totals. You haven't created the worksheet, and you need it quickly. What do you do? Insert Object.

To insert an object, open the **Insert** menu and select **Object**. The Object dialog box appears. You notice two tabs in the Object dialog box. Use the Create New tab when you need to create an object to link or embed (and haven't done so yet). The Create from File tab offers options for linking or embedding an entire file.

To create a new object, select the type of object that you want to insert (for example, an Excel worksheet or a PowerPoint slide). Enter any additional preferences and click **OK**. Windows inserts a placeholder for the selected object and runs the application needed to create the object. By looking at the title bar, you may not realize that Windows has changed applications on you; but if you check out the toolbars and menus, you see that you now have options for creating and manipulating the new object. When you finish creating the object, click anywhere outside it to return to your document.

You can create a new object and embed it in your document.

Select the type of object you want to insert.

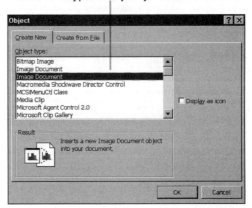

Display As Icon?

The Display As Icon option can come in handy if you are working with shared files on a network. Instead of pasting lengthy inserts into a document, you can insert an icon that the reader can click to display additional information. This is also very useful for sharing files via email.

You can also embed or link an entire file created in another application. To do this, click the **Create from File** tab in the Object dialog box. Click the **Browse** button, use the Browse dialog box to select the file you want to insert, and click **OK**. Select any other options (such as Link to file, Float over Text, or Display As Icon) and click **OK**.

Transforming Word Documents into Presentations and Vice Versa

Although your marketing department and sales force want you to think that presentations are some sort of magical multimedia event, most presentations are nothing more than an outline on slides. Sure, the outline might contain a few graphical decorations and some audio clips, but it's still an outline. Moreover, knowing that it's an outline, you might find some need to transform it into a full-fledged Word document.

Do you have to retype the outline in Word? No way. Just open the presentation in PowerPoint, open the **File** menu, point to **Send To**, and click **Microsoft Word**. The Write-Up dialog box appears, asking how you want the slides and text laid out on Word pages (or if you just want the outline). Click the desired option and click **OK**.

You can also transform an outline that you typed in Word into a PowerPoint presentation. In Word, open the outline you created. Open the **File** menu, point to **Send**

To, and click **Microsoft PowerPoint**. Word converts the outline into a presentation and displays it in PowerPoint.

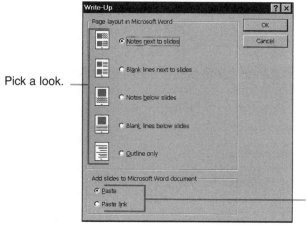

Pick a look.

Specify how you want the slides and text to appear in the Word document.

You can link the Word outline to the slide show.

Publishing Access Reports in Word

Access is a great tool for storing and managing data, but its page layout features are grossly inadequate. Access can slap a title on the report and arrange the data in columns, but that's about it. For more control over the look and layout of your reports, consider transforming the report into a Word document.

To convert an Access report to Word format, first open the report in Access. Then open the **Tools** menu, point to **Office Links**, and click **Publish It with MS Word**. Access exports the report to Word, creating a new document. You can now format the document using Word's advanced formatting tools, and you can add graphics and other objects to enhance the document.

> **Merging Data with Word Documents**
>
> You can also use Access and Word together by inserting field codes in your Word document that pull data from an Access database. (See Chapter 8, "Creating Mailing Labels and Form Letters," for details on how to merge from Word.)

Analyzing Your Access Database in Excel

Although Access is the best tool for storing and extracting data, Excel provides superior tools for performing calculations and analyzing data. If you tried entering formulas in your Access report (as explained in Chapter 21, "Giving Data Meaning with Reports"), you know how difficult it can be to enter the correct formula using the right field codes. It's much easier to do it in Excel with cell addresses and the point-and-click method (as explained in Chapter 11, "Doing Math with Formulas").

Drag and Drop

To copy data quickly from an Access database to an Excel worksheet, simply drag the selected data from a table, query, form, or report in Access and drop it on the Excel worksheet.

In addition, Excel offers scenarios, which enable you to play What if? with a set of values. You can change one or more values to see how the changes affect the net result, and you can create several scenarios to see how they compare.

To send a table, form, query, or report to Excel, first open it in Access. Then open the **Tools** menu, point to **Office Links**, and click **Analyze It with MS Excel**. Access sends the data to Excel and creates a new worksheet for the data. You can now add formulas, format the data, create graphs, and do anything else that you normally do with an Excel worksheet.

Chapter 25

Creating and Publishing Your Own Web Pages

In This Chapter

➤ Churning out Web pages with templates

➤ Saving existing documents as Web pages

➤ Inserting links to other Internet and intranet resources

➤ Transforming PowerPoint presentations into Web pages

➤ Placing your pages on the Web

Nowadays, if you're not on the Web, you're out of the mainstream. Corporations, universities, towns, churches, and individuals are flocking to the Web to express themselves and reach out to customers, members, citizens, and anyone else who might be wandering the Web. Using Web authoring tools, these companies and individuals are beginning to move away from paper publications to more interactive electronic publications on the Web.

As you can imagine, the Microsoft Office applications have also been forced to make the transition from printing on paper to publishing electronically on the Web. Office features several tools that work together with Microsoft's award-winning Web browser, Internet Explorer, to help you create your own Web pages and navigate the Web. In this chapter, you learn how to use these tools.

Internet Explorer 5

Office 2000 comes with a brand new version of Microsoft's Web browser, Internet Explorer 5. To run it, click the Internet Explorer icon on the Windows desktop or click the Launch Internet Explorer Browser icon in the Quick Launch toolbar.

Web Browsing in Office

Assuming that you have an Internet connection and you are using Microsoft Internet Explorer as your Web browser, you can open Web pages directly from the Office applications and use the Web toolbar to navigate the Web. To turn on the Web toolbar, right-click any toolbar and choose Web. However, browsing from Office is a little clunky and typically opens the Web page in Internet Explorer, anyway. Even more useful is Internet Explorer's ability to open Office documents. Use Internet Explorer to browse Office documents on your hard drive or your company network.

Creating Web Pages in Word

For years, you have used desktop publishing programs and word processors to publish on paper. However, when you need to make the transition to publishing on the Web, you may think that you need to learn how to use an entirely new program and fiddle with those complex formatting codes that control the appearance of your Web page.

Fortunately, Microsoft has added some Web page creation tools to Microsoft Word. With these tools, you can easily make the transition to Webtop publishing without having to learn a new program. Word offers two ways to create Web pages: You can transform existing documents into Web pages or use the Web Page Wizard to create a page from scratch. These techniques are discussed in the following sections.

Transforming Existing Documents into Web Pages

If you have a document that already contains most of the text you want on your Web page, don't re-create it, just transform it. To transform a Word document into a Web page, first save the document as a normal Word document so you don't mess up the original. Then open the **File** menu and select **Save As Web Page**. The Save As dialog box appears.

Type a file name for the document, and then select the folder in which you want it stored. To give your page a title other than the file name, click the **Change Title** button and enter the desired page title. (The title appears in the browser's title bar when you or someone else opens the page.) Click **Save**. Word saves the document and converts any Word formatting codes into HTML codes. Skip ahead to "Formatting Your Web Pages," to add a little flair to your document.

Making Web Pages from Scratch with a Wizard

The easiest way to create a Web site from scratch in Word is to use the Web Page Wizard. This wizard displays a series of dialog boxes that lead you through the process of creating a custom Web site consisting of multiple linked pages.

To run the Web Page Wizard, open Word's **File** menu and select **New**. In the New dialog box, click the **Web Pages** tab and double-click **Web Page Wizard**. The wizard leads you through the process of creating a multi-page Web document, allowing you to add, delete, or rearrange pages. Follow the wizard's instructions and click **Next** after entering your preferences in each dialog box.

Of course the page(s) you end up with depend on what you told the wizard to do. The following figure shows a typical Web site that consists of two frames. On the left is a table of contents for your site, and on the right is the default home page. The following sections show you how to modify your Web pages to customize your Web site.

HTML: The Codes Behind the Document

HTML stands for Hypertext Markup Language , which is a coding system used to format documents on the Web. For example, in HTML, you can make text bold by adding the <b> code (start bold) before the text and the </b> code (end bold) after it. Of course, when you're creating a Web page in Word, all you have to do is drag over the text and click the Bold button in the formatting toolbar. Word automatically inserts the HTML codes for you.

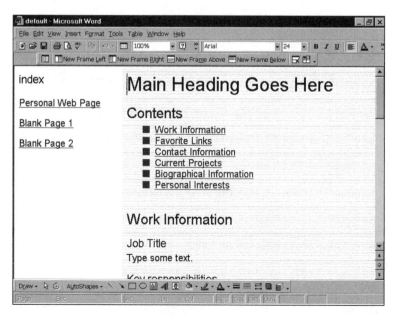

The Web Page Wizard provides the overall structure you need to get started.

Formatting Your Web Pages

In most cases, you can format your text just as you would if you were working on a Word document (see Chapter 4, "Giving Your Text a Makeover"). When you apply formatting to selected text, Word inserts the proper HTML codes for you. The following list provides a quick rundown of additional formatting options, plus a few standard options that are easy to overlook when creating Web pages:

➤ Use the **Style** drop-down list in the Formatting toolbar to apply common Web page styles. For example, apply the **Heading 1** style to the page's title.

➤ Don't forget to use tables to align text. You can create and edit tables on a Web page just as you can in any Word document. Word handles all the complicated HTML table codes for you.

➤ The **Format**, **Theme** command displays a list of predesigned styles for your Web page. The style controls the background, fonts, graphic bullets, horizontal lines, and the appearance of other objects to give your Web page(s) a consistent look and feel. You can also use the **Format**, **Background** options to customize the background.

➤ To insert a horizontal line to divide the contents on your page, position the insertion point where you want the line inserted. Choose **Format**, **Borders and Shading** and click the **Horizontal Line** button. Click the line you want to insert and click the **Insert Clip** button.

➤ Display the Web Tools toolbar for access to additional buttons for inserting objects on a Web page, including movie clips, a background audio clip, and scrolling text boxes. To display the toolbar, right-click any toolbar and choose **Web Tools**.

Previewing Your Page in Internet Explorer

Assuming that you have a Web browser installed on your computer, you should preview your Web page to see how it looks in a browser. (This is sort of like Print Preview for Web pages.) Sometimes, what you see in your Office application is nothing similar to what you get on the Web. Open the **File** menu and click **Web Page Preview**.

Connecting Your Page to Other Pages with Hyperlinks

No Web page is complete without a few links that kick you out to another part of the page or to another page on the Web. All the Office applications have the Insert Hyperlink feature, which enables you to quickly insert links to other documents, files, or pages.

To quickly transform normal text into a link, drag over the text that you want to use as the link and click the **Insert Hyperlink** button in the Standard toolbar. The Insert Hyperlink dialog box appears, allowing you to enter preferences for the link.

Microsoft completely revamped the Insert Hyperlink dialog box in Office 2000. Now, instead of simply prompting you to specify the URL of the page to which you want the link to point, the Insert Hyperlink dialog box provides the following Link To options:

➤ **Existing File or Web Page** lets you point the link to a recently opened file, a page you have recently opened in Internet Explorer, or a Web page address. You can also add a ScreenTip to the link that displays a description of the link when a visitor rests the mouse pointer on the link.

➤ **Place in This Document** inserts a link that points to a heading or bookmark that's on the same page as the link. To use this option, first mark the destination point in the document by applying one of Word's heading styles (Heading1, Heading2, and so on) to a heading or by inserting a bookmark. To insert a bookmark, position the insertion point near the destination, choose **Insert**, **Bookmark**, and type a name for the bookmark.

➤ **Create New Document** inserts a link that points to a document you have not yet created. Type a name for the new document and choose the folder in which you want the document stored. Word creates a new blank Web page. You can then insert text, links, and other objects to complete the page.

➤ **E-mail Address** inserts a link that points to an email address. A person visiting your page can then click the link to run his or her email program and quickly send you a message. The message will automatically be addressed to the email address you specify.

After entering your preferences for the link, click **OK**. When you click **OK**, the selected text is transformed into a link and appears blue (or whatever color you chose for displaying links). As you're creating links, test them to make sure that they work. You don't want to point your visitors down a dead-end street.

You can create links that point to different areas on the same page or to different pages.

Text that will appear as a link

The address of the linked page

Add a ScreenTip to describe the link.

You can choose to link to a recently opened file or Web page.

Working with Frames

Frames provide a structure that allows visitors to your Web site to easily navigate the pages that make up your site. The left frame, for example, contains links that point to other pages at your site. When someone clicks a link, the associated page opens in the right frame; but the contents of the left frame remain onscreen, allowing the person to quickly open other pages.

To resize a frame, drag the edge of the bar that separates the frames. (When you move the mouse pointer over the edge of the bar that's used for resizing the frames, the mouse pointer appears as a double-headed arrrow.) For more frame options, display the Frames toolbar by choosing **View**, **Toolbars**, **Frames**. Use the following buttons on the Frames toolbar to make your changes:

Unlinking a Link

If you decide to remove the link from your page, right-click the link, point to Hyperlink, and click Remove Link.

Table of Contents in Frame creates a new frame with links to headings in the current frame. To create a table of contents, first mark headings in your Web page as Heading1, Heading2, and so on. Then, click the Table of Contents in Frame button to create the new frame.

]**New Frame Left** inserts a blank frame to the left of the current page or frame.

254

New Frame Right inserts a blank frame to the right of the current page or frame.

New Frame Above inserts a blank frame above the current page or frame.

New Frame Below inserts a blank frame below the current page or frame.

Delete Frame removes the current frame. If the Web Page Wizard sticks you with an undesired frame, this is probably the only frame button you'll need.

Frame Properties displays a dialog box that allows you to change the size of the frame, specify a different document to display in the frame, and add borders to the frame.

Creating an Online Presentation in PowerPoint

Although Word seems like the most obvious choice for publishing pages on the Web, PowerPoint offers a more graphical approach, enabling you to transform a slide show into individual linked pages. Visitors to your Web page can advance through the slide show by clicking buttons or other types of hyperlinks. PowerPoint offers a couple ways to create Internet presentations:

➤ If you have already created the presentation that you want to use, save it as an HTML file. Open the presentation in PowerPoint, open the **File** menu, and select **Save As Web Page**. In the Save As dialog box, click the **Publish** button. Enter your preferences and click **Publish**.

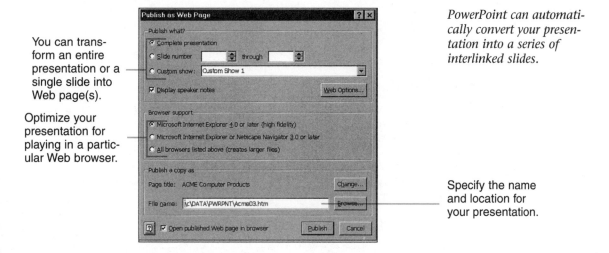

PowerPoint can automatically convert your presentation into a series of interlinked slides.

You can transform an entire presentation or a single slide into Web page(s).

Optimize your presentation for playing in a particular Web browser.

Specify the name and location for your presentation.

➤ Use the AutoContent Wizard when you start PowerPoint (as explained in Chapter 15, "Slapping Together a Basic Slide Show"). In the third AutoContent Wizard dialog box, the wizard provides five output options for the slide show. Select **Web Presentation**.

After you create your Web presentation, you can insert links to other slides in the presentation using the Animation Settings option. Select the object or text that you want the user to click to move to another slide (the next slide or any slide in the presentation). Right-click the selected text or object and click **Action Settings**. The Action Settings dialog box appears. Click the **Mouse Click** tab if it is not already in front. Click the **Hyperlink To** option to turn it on. Open the **Hyperlink To** drop-down list and select the slide to which you want this object or text to point. You can select the first or last slide, the next or previous slide, or click **Slide** and pick the specific slide to which you want this link to point. (You can also choose to point a link to another file, a page on the Web, or another PowerPoint presentation.) Click **OK**. (To learn more about inserting hyperlinks that point to other pages on the Web, see "Connecting Your Page to Other Pages with Hyperlinks," earlier in this chapter.)

Placing Your Pages on the Web

When you have completed your Web page, you must place it on a Web server so that other people can open and view it with their Web browsers. In the past, the only way to place a page on a Web server was to use a separate FTP (File Transfer Protocol) program. Now, Office provides a couple tools that allow you to save your Web page(s) directly to a Web folder or a folder on the FTP server simply by using the File, Save As command.

The following sections lead you through the process of finding a home for your Web page(s) and setting up Office to upload your Web page and any associated files to the Web.

Finding a Home for Your Page

If you work at a big corporation or institution that has its own Web server, lucky you. You already have a Web server on which to store your Web pages. Just ask your Web administrator for the path to the server and write it down.

For the less fortunate, the best place to start looking for a Web server is your Internet service provider. Most providers make some space available on their Web servers for subscribers to store personal Web pages. Call your service provider and obtain the following information:

➤ Does your service provider make Web space available to subscribers? If not, maybe you should change providers.

➤ How much disk space do you get, and how much does it cost (if anything)? Some providers give you a limited amount of disk space, which is usually plenty for one or two Web pages, assuming you don't include large audio or video clips.

➤ Can you save your files directly to the Web server or do you have to upload files to an FTP server?

➤ What is the URL of the server to which you must connect to upload your files? Write it down.

➤ What username and password do you need to enter to gain access to the server? (This is typically the same username and password that you use to connect to the service.)

➤ In which directory (folder) must you place your files? Write it down.

➤ What name must you give your Web page? In many cases, the service lets you post a single Web page, and you must call it **index.html** or **default.html**.

➤ Are there any other specific instructions that you must follow to post your Web page?

➤ After posting your page, what will its address (URL) be? You'll want to open it in Internet Explorer as soon as you post it to check it out.

Setting Up a Web Folder

If a local Web server is available (on your company's intranet) or your service provider allows you to publish your Web pages directly to a folder on its Web server, you should first set up a Web folder in My Computer. Take the following steps:

1. Run My Computer, double-click the **Web Folders** icon, and then double-click the **Add a Web Folder** icon.

2. In the **Type the Location to Add** text box, type the address of the Web server, complete with a path to the directory in which you want your new folder created (for example, `http://www.internet.com/public`).

3. Click the **Next** button.

4. Type a name for the folder in which you intend to publish your Web pages.

5. Click the **Finish** button.

To save your Web page(s) to your Web folder, choose the **File**, **Save As Web Page** command. Then, click the **Web Folders** icon, double-click the Web folder you just set up, and click the **Save** button.

You may be able to save your Web page(s) directly to a folder on the Web server.

2. Double-click the folder you just set up.

1. Click the Web Folders icon.

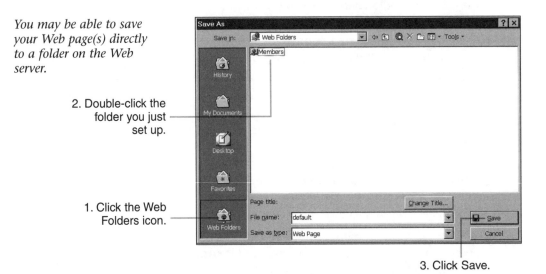

3. Click Save.

Uploading Files to an FTP Server

Many Internet service providers still require that you upload Web pages to an FTP server in order to place them on the Web. Fortunately, Office simplifies the process, allowing you to perform FTP uploads with the File, Save As Web Page command. Take the following steps:

1. Open the page in the Office application you used to create it.

2. Open the **File** menu and select **Save As Web Page**.

3. In the Save As dialog box, open the **Save In** drop-down list, and click on **Add/Modify FTP Locations**. This opens a dialog box prompting you to enter the address of the FTP site, your username, and your password.

4. Enter the requested information and click **Add**. (In the Name of the FTP Site text box, type only the address of the FTP site. Don't include the path to the folder.)

5. Click **OK**. This returns you to the Save As dialog box, which now contains the address of the FTP site.

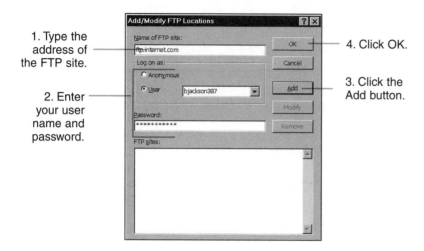

1. Type the address of the FTP site.

2. Enter your user name and password.

4. Click OK.

3. Click the Add button.

You can set up your Office applications to save Web pages directly to an FTP server.

6. Click the address and click **Open**.

7. If you are not connected to the Internet, the Connect To dialog box appears; click **Connect**. Once you are connected, the Save As dialog box lists the directories (folders) on the remote computer.

8. Change to the folder in which your service provider told you to save the Web page file, and then click the **Save** button.

Edit Any Page

You can open a Web page in Internet Explorer and then choose to edit it in Word. First, open the page in Internet Explorer, and then choose File, Edit with Microsoft Office Component . This opens the Web page as a read-only document. Use the Save As command to save the document to a folder on your hard drive so you can save any changes you enter.

Managing Your Web Site with FrontPage

Although the Web page creation and publication tools in Word, Excel, PowerPoint, and Access are sufficient for most beginning users, Office 2000 includes an industrial-strength Web-management program, called FrontPage. With FrontPage, you can further customize existing Web pages, create new Web pages, modify linked pages, and control the structure of a complex Web site (which FrontPage refers to as a *web*).

To run FrontPage, click the Windows **Start** button, point to **Programs**, and click **Microsoft FrontPage**. The Microsoft FrontPage window appears, as shown in the following figure. As you can see, it looks very similar to the Microsoft Word window and contains many of the same menus and toolbar buttons. What's unique about the FrontPage window is that it contains a Views bar at the left. This bar contains the following buttons:

➤ **Page** displays the current Web page. Use this view to add text and objects to a page, format your page, insert links, and perform other Web-page related tasks. In Page view, three tabs appear below the work area: Normal (for displaying the formatted Web page), HTML (to display the HTML tags that control the layout and formatting), and Preview (to display the page as it will appear in a Web browser).

➤ **Folders** displays a list of folders and files that make up your Web site, allowing you to quickly rearrange the folders and files just as if you were using Windows Explorer. As you drag Web pages and other files from one folder to another, FrontPage automatically adjusts the hyperlinks so they point to the correct files.

➤ **Reports** displays a site summary that acts as an inventory of the contents of your Web site, including the number of files and their sizes, the number and type of hyperlinks, the number of incomplete tasks, and any problems, such as hyperlinks that point to non-existent pages or other files.

➤ **Navigation** displays a graphic representation of the structure of your Web site, giving you a bird's-eye-view of your site and allowing you to quickly restructure the site. In Navigation view, you can even create a navigation bar to place at the top of every page; users can click links on the bar to jump to specific opening pages.

➤ **Hyperlinks** shows a list of pages linked to the current Web page, so you can verify that the links on a page are working properly.

➤ **Tasks** acts as a project-management tool for your Web site. You can create a list of tasks, assign tasks to individuals or workgroups, check the status of each task, associate each task with a file, and mark a task as completed when it's done.

1. The Views bar.   3. Click the page you want to work on.

Use FrontPage to fine-tune your Web pages and manage your Web site.

```
┌─────────────────────────────────────────────────────────────┐
│ Microsoft FrontPage - C:\My Webs\myweb              _  □  ×  │
│ File  Edit  View  Insert  Format  Tools  Table  Frames  Window  Help │
├─────────────────────────────────────────────────────────────┤
│ Normal  ▼  (default font)   ▼  Normal  ▼  B  I  U  ≡ ≡ ≡ ...  │
├──────┬──────────────────┬───────────────────────────────────┤
│Views │ Folder List      │ index.htm                        × │
│      │ ⊟ 🖿 C:\My Webs\my│  ┌─────────────────────────────┐  │
│ 📄   │   ⊞ 🖿 _private   │  Home   Feedback  Contents  Search│
│Page  │   ⊞ 🖿 images     │                                   │
│      │     📄 feedback.htm│         Home          ───────────┼─ 4. Work on individual
│ 📁   │     📄 index.htm  │                                   │   pages here.
│Folders│     📄 news.htm  │ [Edit the properties for this Navigation Bar to display hyperl│
│      │     📄 pr01.htm   │ here]                             │
│ 🗐   │     📄 pr02.htm   │                                   │
│Reports│     📄 pr03.htm  │                                   │
│      │     📄 prod01.htm │ ✦   ┌──────────────────────────┐ │
│ 🗂   │     📄 prod02.htm │     │Comment: Write an introductory│
│Navigation│  📄 prod03.htm│     │paragraph for your home page here.│
│      │     📄 products.htm│    │This is like the front door to your home│
│ 🔗   │     📄 search.htm │ News│on the Internet. Invite visitors to step in│
│Hyperlinks│  📄 serv01.htm│     │and have a look around.   │ │
│      │     📄 serv02.htm │     └──────────────────────────┘ │
│ 📋   │     📄 serv03.htm │ Products                          │
│Tasks │     📄 services.htm│                                  │
│      │     📄 toc.htm    │ Services                          │
│      │ ◄        ►        │ \Normal/HTML/Preview/ ◄           │
├─────────────────────────────────────────────────────────────┤
│                              ■ ⏱ 4 seconds over 28.8         │
└─────────────────────────────────────────────────────────────┘
```

2. In Page view, click a tab to
specify the desired page view.

Creating a New Web Site

Although a Web site can consist of a single page, more complex sites may contain dozens of pages stored in related folders or directories on the server. To ensure that you are starting with a sound structure, use one of the FrontPage templates or wizards to create the overall structure for your Web site:

1. Open the **File** menu, point to **New**, and click **Web**.

2. Click the icon for the type of Web you want to create and click **OK**. If you clicked an icon for a template, FrontPage automatically creates the web. If you clicked an icon for a wizard, FrontPage runs the Wizard.

3. If you clicked an icon for a web wizard, follow the wizard's instructions and enter your preferences.

Once FrontPage has created the web, click the Page button in the Views bar to start editing the pages that comprise the web. A folder list appears to the right of the Views bar displaying a list of pages. Click the icon for the page you want to view and then edit and format the page in the Page view window, as shown in the previous figure.

Making Pages

In addition to helping you manage the overall structure of your Web site, FrontPage offers powerful features for creating individual pages and includes a wide selection of Web page templates from which to choose. To create a new Web page using a template, take the following steps:

1. Open the **File** menu, point to **New**, and click **Page** (or press **Ctrl+N**). The New dialog box appears, presenting icons for a wide variety of Web pages.

2. Click the desired icon and click **OK**. FrontPage creates the page and displays it in the Page view window.

3. Edit and format the page as desired.

4. To save the page as its own document file, open the **File** menu and click **Save**.

5. Type a name for the Web page.

6. To give the page a title that differs from the filename, click the **Change** button, type a title for the page, and click **OK**.

7. Click the **Save** button. The name of the new page appears at the bottom of the Folder List.

Formatting and Editing Pages

The tools for editing and formatting pages in FrontPage are very similar to those used in Word. Use the same steps explained earlier in this chapter. To place more complex objects on your Web page, such as a hit counter, table of contents, or scrolling marquee, click the Insert Component button on the Standard toolbar and choose the desired component.

Verifying Hyperlinks

When you create a Web site that consists of multiple pages, it's easy to lose track of the overall structure of the site and how the pages are interconnected. To help, FrontPage can display your Web site in Hyperlinks view, as shown in the following figure. To switch to this view, click the **Hyperlinks** button in the Views bar. In Hyperlinks view, you can perform the following tasks:

➤ Click the plus sign next to a page icon to view pages that link to this page.

➤ Click the minus sign next to a page icon to collapse (hide) the list of pages that link to this page.

➤ To give a page center stage and see more clearly how other pages link to it, right-click the page's icon and choose **Move to Center**.

➤ To delete a page and remove any links to it, right-click the page and choose **Delete**.

➤ To open a page, double-click its icon or right-click the page and choose **Open**.

1 Click a plus sign to view pages that link to this page.

3 Right-click a page for additional options.

In Hyperlinks view, FrontPage provides a graphic representation of how your Web pages are linked.

2 Click a minus sign to hide the links for this page.

Publishing Your Web

Perhaps the coollest, most useful feature of FrontPage is that it allows you to transfer your entire Web site from your hard drive to the Web server as a single unit. To publish your web to the server, take the following steps:

1. Open the **File** menu and click **Publish Web**. The Publish Web dialog box appears.

2. Type the address of the Web or FTP server on which you want your web placed. If typing the address of a Web server, start with http://. If typing the address of an FTP server, start with ftp://. (If you don't have a Web service provider, you can click the WPP's button and shop for one on the Web.)

3. Click the **Publish** button.

4. Type your username and password, if required to log on, and click **OK**. FrontPage uploads all the folders and files that make up your Web site to the specified Web or FTP server.

263

Web Servers Have Some Limitations

Many service providers that offer Web publishing support have strict rules for naming files and creating folders. Before you do much work with FrontPage, make sure you know the rules, so you can work around them.

Chapter 26

Macros for Mere Mortals

In This Chapter

➤ Define macro in 25 words or less

➤ Record macros for the tasks that you perform frequently

➤ Assign keystrokes to macros

➤ Sew some macro buttons on your Office toolbars

You probably already have a few favorite shortcut keys. You can bypass the Office application menus by pressing Ctrl+S to save a document, Ctrl+P to print, and Ctrl+B to boldface text. But you secretly wish that Microsoft had built in a few more shortcuts for step-heavy operations that you perform frequently.

To make your wishes come true, you can create your own shortcut keys and buttons using *macros*. A macro is a recorded series of commands that you can play back in Office applications by selecting the macro's name from a list or by pressing a keystroke or clicking a button that you assigned to the macro. In this chapter, you learn how to record commands using the macro recorder and how to name and run your macros.

Roll 'em: Recording a Macro

The easiest way to create a macro is to use the macro recorder, which is available in all the Office applications. The steps for recording macros, however, vary slightly among the Office applications. (In Access, the procedure for recording macros is much more complex; check the Access help system for details or ask your Office Assistant to lend a hand.)

The following steps show you how to record a macro in Microsoft Word:

1. Open the **Tools** menu, point to **Macro**, and choose **Record New Macro**. The Record Macro dialog box appears, prompting you to name the macro.

2. Type a name for your macro, up to 80 characters (no spaces). The macro name must start with a letter—never a number. The macro recorder supplies a default name—Macro1, Macro2, and so on, as you keep recording macros—but nondescriptive names such as this aren't very helpful when you're trying to remember which macro did what.

3. Open the **Store Macro In** drop-down list and choose to store the macro in the current document or in **All Documents (Normal.dot)** to make the macro available in all your documents. At this point, you can assign the macro to a keystroke or create a toolbar button for it. (See "Assigning Shortcut Keys for Quick Playback" and "Making Buttons for Your Macros" later in this chapter for details.)

4. Click in the **Description** text box and type a brief description of the macro's function (the task it performs).

Do You Need a Macro?

Office includes shortcut keys and buttons for the most commonly entered commands. Before creating your own macro to automate a task that you commonly perform, check the help system to determine if Office already offers a shortcut for that task. Also, ask yourself whether you can use an easier feature, such as AutoCorrect or AutoText, instead of using a macro.

Where Should I Store It?

When recording a macro in Excel, it's a good idea to store it in the Personal Macro Workbook. This keeps all your macros in one place and makes them available in all workbooks. In PowerPoint, macros can be recorded only for specific presentations (the presentation must be open in PowerPoint when you start recording).

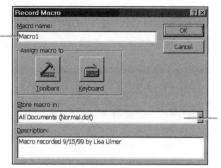

Name your macro.

The Record Macro dialog box in Word.

Store the macro in Normal.dot to make it available in all your documents.

5. Click the **OK** button. A small toolbar appears with buttons for stopping and pausing the recording (in Excel and PowerPoint, you don't get a pause button).

Why Pause?

Use the Pause Recording button to test commands before recording them. If you're not sure what a particular command is going to do, click the **Pause Recording** button, enter the command to test it, and then click the **Undo** button. If the command did what was expected, click the **Resume Recorder** button and enter the command again to record it. You can also pause recording if you need to refer to another document, check a file name, or perform some other operation that you don't want to be recorded as part of the macro.

6. Perform the task whose steps you want to record. You can choose menu commands and press keystrokes to enter commands, text, or objects. You cannot, however, move the insertion point or select text using the mouse; you must use the arrow keys to move and Shift+arrow keys to highlight text.

7. When you are finished performing the steps, click the **Stop Recording** button.

Excel Exceptions

Excel macros automatically record any cell selections using absolute references. If you want to use relative references, click the **Relative Reference** button on the Stop Recording toolbar. You can click this button repeatedly to switch back and forth from absolute to relative references.

As you perform the task, the macro recorder records the commands that you enter.

When you are done performing the task, click the Stop Recording button.

Pause Recording

Enter commands as you normally would.

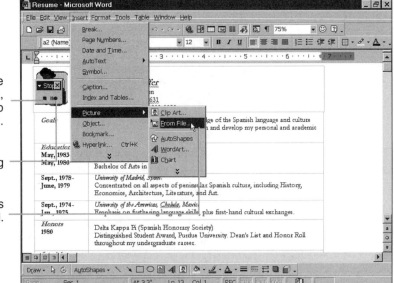

Playing Back a Recorded Macro

When you record a macro, its name is added to the list of macros that you have recorded. To play the macro (and perform the steps recorded in that macro) open the **Tools** menu, point to **Macro** and choose **Macros**, or press **Alt+F8**. A list of available macros appears. Click the name of the macro that you want to run and click the **Run** button.

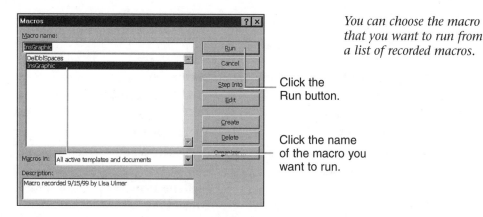

You can choose the macro that you want to run from a list of recorded macros.

Click the
Run button.

Click the name
of the macro you
want to run.

Although selecting a macro from a comprehensive macro list is a foolproof way to find and play the macro, it is hardly the most efficient. If you find yourself frequently playing back the macro, consider assigning a shortcut keystroke to the macro or adding a button for the macro to one of your toolbars. The following sections show you just what to do.

What's It Doing to My Document?

Before running your macro for the first time, save your document. If the macro goes whacko and messes up the document, close the document without out saving the changes. To stop a macro before it does too much damage, press **Ctrl+Break** and then use the Undo feature to try to recover from the disaster. If, however, the macro includes a File, Save command, you may be out of luck.

Assigning Shortcut Keys for Quick Playback

Shortcut key combinations are by far the most efficient way to enter commands in your Office applications because you don't have to move your fingers from the keyboard to enter the command.

Hey, Ctrl+P Doesn't Print My Document!

When assigning shortcut key combinations, be careful not to assign a macro to a keystroke that the application already uses, such as Ctrl+P (for Print) or Ctrl+S (for Save).

To assign a shortcut key combination to one of your macros in Word, take the following steps:

1. Open the **Tools** menu and choose **Customize**.
2. Click the **Keyboard** button.
3. Under **Categories**, click **Macros**. A list of available macros appears in the Macros list.
4. Click the macro to which you want to assign a shortcut key combination.
5. Click the **Press New Shortcut Key** text box and press the key combination that you want to use for this macro. A message appears below this text box indicating if the keystroke is already in use. If the keystroke is in use, press the **Backspace** key and press a different key combination.
6. Click the **Assign** button.
7. Click the **Close** button.

What About PowerPoint and Excel?

PowerPoint doesn't support shortcut keys for macros. Excel has a different method for setting up shortcuts. Choose **Tools, Macro, Macros**. Select the macro and click **Options**. In the **Shortcut Key** box, type the keyboard character to use for the shortcut. You can use **Ctrl+*character*** or **Ctrl+Shift+*character***.

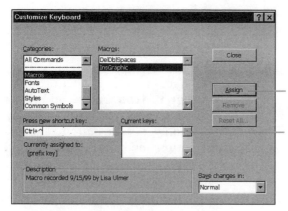

You can assign a shortcut key combination to a macro.

Click the Assign button.

The keystroke that you press appears here.

Making Buttons for Your Macros

The Office toolbars are great time-savers. Instead of having to flip through a series of menus and submenus, you simply click a button in one of the toolbars or choose the desired option from one of the drop-down lists. These toolbars can give you quick access to your macros as well. To add a macro to one of the Office toolbars, take the following steps:

1. Make sure that the toolbar on which you want to place your macro button is displayed. (Choose **View**, **Toolbars** to display a list of available toolbars.)

2. Open the **Tools** menu and choose **Customize**.

3. Click the **Commands** tab.

4. In the Categories list, click **Macros**. A list of available macros appears in the Commands list. (Excel provides only two options: Custom Button and Custom Menu Item.)

5. Drag the desired macro (or the Custom Button in Excel) from the Commands list over the toolbar on which you want it to appear, drag it to the desired location (watch for a dark I-beam pointer that shows where the button will appear), and release the mouse button. The button appears on the toolbar. (Leave the Customize dialog box open to perform the next steps.)

Check This Out

Additional Keystrokes

For more keystroke options, hold down a key combination and then release it and press another key. A comma appears after the first keystroke, and the second key or keystroke that you pressed is tacked onto the end (for example, Ctrl+Shift+X,L). To enter this keystroke, you press Ctrl+Shift+X, release the keys, and then press L.

271

Remove a Toolbar Button

To remove a button from a toolbar, display the Customize dialog box and then drag the button off the toolbar.

6. To change the name of the button, right-click it, drag over the entry in the **Name** text box, and type a new name for the button.

7. To add an image to the button, point to **Change Button Image**, and click the desired image. If you want to display the image only, not the button name, right-click the button and choose **Default Style**.

8. If you're doing this in Excel, right-click the button and choose **Assign Macro**. Select the desired macro from the list and click **OK**.

9. When you are done, click the **Close** button in the Customize dialog box to close it.

Saving Your Macros

When you create a Word macro, the macro is saved automatically when you save or close the document in which you created the macro. You're cool. If you create the macro in the Normal.dot template, however, so that it's available to all documents, the macro isn't saved with the File, Save command. What if the power goes out before you close Word and save those precious macros? Sorry, they're gone. To save your document and Normal.dot, **Shift**+click **File** in the menu bar and choose **Save All**. This saves all open documents plus Normal.dot.

No Need to Shift when You Click

If you plan to do a lot of customizing in Word, add the Save All command to your File menu so that it will be there even if you forget to hold down the Shift key while clicking File. Choose **Tools**, **Customize**, click the **Commands** tab, click **File** in the **Categories** list, click **Save All** in the **Commands** list, and drag it out of the dialog box and over your File menu. The menu drops open. Position the Save All command where you want it and let go. Then just choose **File**, **Save All** when you want to save all open documents plus Normal.dot.

You face the same problem when you create macros in Excel. The macros are not saved until you save the workbook or exit Excel. If you create your macros in the Personal Macro Workbook, choose **Window**, **Unhide** and unhide Personal.xls. Then choose **File**, **Save** to save the macro workbook. If you don't save Personal.xls as you're going along, Excel prompts you to save it before exiting.

Chapter 27

No-Brainer Publications with Microsoft Publisher

In This Chapter

➤ The five-second publication

➤ Answering the PageWizards' questions

➤ A little customizing goes a long way

➤ Some basic tools you should know about

➤ A few wizardly tricks of your own

Although your local print shop will gladly "fulfill your every publishing need," they will also charge you an arm and a leg to create publications that don't quite match what you had in mind. In addition, they might not be able to meet your tight deadlines—they usually have to "fit you in," which translates to "maybe sometime next week."

To save some money, get the job done on time, and let your own creative vision drive your publications, use Microsoft Publisher. Publisher comes with a coven of Wizards for creating newsletters, brochures, mailing labels, letterhead, business cards, and even resumes. You just fire up a Wizard, answer a few questions, and you have a custom publication, carefully laid out for you. In this chapter, you learn how to use Publisher to "fulfill your every publishing need" on *your* schedule and for a few pennies per printout.

Conjuring Up Quick Publications with PageWizards

With Microsoft Publisher, you never have to start with a blank page. On startup, Publisher displays a collection of PageWizards for creating everything from greeting cards to resumes. You simply click the desired publication and click **OK**. Each PageWizard displays a series of dialog boxes that ask you questions about how you want the text laid out and allow you to replace existing text with your own messages. (To access the PageWizards later, choose **File**, **New** , or press **Ctrl+N**, and click the **Publications by Wizard** tab.)

Publisher offers a wide selection of prefab publications.

3 Click the desired style.

1 Click the Publications by Wizard tab.

2 Click the desired publication type.

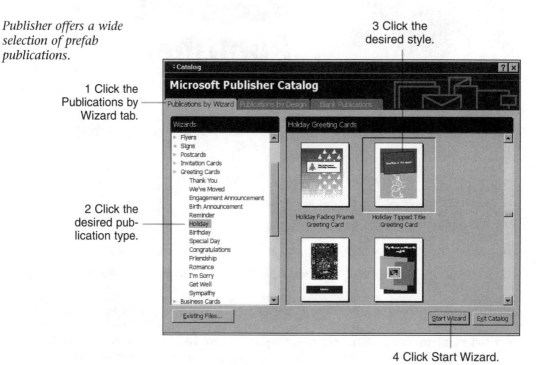

4 Click Start Wizard.

If you know your way around a dialog box, dealing with a PageWizard is a snap. In each dialog box, you enter your preferences and click **Next**. In the final dialog box, click **Finish**. The PageWizard then announces that you've done everything you needed to do and offers to create the publication. Click **Create It**, and then sit back and watch as the PageWizard does its paste-up work.

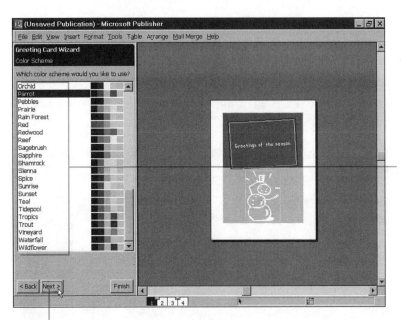

Answer the PageWizard's questions and enter your preferences.

1 Enter your preferences.

2 Click Next.

At this point, all you need to do is click the **Print** button. However, you may want to replace some of the clip art, add text, or rearrange items before you print. The following sections explain your options.

Web Work

To create a page for publication on the Web, run the Web Site PageWizard. You can tweak your Web pages just as you do with standard paper publications. However, Publisher offers a few additional tools for inserting *hyperlinks* (that point to other Web pages and resources), previewing your pages in your Web browser, and publishing your pages electronically on the Web. There are also a few design no-no's you should be aware of when creating your Web pages. See Chapter 25, "Creating and Publishing Your Own Web Pages," for details.

When Publisher is done slapping together your publication, Publisher displays it in the work area on the right. To the left of the work area is the Wizard pane, where you can change the overall design, layout, color scheme, and other settings that control your publication. To make a change, click the desired category in the Wizard list at the top, and then click the desired setting or enter the requested information at the bottom. You can hide the Wizard pane at any time by clicking the **Hide Wizard** button below the pane.

The Wizard hangs around to help you tweak the publication's overall design and layout.

1 Click the desired step in the Wizard.

2 Follow the Wizard's instructions or enter the desired setting.

3 To hide the Wizard pane, click this button.

Basic Stuff You Ought to Know

Your first glance at the publication that the PageWizard created might just turn you to stone. The page is dinky, the graphics look sloppy, and the text looks as if the PageWizard was trying to fit it on the head of a pin. Before you can do anything, you need to know how to zoom in and out and flip from one page to the next.

First, zoom in. Open the **Zoom** drop-down list in the standard toolbar and choose the desired zoom percentage—75% is usually sufficient. Just below the work area are the page flippers. Click the icon for the desired page to quickly display it. You already know how to use the scrollbars; you'll get plenty of scrollbar practice in Publisher.

Choose the
desired zoom
percentage.

*Before you can start work-
ing, make sure you can
see everything.*

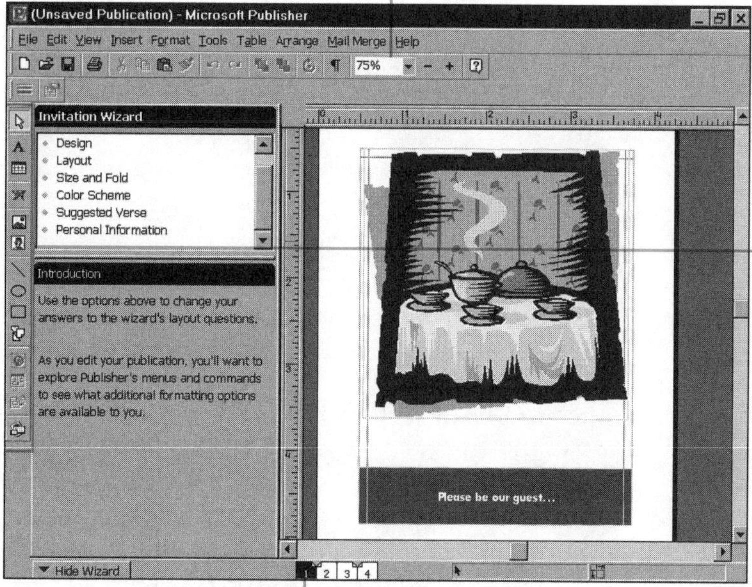

Tools for inserting
objects

Use the Page
Navigation buttons
to flip pages.

Once you have everything in plain sight, you're ready to fiddle with the publication. However, there are a few additional things that might not seem obvious at first:

➤ Every fifteen minutes, a dialog box pops up on your screen, reminding you to save your work. Reply the first time and save your file, but if this dialog box becomes too annoying, turn it off. Choose **Tools**, **Options**, click the **User Assistance** tab, and click **Remind to Save Publication** to remove the check mark.

➤ The **Undo** button doesn't have a drop-down list as in Word, but it can undo more than one action (unlike previous versions of Publisher).

➤ You will encounter two types of text boxes, normal and WordArt, that may look the same. To edit text in a normal text box, click in the text box to position the insertion point and type your changes (just pretend that you're working in Word). For WordArt "text boxes," double-click the box to display a dialog box for editing the text. Edit your text and click **OK**.

➤ The dotted lines are page layout guides. They don't print. See "Page Layout Tools You Can't Live Without," later in this chapter, for details.

➤ Some publications have a text frame off to the side that displays information about the publication. This won't print. In fact, nothing placed on the gray area outside the page will print. You can drag objects onto this work area as you lay out your pages.

➤ A greeting card may have a graphic on the first page that looks as though it doesn't fit on the page. Don't worry about it. Publisher does this wrap-around thing with the graphic so it prints on both the front and back of the card. It's actually pretty cool.

Frames

Every object on a Publisher page is a *frame*. Text is contained in a text frame, images hang out in picture frames, and WordArt objects are held in WordArt frames. Frames make it easy to rearrange objects on a page.

Making New Pages

If you created a greeting card, you probably don't want to add any pages to it. It consists of four pages that print on a single sheet of paper. However, if you're working on a newsletter, resume, or some other document that might need to spread out on two or more pages, you'll have to add pages to your publication.

To add a page, flip to the page where you want the new page inserted. Open the **Insert** menu and choose **Page** or press **Ctrl+Shift+N**. The Insert Page dialog box appears. Enter the desired number of new pages, specify where you want them inserted (Before or After Current Page), and select the desired setting under Options: **Insert Blank Pages, Create One Text Frame on Each Page,** or **Duplicate All Objects on Page ___.** Click **OK**, and Publisher slaps in the specified number of pages.

Working Faster with Grainy (or No) Pictures

Nothing can slow down your computer more than graphics. They take a great deal of memory and processing power to display right, and will slow your scrolling and frame work down to a crawl.

To speed things up, you can hide the graphics or display them in a lower resolution. Open the **View** menu and choose **Picture Display**. In the Picture Display dialog box, choose the desired option: **Detailed Display** (high-quality, but slow), **Fast Resize and Zoom** (fast, but grainy pictures), or **Hide Pictures** (white placeholders that don't even show the picture)

Customizing a Prefab Publication

Some head hunter just called to inform you of a mind-boggling job offer—high pay, good benefits, four weeks vacation, company car. You need a great looking resume and you need it quick. You fired up the Resume PageWizard and answered all the questions. Now what? Here's a bare-bones list of what you need to know:

➤ Click in a text frame (box) to position the insertion point and then type your additions. You can drag over text to highlight it and then type to replace it.

➤ To format text, highlight it and use the Formatting toolbar buttons or the Format menu options just as you do in Word (although the paragraph formatting options are limited). See Chapter 4, "Giving Your Text a Makeover," for details.

➤ To select a frame, click it. Handles (small black boxes) appear around the frame. Drag a handle to resize the frame. Drag an edge of the frame to move the frame. When you move the mouse pointer over an edge of a frame, the pointer appears as a moving van. Cute, huh?

➤ If you type more than a text frame has room for, an Overflow button (with three dots on it) appears at the bottom of the frame, indicating that the text doesn't fit. You have three options: resize the text box, make the text smaller, or spill the text into an empty text frame (click the Overflow button and click inside the empty text frame).

➤ To replace an image, double-click the existing image and choose a different clip art image.

➤ To insert a new picture, text, table, or WordArt frame, click the button for the desired object in the left toolbar. Position the mouse pointer over the page where you want the upper left corner of the object placed and then drag down and to the right. Release the mouse button.

➤ You can lay frames on top of each other, sort of like a stack of pancakes. However, selecting the frame at the bottom is as difficult as eating the pancake at the bottom of the stack. To dig up a buried frame, click the frame that's lying on top of it, and click the **Send to Back** button.

Destacking Frames

Another way to dig a frame out of a pile is to drag frames to the gray area surrounding the page. This is the F. When you decide where you want to place the frame, drag it back over the page and drop it.

If you can manage frames, you know most of what you need to know to customize your publication.

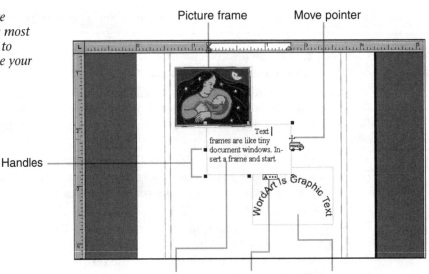

Picture frame   Move pointer

Handles

Text frame Overflow button WordArt frame

Email Right from Publisher

To email your publication to someone, open the **File** menu, choose **Send**, and follow the onscreen instructions. (If you are emailing a multi-page publication that contains a great deal of artwork, sending the publication via email may take several minutes.) If you installed Symantec WinFax Starter Edition, as explained in "Sending Faxes with Microsoft Fax," in Chapter 23, "Managing Your Email," you can fax the publication. When the Message window appears, open the Send drop-down list, choose **Symantec Fax Starter Edition**, and follow the instructions in Chapter 23.

Sure, there's much more you can do to customize your publication, but you want to get that resume out in a hurry. Be sure to proofread it before you send it. And good luck!

Page Layout Tools You Can't Live Without

I mentioned the blue and pink dotted lines earlier in this chapter. What are they for? The pink box indicates the page margins. Try to stay within the margins, so your objects won't stretch out to an area that your printer can't print on. The blue lines are *grid lines* that help you position frames more precisely on a page. When you drag the edge of an object near a grid line, the edge snaps to the gridline, as though the gridline were magnetic.

To adjust the margins and turn on gridlines, open the **Arrange** menu and choose **Layout Guides**. Enter the desired page margins (in inches), select the number of columns and rows you want to use in the grid, and click **OK**.

To move a gridline, open the **View** menu and choose **Go to Background** or press **Ctrl+M**. This displays the margins and gridlines. Hold down the **Shift** key, and move the mouse pointer over a gridline (or margin line) so the pointer displays "Adjust." Drag the gridline to the desired position. As you drag, a light gray line appears in the ruler at the top or left side of the viewing area, showing you the exact position of the line. Release the mouse button and Shift key. (To return to the foreground, press **Ctrl+M** or choose **View**, **Go to Foreground**.)

Shift+drag a gridline
or margin line to the
desired position.

You can adjust the grid-line positions in the Background.

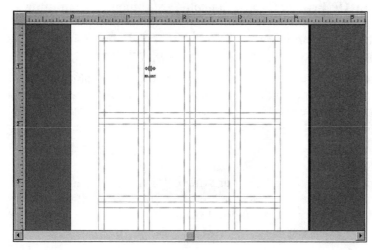

Although those sticky gridlines sure help when it comes to aligning objects, they can also get on your nerves. To turn off the snap-to feature, open the **Tools** menu and choose the desired **Snap to** option: **Snap to Ruler Marks**, **Snap to Guides**, or **Snap to Objects**. (You can toggle the Snap to Guides option by pressing **Ctrl+W**; what the W stands for, I have no idea.)

Printing Professional-Looking Publications

Modern desktop printers are capable of generating high-quality publications economically, and they give you complete control over the printing schedule. When you need a publication in a hurry, there's no better way to produce it than by printing it. However, if you need to print large quantities of full-color catalogues, three-fold brochures, menus, or other professional publications, a full-service printing shop is much better equipped to handle the job.

But where do you start? What are your options? The following sections provide the information you need to print your publications yourself and prepare your publications to have a professional printer produce them.

Checking Out Your Printing Options

Faced with the decision of how to mass produce your publications, you should consider two things—cost and quality—and try to balance these two considerations to make the best business decision. Before you decide, read through the following list of printing options:

Strict Budget: Go grayscale, medium resolution (600 dpi). Grayscale is sort of like black-and-white TV, which uses black, white, and various grades of shade to display images. (To add color cheaply, print on colored paper.)

Colorful, but a Little Pricey: Choose full-color, continuous tone printing at low to medium resolution (300 to 600 dpi), assuming the printing shop offers this option. This isn't the best option for printing full-color photos, but it's great for printing text and computer graphics using a desktop printer.

Money Is No Object: Choose full-color, high-end printing at resolutions of 1200 dpi. If your publication includes crisp color photos and you need high-quality print, high-end printing is the only way to go. This option requires that you send the publication to the printing shop on disk or via modem.

Compromise Solution: To stay within budget and yet create high-quality publications, use *spot-printing* or *two-color* output. With spot printing, most text and graphics are printed in grayscale, but another color is used for headings or other objects, such as sidebars. Because you are using only one additional color, spot-printing is much less expensive than full-color.

Do It Yourself with Your Desktop Printer

Your printer can handle most of your publication needs and should be able to produce fairly high-quality printouts, assuming you use high-quality paper. Load the paper into your printer, turn it on, and choose **File**, **Print**. Enter your printing preferences and click the **OK** button.

Two-Color Output for the Budget Conscious

An inexpensive way to add color to a document is to use spot-color (also called two-color) printing. To print a publication that uses spot color, the printer must create two sets of printer plates for each page. One plate prints everything that appears black (typically the running text), and the other plate applies the color.

In most cases, the imagesetter will create the actual color separations and output them on film for application to the printing plates. However, you must format the objects that you want to appear in the second color. Take the following steps:

1. Open your publication.
2. Open the **Tools** menu, point to **Commercial Printing Tools**, and click **Color Printing**.

3. Click **Spot Color(s)** and click the **Change Spot Color** button.

4. Open the **Spot Color 1** drop-down list and choose the color you want to use. (You can specify a different color at the printing shop, but try to pick something close.)

5. To use another color, click the **Spot Color 2** check box and choose a color for the second color. (Using another color adds to the printing costs, of course.) Click **OK** to return to the Color Printing dialog box.

6. Click **OK** to save your changes. Publisher automatically applies the second color to some of the objects in your publication.

7. 🖌️ To have a frame's background print in the second color, select the frame, click the **Fill Color** button, and choose the second color or a shade of it. (In spot-color publications, the available colors are limited to black, shades of gray, the specified second color, and shades of the specified color.)

8. To make a picture, text, or WordArt object print in the second color, take one of the following steps:

   Picture: Right-click the picture, point to **Change Picture**, and click **Recolor Picture**. Select the second color and click **OK**.

   WordArt: Right-click the WordArt object, point to **Change Object**, and click **Recolor Object**. Select the second color and click **OK**.

   Text: Highlight the text, click the **Font Color** button, and choose the desired second color or shading.

To print your document, choose **File**, **Print**, select **Print Separations**, and then click **OK**. Publisher prints each page as two pages: one containing all the grayscale text and objects and a second page containing all the color text and objects. When the printing shop returns a proof of your publication, match it against your proof to verify the color separations.

Printing to a File for Outside Printing

If you're outputting your publication to a file to send it to the printing shop on a floppy disk or via modem, the process is a little complicated. First, find out from the printing shop which printer you should use. You may have to install another Windows printer driver (**Start**, **Settings**, **Printers**, **Add Printer**).

When you have the correct printer installed, you can use the Pack and Go Wizard to print your publication to a file on your hard drive or transfer your publication to a set of floppy disks. Here's what you do:

1. Save your publication as you normally save a document.

2. Open the **File** menu, point to **Pack and Go**, and click **Take to a Commercial Printing Service**. The first Pack and Go Wizard dialog box appears, describing what the Wizard can do.

285

3. Click **Next**.

4. Choose the drive and folder in which you want the output stored. (If you are transferring the publication to a set of floppy disks, make sure you have several freshly formatted disks on hand.) Click **Next**.

5. Choose the desired options for embedding fonts and graphics in your publication and click **Next.**

6. Click **Finish**. The Pack and Go Wizard transfers your publication into a file or set of files and includes a file called Unpack.exe, which you run to extract the file(s) that make up your publication.

Speak Like a Geek: The Complete Archive

absolute cell reference   In an Excel worksheet formula, a cell address that does not change when you move or copy the formula. (See also *relative cell reference*.)

Access   The database application included with Microsoft Office 97 Professional. Access enables you to create forms, use the forms to enter data, and create reports with stored data.

action button   On a PowerPoint slide, a button that appears on the slide and enables the person viewing the slide show to perform some action, such as advancing to the next slide.

address   A combination of a column letter and row number that specifies the location of a cell in an Excel worksheet. For example, the address of the cell in the upper-left corner of the worksheet is A1. Addresses are commonly used in formulas to pull values into the calculation.

appointment   In Outlook, a scheduled time at which you need to do something but that does not require the time of another co-worker (for example, lunch with your spouse, a dentist appointment). Contrast to *meeting*.

argument   The part of a function statement in an Excel worksheet that tells the function which values to use in the calculations. For example, in =AVG(A1..K15), AVERAGE is the function, and (A1..K15) is the argument.

AutoContent Wizard   In PowerPoint, a series of dialog boxes that creates a prefab presentation for advertising a product, presenting a sales pitch, training new employees, and so on.

AutoCorrect   A feature that automatically corrects typos and misspellings as you type.

AutoFit   An Excel feature that makes a column wide enough to fit the widest entry in that column. Think of AutoFit as spandex for spreadsheets.

AutoFormat   An Excel feature that beautifies your worksheets without making you do too much. AutoFormat adds shading, cell borders, and other fancy formatting to your worksheet. Word has this feature, too, for use on tables.

AutoText   A feature that enables you to create shorthand entries for text that you commonly type. For example, you can create an AutoText entry that inserts "Microsoft Office Shortcut Bar" whenever you type MOSB and press the F3 key.

bookmark   1. A Word feature that inserts a tag in your document so you can quickly jump back to that spot later. 2. In a Web page, a code that allows you to point a link to a specific location on the page.

border   A box around text, a picture, or some other object. You can change the color, thickness, and style of borders to give them a different look.

browser   See *Web browser*.

build   An animated effect in a slide show that introduces elements on a slide one at a time. You can create a build, for example, that assembles a bulleted list one bullet at a time.

cell   The rectangle formed by the intersection of a column and a row in an Excel worksheet. You type text labels, values, and formulas in cells to create a worksheet.

chart   Another name for a graph.

circular reference   In a worksheet, a formula that references the same cell that contains the formula. This results in an error; and Excel slaps your hand and displays a dialog box saying, "Can't do that."

client   A program that receives copied, linked, or embedded data from other programs. The term client is also used to describe your computer when you are connecting to a server computer on a network or on the Internet.

clip art   A collection of predrawn images that you can use to decorate your documents even if you have no artistic talent.

Clipboard   A Windows storage area in which data is temporarily stored when you cut or copy it. With the addition of Office 2000, the Clipboard can store a series of cut or copied chunks of data.

column   In a table or worksheet, a vertical arrangement of data. Columns intersect with rows to form boxes, called *cells*, into which you type entries. See also *newspaper columns*.

conditional formatting   A cell-formatting option in Excel that changes the way a cell or its content appears based on the value in that cell. For example, you can format a cell so that it displays the value in black when the value is positive or in red when the value is negative.

contiguous   A fancy term for *neighboring*. On a worksheet, for example, all cells that are next to each other are said to be contiguous.

control   A graphical object on an Access form or report that enables a user to enter data, execute a command, or display data. Common controls include text boxes, option buttons, and check boxes.

control source   The field from which a control on a form or report obtains data entries. For example, you can place a Product Name field on your report that extracts data from a source, such as the Product Name field in the Products table.

cursor   Another name for the vertical line that indicates where text is inserted when you start typing. The preferred name is *insertion point*.

data   Information a computer stores and works with.

database   A computer program used for storing, organizing, and retrieving information. The term is also used to describe any collection of data.

datasheet   A mini-worksheet/table that makes it easy to enter data that you want to graph or include in a database. In Access, you can view a table or form in Datasheet view for quicker data entry.

data source   A file from which you extract data entries. If you create a form letter in Word that extracts names and addresses from an address book, for example, the address book is the data source. (See also *main document*.)

desktop   The area on your Windows computer screen from which you can open programs, remove files with the Recycle Bin, and view or manage other resources.

destination document   The file into which you paste data that has been cut or copied from another document.

dialog box A typically small window that an application displays when it needs more information to perform a required task.

document The file that you create when you work in any of the Office applications. These files include Word documents, Excel workbooks, PowerPoint presentations, and Access databases.

drag and drop To copy or move data simply by selecting it and dragging it with the mouse from one place to another in the same document or in different documents.

email Short for electronic mail, a system that enables users to exchange messages and files over network connections, the Internet, or via modem.

embed To copy data from a document in one application and paste it into a document created with another application, while retaining a link to the application in which the data was created. If you embed an Excel worksheet into a Word document, for example, you can double-click the worksheet in the Word document to run Excel and edit the worksheet.

event In Outlook, an activity that takes one or more days as opposed to a block of time during one day.

expand A Word outlining feature that enables you to bring text back into view after you collapse an outline.

Excel A spreadsheet program made by Microsoft. You can use Excel to organize numbers and other data, perform complex mathematical operations, and much more.

favorites A list of Web pages you really like. You add favorites to the Favorites menu, and then you can quickly return to those pages later by selecting them from the menu.

field On a fill-in-the-blank form, the blank. In a database, you create forms for entering data. Each form has one or more fields into which you type data. A collection of field entries makes up a record.

field code A tag that Word inserts in a document to extract data from another source. For example, the date field code inserts the date from your computer's internal clock. Word also uses field codes to pull information into a form letter, generate a table of contents, and create numbered lists.

file A collection of data saved to disk under a specific name. Whenever you save a document, the application stores it in a file on a floppy disk, a hard disk, or a network drive.

fill   The background color used for a cell in a Word table or Excel worksheet, or for a drawing object.

fill handle   A little black box that appears just outside the lower-right corner of a selected Excel worksheet cell. You can drag the fill handle to copy the entry from the selected cell into a string of neighboring cells.

fill series   A string of related values that you can insert quickly into neighboring cells in an Excel worksheet. For example, Excel has a fill series that consists of the names of the week. To insert the names into a series of cells, all you have to do is type Monday in the first cell, and then drag the fill handle on the cell over six neighboring cells. When you release the mouse button, Excel inserts the names of the remaining six days of the week.

filter   To extract related records from a database. If you had a phone book full of names and addresses, for example, you could use a filter to pull out the records Smith through Smythe.

font   A set of characters sharing the same design.

foreign key   An access field that establishes a relationship to another table. In most cases the two tables have fields of the same name. The *primary key* in one table supplies information to the foreign key field in the other table. For example, you might have a Customer table that supplies the Customer ID to the Orders table. (See also *primary key*.)

form   A fill-in-the blanks page common on Web pages and in Excel and Access databases. In databases you fill out a form to enter a record. (See also *record*.)

formatting   Changing the appearance or layout of a page or of selected text. Formatting includes changing margins and picking different font styles.

formula   A mathematical statement in a table or worksheet that tells the application how to perform calculations on a set of values. Formulas typically consist of cell addresses that pull values from specific cells and mathematical operators that specify which operations to perform. For example, =(C1+C2+C3)/3 determines the average of the values in cells C1 to C3.

frame   A light gray box that appears around a text box in PowerPoint or Word and keeps any text and graphics together.

function   A ready-made formula that performs a mathematical operation on a set of values. The simple function SUM, for example, determines the total of a set of values. A more complicated function might determine a payment on a loan given the loan amount, the term, and the interest rate.

grammar checker   An editing tool built into most word processors and rarely used by any person for any real good. Microsoft Word has a grammar checker, so you can see firsthand what I mean.

graph   See *chart*. Although most people call them graphs, Microsoft insists on calling them *charts*.

graphics   Electronic art and pictures. A graphic can be a drawing created on the computer, an image scanned in for digital manipulation (clip art), or various shapes, lines, and boxes created with the computer.

gridlines   Nonprinting lines in a table or worksheet that display the boundaries of cells. Not to be confused with *borders*, which actually do appear in print.

group   To select and treat a collection of graphic objects as a single object. If you have several drawn objects that compose a single graphic, grouping is useful for moving and resizing the objects as a unit. (See also *ungroup*.)

handles   Tiny squares that surround a selected graphics object or text box. You can easily change the size or dimensions of an object by dragging one of its handles.

handouts   PowerPoint pages that you can print for distribution to your audience.

home page   1. The Web page that your Web browser loads whenever it starts. 2. The opening page at a Web site. A home page typically contains a brief introduction to the site along with links to other pages at the site.

HTML   Short for Hypertext Markup Language, a set of codes (called *tags*) that insert graphics, links, audio clips, and other objects on a Web page and tell your Web browser how to display the page. You don't actually see these codes when you view a Web page, unless the Web page creator didn't know what he was doing.

hyperlink   Text, graphics, icons, or other items in a document that link to other areas in the document or to pages, files, and other resources outside a document. Hyperlinks are commonly used on Web pages to link one Web page to another.

insertion point   A blinking vertical line that indicates where text will appear when you start typing or where an object will be inserted.

IntelliMouse   A three-button pointing device from Microsoft. The middle button on the IntelliMouse is a little gray wheel that you can spin to scroll through a document. You can use this button for other tasks, as explained in Chapter 1.

Internet   A global system of interconnected networks that makes it possible for anyone with a computer and a modem or other network connection to open multimedia Web pages, exchange email, chat, and much more.

Internet Explorer   A popular Web browser that Microsoft is just giving away. Can they afford to do that? (See also *Web browser*.)

intranet   An internal network (in a corporation, university, or other institution) that uses Internet technologies to make it easier to navigate the network.

journal   In Outlook, a diary that keeps track of your work, including the documents you create and email messages you send and receive. You can also enter information about important phone calls (for legal purposes) and record personal information.

labels   Entries in an Excel worksheet that are typically used to indicate the meaning of other entries, such as values. Labels usually appear at the tops of columns and to the left of rows.

leader   A string of characters that lead up to the text at the tab stop.

legend   A little box that displays color codes for your charts (graphs). On road maps you've no doubt seen legends that show the mileage scale and differentiate between side roads and main drags.

link   1. To copy data from a source document and paste it into a destination document while retaining a live connection between the two documents. Whenever you edit the data in the source document, the changes appear automatically in the destination document. For example, if you paste an Excel worksheet as a link into a PowerPoint presentation, whenever you edit the worksheet the changes appear in your presentation. 2. On a Web page, highlighted text or icons that you click to open associated Web pages (see *hyperlink*).

macro   A series of recorded commands, keystrokes, and/or mouse moves that you can play back by entering the macro's name, clicking a button, or pressing a special key combination.

mail merge   A feature that extracts data (such as names and addresses) from one document and automatically inserts it into another document (such as a form letter) to create a collection of unique documents.

main document   The primary document of the two documents you are merging. In a mail merge operation, the letter is the *main document* and the address book is the *data source*. (See also *mail merge*.)

maximize   To enlarge your window to fill the entire screen. Or, to pay 69 cents extra to move up to a large order of fries and a Biggie Coke.

meeting   An event that you do with other people at your work, excluding complaining about the boss, betting on the NCAA basketball tournament, and sneaking out for a cigarette. Meetings require that you coordinate a time block with your fellow drones.

memory   The computer's electronic storage area. Memory used to be measured in kilobytes; but with the advances in operating systems and applications, it is now measured in megabytes. And your computer had better have at least 16 megabytes if you want to use Office.

menu   A list of commands that you can choose by clicking them with your mouse. Menus can drop down from a menu bar or pop up on your screen when you click with the right mouse button. You can usually get a menu to disappear by clicking something other than the menu.

minimize   To reduce your window to a button on the taskbar.

mixed reference   In a spreadsheet formula, an absolute cell reference, such as $A3, that tells the formula to always refer to a cell in column A, but that when copying the formula to another cell, the row number can change.

narration   In a PowerPoint presentation, a voice recording that plays during the presentation.

network   A group of computers connected with high-speed data cables for the purpose of sharing hardware, software, data, and communications.

newspaper columns   A formatting option for text that causes it to display two or more columns of text on a page. The text runs from the top of the first column to the bottom and continues at the top of the next column, as in a newspaper or magazine.

Office Assistant   An animated character that pops up on your screen and offers help whenever you start an Office application or try to perform a somewhat complex task.

OLE   Short for *object linking and embedding*, OLE is a technology that enables different types of documents to freely share data. (See also *embed* and *link*.)

online   To be connected to another computer or network of computers.

order of operations   The sequence in which Excel performs a series of calculations, also called *precedence*. Excel performs all operations enclosed in parentheses first, next exponential equations, multiplication and division, and, finally, addition and subtraction.

outline level   A Word feature that enables you to specify how you want the headings in your document treated. By specifying an outline level for each heading, you can collapse the outline to view only the headings and then restructure your document simply by moving the headings.

Outlook   The personal information manager/email application that comes with Office. With Outlook, you can keep track of appointments and special dates, prioritize your list of things to do, manage your email, keep an address book and journal, and even write yourself personal reminder notes.

page break   A printing code that indicates where a page ends and a new page begins. Office applications automatically insert page breaks based on the margins and the paper size. You can, however, insert manual page breaks to divide pages as desired.

pane   A portion of a window that displays different data in the same document. Panes are useful if you are working in one part of the document and need to refer to information in a different part of the document.

pattern   A design typically used as the background for a page, graphic, table, or cell.

PowerPoint   The Office slide show program. With PowerPoint, you can create onscreen presentations, transfer your presentations to 35mm slides, or print them on paper or overhead transparencies. You can even create talkies by recording a voice narration.

presentation   Fancy name for a PowerPoint slide show.

primary key   In an Access table, a field that supplies entries to a corresponding field in another table. (See also *foreign key*.)

print area   A portion of an Excel worksheet that you want to print. Because worksheets can become quite long and wide, you might want to print only a portion of the worksheet.

program   A special set of instructions written for the computer, telling it how to perform some useful task. You hear the words *program*, *software*, and *application* used interchangeably; they all mean the same thing.

query   A set of instructions that tells Access which data to extract from a database, how to sort the data, and how to arrange it. You use queries to pull data from one or more tables or from various databases to create reports.

range   In an Excel worksheet, a group of neighboring cells or a set of cell blocks.

recalculation   To run the formulas in a worksheet again after changing a value. By default, Excel automatically recalculates the formulas. If you turn off AutoRecalculation, you can have Excel recalculate formulas by pressing F9.

record   A collection of fields making one complete entry in a database. Think of a Rolodex as a database. Each card on that Rolodex is a record.

relative cell reference   In an Excel worksheet formula, a cell address that changes when you paste the formula into a different cell. Unless you specify otherwise, Excel makes all cell references in formulas relative, so that when you copy a formula into a different cell, the addresses automatically adjust to perform the calculations on a different set of data. If you don't want a cell address to change, you must mark it as an *absolute cell reference*.

report   An Access and Excel feature that extracts data from one or more databases or tables, arranges the data attractively on a page, and (optionally) performs calculations on the data. You typically use reports to analyze data and present it in a meaningful format.

ruler   A ribbon, typically displayed above and/or to the left of the document viewing area, that you use to change margins, indent paragraphs, and set tab stop positions.

scenario   In Excel, a set of values that you can plug into a worksheet to see how these values affect the end result. When you play with sets of values in this way, you are said to be playing *What-if?*

scrap   Selected text, graphic, or other object that you dragged from a document and placed on the Windows desktop. Scraps enable you to quickly move and copy data from one document to another.

ScreenTip   Formerly known as ToolTip, a ScreenTip is a brief description of an object, button, or option that pops up whenever you rest the mouse pointer on the object.

section   In a Word document, a part of the document that has the same format settings for headers, footers, and columns. By default, every document has one section. If you change the section formatting for part of the document, you create a new section.

selection box   An outline that appears around a cell or block of cells in an Excel worksheet when the cell(s) are selected.

server   On a network or on the Internet, the computer that your computer (the client) connects to and uses to access information, use applications, or share resources.

Shortcut Bar   A strip of buttons that make it easy to access the Office applications and perform specific tasks, such as creating a new document or recording an appointment. After you install Office, the Shortcut Bar appears whenever you start your computer.

shortcut keys   Keypress combinations that enable you to bypass a menu or command sequence.

slide master   A PowerPoint slide that works in the background to control the color and formatting for all the slides in a presentation. You can override the master slide settings on individual slides. (See also *title master*.)

source document   The file from which you copy or cut data to insert into another document. If you copy data from a source document and paste it as a link into another (destination) document, whenever you edit the source document, your changes appear in the destination document.

split box   A small bar, typically at the top of the vertical scrollbar or the right end of the horizontal scrollbar, that enables you to divide a document window into two panes. (See also *pane*.)

spool   A printing technology that sends print instructions to the hard disk and then feeds the instructions to the printer so that you can continue working while the printer prints your document.

spreadsheet   A program made to imitate a ledger's rows and columns that you use to organize and display data. You can use spreadsheets to arrange data in rows and columns, to perform calculations on numerical entries, and to analyze data through charts.

style   A collection of format settings that you can apply to a paragraph or to selected text. If you change one or more format settings in a style, the changes affect all the text that you formatted with that style.

syntax   The taxes levied on cigarettes, alcohol, and other items that the government deems harmful to your health or moral well-being. Also, the format in which you must enter a formula or function in order for it to work properly. Think of it as grammar for numerical sentences.

table   A structure that organizes data in rows and columns. Tables are commonly used in Word documents and on Web pages to help align text without having to enter awkward tab settings.

taskbar   The bar at the bottom of your Windows desktop that enables you to switch back and forth between applications or launch new programs with the Start button.

template   A pattern for a document that controls fonts, sizes, and other format settings.

text box   1. A blank space in a dialog box into which you can type a setting, such as the margin width. 2. A rectangular area on a page into which you can type text. Text boxes are excellent for newsletters and for adding sidebars and other chunks of text that do not fit in the normal flow of your document.

timings   A PowerPoint feature that enables you to control the amount of time each slide remains onscreen during an online presentation.

title master   A PowerPoint slide that works in the background to control the formatting for the titles and subtitles on each slide in the presentation. (See also *slide master*.)

toolbar   A strip of buttons that usually appears at the top of an application's window just below the menu bar. With a toolbar, you can bypass the pull-down menu commands by clicking a button.

ungroup   To separate several drawing objects that you have grouped together to act as a single object. To delete or modify a single object, you must first ungroup the objects. (See also *group*.)

values   Numerical entries in a worksheet[md]as opposed to *labels,* which are text entries.

Web   Short for the World Wide Web, a collection of pages that are stored on computers all over the world and are linked to one another with hyperlinks. Your Office applications offer many new features that help you create your own pages for publication on the Web or download new features or updates online.

Web browser   An application that opens and displays pages on the World Wide Web. In addition to displaying the text that makes up those pages, most Web browsers can display graphics and play audio clips. Microsoft's Internet Explorer is a popular Web browser.

wizard   A series of dialog boxes that leads you through the process of performing a complicated task. Office applications offer wizards as a quick way of creating documents. The Letter Wizard in Word, for example, can help you create a properly formatted business letter.

Word   The Office word processor.

word processor   An application that enables you to slice, dice, and mince your words and phrases, add graphics to your pages, and perform all other tasks required to create a printed publication.

word wrap   A feature in all word processing programs that automatically moves the insertion point to the next line when you reach the end of the current line, as opposed to a typewriter where you must hit the carriage return to start a new line.

workbook   A collection of Excel worksheets. Each file that you create in Excel is a workbook.

worksheet   A page in an Excel workbook on which you enter data.

wrap   See *word wrap*.

Index

313

O

317

319

321

327

Other Related Titles

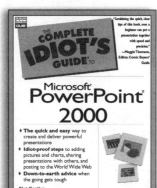
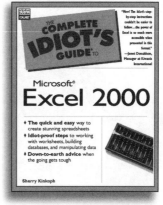
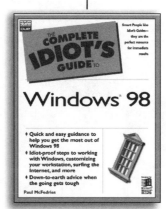